WITHDRAWN

P9-DFE-509

ILLINOIS CENTRAL COLLEGE
JA79.E82
STACKS
Ethical issues in government /

A12900 728478

JA 79 .E82

Ethical issues in government
/

Illinois Central College
Learning Resources Center

Ethical Issues
in Government

 **PHILOSOPHICAL MONOGRAPHS**

Joseph Margolis,
General Editor
Temple University
Philadelphia, Pa. 19122

Assistants to the Editor

Tom L. Beauchamp
Georgetown

Judith Tormey
Temple

Donald Harward
Delaware

Editorial Advisory Board

Kurt Baier
Pittsburgh

Michael Lockwood
Oxford

Stephen F. Barker
Johns Hopkins

Ernan McMullin
Notre Dame

Panayot Butchvarov
Iowa

Harold Morick
SUNY, Albany

Norman Care
Oberlin

Terence Penelhum
Calgary

V. C. Chappell
Massachusetts, Amherst

Jerome Shaffer
Connecticut

Keith Donnellan
California, Los Angeles

H. S. Thayer
CUNY

Jerry Fodor
MIT

Zak Van Straaten
Witwatersrand

Donald Gustafson
Cincinnati

Richard Wasserstrom
California, Los Angeles

Ethical Issues in Government

I.C.C. LIBRARY

Edited by

Norman E. Bowie

72050

Philosophical Monographs
Third Annual Series
Temple University Press, Philadelphia

Library of Congress Cataloging in Publication Data
Main entry under title:

Ethical issues in government.

(Philosophical monographs)
Includes index.
1. Political ethics—Addresses, essays, lectures. I. Bowie, Norman E., 1942–
II. Series: Philosophical monographs (Philadelphia)
JA79.E82   172'.2   80-22217
ISBN 0-87722-165-0

Temple University Press, Philadelphia 19122
© 1981 by Temple University. All rights reserved
Published 1981
Printed in the United States of America

To my undergraduate professors
Joseph D'Alfonso and James Miller

Contents

Preface

The decade of the seventies witnessed the rebirth of normative ethics. The focus of that rebirth seemed to be on professional ethics. Medical ethics led the way, but engineering ethics, nursing ethics, business ethics, and legal ethics have followed. This volume addresses some of the issues that fall under the term "government ethics". Specifically, it addresses the following questions: Should legislators serve constituents or conscience? What are the proper bounds of government regulation? Is cost-benefit analysis an ethically acceptable tool for public policy decisions? What is the government's obligation to inform the public? Of course, these questions in no way exhaust the list of questions that might properly be considered in a volume on government ethics. Rather, they are meant to be representative of the *types* of questions that arise in most areas of applied ethics.

The constituents versus conscience issue (Part I) provides an ethical dilemma—or what, on at least a first glance, appears to be an ethical dilemma. The analysis of ethical dilemmas is one of the main focuses in the renewed interest in normative ethics.

The issue of the proper bounds of government regulation (Part II) raises some of the problems of constitutional design—problems that received their impetus for close examination with the appearance of John Rawls' *A Theory of Justice*. In discussing the proper bounds of government regulation, contemporary normative ethics is linked to traditional political philosophy and further back to nineteenth-century political economy.

A scrutiny of cost-benefit analysis as an instrument for policy decisions (Part III) continues the traditional debate between moral philosophers of a utilitarian bent and their deontological critics. The actual use of cost-benefit analysis (and related tools like risk assessment) provides data and information that move the traditional debate in new directions. In particular, it gives moral philosophers some pause: Just what should be expected of a justifiable normative ethical theory?

Finally, the specific question of the government's responsibility to inform the public (Part IV) enables us to apply the results of some of these broader, more general analyses to a specific problem. For example, to answer the question of the government's obligation to inform the public requires that we have some notion of what constitutes good government.

If the reader looks at the articles in this volume from the perspective outlined above, he or she will not only achieve a more technical understanding of some of the problems that arise in a discussion of ethical issues in government but will also see how those issues cohere within the general traditional discussions of normative ethics.

All the articles appearing in this volume were specifically prepared for this anthology. They have not appeared in print elsewhere. Many of the papers are revised versions of papers presented at a conference, "Ethical Issues in Government," held November 8–9, 1979, at the John M. Clayton Center, University of Delaware. Support for that conference was provided by the Delaware Humanities Forum and the Exxon Education Foundation.

The editor expresses his appreciation to his secretarial staff, Mrs. Marguerite Baker and Mrs. Sandy Manno, and to the general editor, Joseph Margolis.

Contributors

Elizabeth L. Beardsley is professor of philosophy at Temple University and author of several papers in philosophy of language, ethical theory, and political and legal philosophy.

Tom L. Beauchamp is associate professor of philosophy at Georgetown University and author of *Philosophical Ethics* (1981), as well as editor or co-editor of eight books in contemporary ethical issues.

Lawrence C. Becker is associate professor of philosophy at Hollins College and author of *Property Rights: Philosophic Foundations* (1977).

Hugo Adam Bedau is professor of philosophy at Tufts University and author of *The Courts, the Constitution, and Capital Punishment* (1977), as well as editor or co-editor of four books.

David Braybrooke is professor of philosophy at Dalhousie University, Halifax, Nova Scotia, author of three books, and editor of *Philosophy in Canada*—a monograph series.

John Byrne is associate professor in the College of Urban Affairs at the University of Delaware. He has published seven articles in the fields of policy formulation, energy use, and cost-benefit analysis.

Peter A. French is professor of philosophy at the University of Minnesota at Morris and the editor of *Midwest Studies in Philosophy*. He is the author of seven books and twenty professional papers, primarily in ethical theory and applied ethics.

Holly Smith Goldman is associate professor of philosophy at the University of Illinois at Chicago Circle. She has published numerous articles on ethics in professional journals and volumes.

James O. Grunebaum is associate professor of philosophy at State University College at Buffalo and has published several articles on ownership.

Gerald C. MacCallum, Jr., is professor of philosophy at the University of Wisconsin and has published widely in political philosophy and metaphysics.

Eric Mack is associate professor of philosophy at Tulane University and author of numerous articles on moral, political, and legal philosophy.

Joseph Margolis is professor of philosophy at Temple University and author of *Art and Philosophy* (1979).

Rex Martin is professor of philosophy at the University of Kansas and author of *Historical Explanation: Re-enactment and Practical Inference* (1977) and several articles in political philosophy and philosophy of law.

Lisa H. Newton is professor of philosophy at Fairfield University and has published several articles in political philosophy, ethical theory, and professional ethics.

Vincent Vaccaro is a personnel management specialist with the Naval Supply Systems Command in Washington, D.C.

Ethical Issues
in Government

Part I

Should Legislators Serve Constituents or Conscience?

Traditional discussions of the constituent or conscience dilemma often distinguish two contrasting theories of representation. The delegate theory, closely associated with James Mill, sees the representative as a kind of substitute for his or her constituents. He or she takes the place of the constituents in the legislative assembly halls. Looked at from this perspective, the delegate theory implies that the legislator must choose the constituent side of the dilemma. On the other hand, the trustee theory, closely associated with Edmund Burke, sees the representative as having a duty to preserve the institutional values of the society and/or to protect the individual interests of his or her constituents. The legislative activity of the trustee legislator is directed toward a political goal or ideal that is not necessarily identical with the immediate individual wants of the constituents. So long as the legislator's conscience embodies this ideal, any conflict between conscience and constituent must, on the trustee view, be decided in favor of conscience.

In our opening essay Peter French sides with Edmund Burke and against James Mill as he subjects Mill's delegate theory of representation to critical scrutiny. After explaining Mill's theory, he provides three arguments against it: First, the delegate theory robs the legislator of his judgment and, hence, of his autonomy. Second, the delegate theory commits the legislator to vote for a majority-preferred position over one that is morally correct (and French does not see how such a position could be morally justified). Finally, a representative operating under the delegate theory cannot completely escape being held accountable for the unhappy consequences that

3

result from a bill he or she voted for. French concludes with a sympathetic analysis of Burke's theory of representation.

Although the authors in this section differ as to how they would resolve the dilemma of constituent versus conscience, they all agree that any conclusion as to how one resolves the dilemma depends, in part, on what the person builds into the terms "conscience" and "constituent." Consider Gerald MacCallum's chapter. MacCallum doubts that, once the terms "constituent" and "conscience" are properly understood, you will find many genuine dilemmas between the legislator's conscience and the interests of his or her constituents. "Have legislators a moral obligation to serve conscience?" Mac-Callum asks. So long as the conscience is neither erroneous nor over-scrupulous, the answer is yes. The reason for the affirmative answer is that if something *really is* morally obligatory, it will be obligatory for that kind of conscience. Have legislators a moral obligation to serve constituents? The answer to this question depends, in part, on the responsibilities given to legislators and on what counts as a constituent. In other words, how one should represent his or her constituents depends somewhat on the political system the legislator is operating under. Having sorted the dilemma into two distinct questions, should a conflict between a correctly informed conscience and pursuit of politically legitimate interests of constituents arise, the legislator should opt for conscience.

If French and MacCallum ultimately come down on the side of conscience, Lisa Newton and James Grunebaum ultimately come down on the side of the constituents. However, Professor Newton distinguishes three ways in which constituents can be benefitted. A legislative action can benefit a constituent's *good* in terms of health, knowledge, and sensitivity; his or her *interest* in terms of wealth or goods; and his or her *preference* in terms of how constituents would respond to a questionnaire. Using the principle of "respect for persons," Newton argues that a legislator should seek to benefit constituents in terms of their interests rather than their preferences. However, if a legislator's conscience seeks the constituent's good and if the constituent's good and interest conflict, the legislator ought to seek the constituent's interest rather than follow conscience and seek the constituent's good.

Using a strategy similar to Newton's, James Grunebaum proposes a rationally justified principle for choosing when the representative ought to represent the interests of those whom he represents. Grunebaum distinguishes between basic needs and secondary wants. Basic needs are wants that one must fulfill if one is to want anything at all—food, clothing, shelter, love, and so forth. Secondary wants are those things that do not affect the satisfaction of basic needs. Mistakes regarding basic needs are possible, while mistakes about non-basic wants are not. Grunebaum then concludes that a representative should promote the basic needs of constituents, whatever the constituents want; but where basic needs are not at issue, the representative should promote whatever his or her constituents want. Finally, Grunebaum considers the situation where what is "in" the constituency's interest is a policy that will promote the secondary wants of the members and they do not want it.

Holly Goldman shows that those who argue that a legislator should benefit constituents by voting in accordance with constituent preferences because such voting best supports democracy are mistaken. Goldman begins her discussion by distinguishing two concepts of democracy: accordance democracy, in which policies accord with the people's preferences, and control democracy, in which policies not only accord with but are actively controlled by the people's preferences. A representative who votes in accord with the people's preferences necessarily brings his or her system closer to the ideal of an accord democracy. But a representative who votes in accord with popular preferences does not bring his or her system closer to the ideal of control democracy unless that vote is independently motivated by regard for sanctions the people would deploy if a different vote had been cast. Citing the benefits of the democratic decision-making process, Goldman concludes by arguing that control democracy is intrinsically superior to accord democracy.

Although Goldman does not discuss this issue, her arguments on behalf of control democracy raise some important points for the question at hand. Assuming that Goldman is right, could one not argue that the greater and more efficacious the constituent control, the more justified a legislator is in following conscience over constituent preference?

Finally, Elizabeth Beardsley approaches the conscience versus constituent dilemma by considering whether the morality of its citizens is an appropriate area of concern for a government. She begins with the relatively uncontroversial claim that citizens have rights to security in their persons and property and that legislators have obligations to protect those rights. One means for protecting those rights is by strengthening the morality of at least some citizens. Since such an action would be in conformity with an obligation of legislators, this action should also be in conformity with legislators' consciences. This action would also be in the interests of the constituents even if it were not in the expressed interest of those constituents whose morality the legislators were trying to strengthen. In this case the expressed interests of those latter constituents are made subservient both to the interests of the constituents and to the conscience of the legislator.

PETER A. FRENCH

1 Burking a Mill

I

To burke. To murder someone by suffocation so as to leave the body intact and suitable for dissection. To suppress quietly and unceremoniously.

The Burke for whom the verb is named was William, that infamous wholesaler of cadavers to the surgeons of early nineteenth-century Edinburgh, the same Burke who now has an honored place in Madame Tussaud's Chamber of Horrors. It was not Edmund, the philosopher-politician of the latter half of the eighteenth century, who has no place in the wax museum in Marylebone Road at all. The Mill I have an interest in burking is not the famous John Stuart but his somewhat less famous father, James. (I suppose it should be noted that neither Mill is honored with an effigy in Tussaud's.)

I shall construct a series of arguments that are not dependent upon or derivative of Burke's account of representation, though they were provoked and inspired by Burke, arguments that I find persuasive against a Millian delegate theory. I do not wholeheartedly share many of Burke's foundational political views, but I hope to provide some strong reasons for adopting a position on legislative style that is clearly Burkean and that may also lend some credibility to a possible interpretation of Burke's most controversial views on government.

II

In the *Second Treatise of Government*, John Locke writes of a legislature as being a "fiduciary power to act for certain ends."[1] He maintains that insofar as the government is representative, legislators should in some way be bound to the will of their constituents. His

7

reason for holding this view is, though rather paradoxically I think, based on the principle that no one has the power to place himself under the "Absolute Will and arbitrary Dominion of another."[2] This law of self-preservation dictates, Locke seems to think, that legislators act only as agents of the "Power of the People," representing the people by making their will present in the legislative process, and are to be held accountable to the people as any fiduciary would normally be held accountable to his principal. Locke adds that "the Community perpetually retains a Supream Power of saving themselves from the attempts and designs of any Body, even of their legislators, whenever they shall be so foolish, or so wicked as to lay and carry on designs against the Liberties and Properties of the Subject."[3] For Locke, this fiduciary relationship is the cornerstone of the doctrine of the supremacy of the legislative branch of government. If the legislature is directly accountable to the electorate, and the right of self-preservation for each citizen is inalienable and nonnegotiable, then each citizen theoretically maintains control of his preservation by controlling his lawmaker so long as the legislature is the supreme governmental power. (This, of course, is pure fiction because the theory of popular sovereignty is also conjoined with a majority rule principle. Hence, not every citizen has control of his legislator; only those in the majority do. This point is not lost on Burke.) The supremacy of the legislature for Locke is provisional, being dependent upon its continued incorporation to the ends, if not the will, of *the people* in the matters it legislates.

It would be, I think, an injustice to Locke to characterize the fiduciary relationship he has in mind as being one of a "bound agent," as many of the populists would prefer it, rather than a "free agent." The power of the legislator and the scope of his actions clearly are to be limited by the ends of the people, but it is instructive that Locke uses the notion of trust to characterize the relationship, implying a form of free agency. What Locke intended with respect to type of agency is not settleable for, unfortunately, Locke does not comment on the subject of instructions. Nonetheless, it seems from what Locke says about removal and the like that he would not have treated the legislator as bound on particular issues to the instructions of the majority of his constituents. The ends of the people set the parameters on legislative behavior but the people are not given the effective power to dictate specific legislative actions.

III

In his *Essay on Government*,[4] James Mill, after restating the Benthamite's creed that the only true end of government is the attainment of the greatest happiness for the greatest number of people (which for him was the great and growing middle class), argues that only a fully representative system can achieve that end. Obviously, government cannot be democratic in the classical sense, Mill allows, because "the people as a body cannot perform the business of government for themselves"; hence, the "goodness of government" depends upon "the right constitution of checks" that assures the identification of the people's happiness with the legislator's decisions. The legislator "must have an identity of interest with the community." How is that identity to be ensured? "If things were so arranged that, in his capacity of representative, it would be impossible for him to do himself so much good by misgovernment as he would do himself harm in his capacity of member of the community, the object would be accomplished."[5]

The legislator is to be seen then as having two aspects, that of representative, able to wield a certain amount of power, and that of common citizen, liable to be the victim of the misuse of legislative power. The power that is to be placed in the legislature is essential to guard against usurpations and other forms of malfeasance that might be practiced by the executive or the judiciary. There is a critical point beyond which that power ought not to be limited, for to limit it so as to ensure no legislative misgovernment is likely also to render it so weak as to destroy its capacity to check other government activities. If, Mill reasons, the amount of legislative power ought not to be diminished, then the only way to ensure the utilitarian ends of government is to limit the duration of the period of time anyone can exercise that power:

> The smaller the period of time during which any man retains his capacity of representative, as compared with the time in which he is simply a member of the community, the more difficult it will be to compensate the sacrifice of the interests of the longer period by the profits of misgovernment during the shorter.[6]

Mill, however, recognized that limiting the duration of legislative service is inadequate to fully ensure that the greatest happiness of the majority will be promoted unless there is "a conformity between the conduct of the representatives and the will of those who appoint them,"[7] and then only if those who appoint them, the electors, are themselves fully representative of the people. What could be more representative than full enfranchisement and a mandated legislator?

Millian legislators are to see themselves as delegates or ambassadors of their electors. Should they stray from the path of representation of the will of the electors, they can expect to be turned out of office in the very near future. Either they promote the interests of the majority of the electors—as the majority understands their own interests—or they will have to seek another line of work. De facto, the Millian delegate binds himself to the instructions of his constituents. He willfully accepts mandate. He represents the majority by translating their will into legislative votes. The whole system in its pure form is most appealing; it is unfortunate that it is morally flawed.

IV

One flaw in any delegate theory of representation is, as Burke noted, that it robs the legislator of his judgment. It makes his rationality subservient to the "collective will" of the majority of his constituents. By doing so, it obligates the legislator to sacrifice his autonomy, what many philosophers regard as a condition of his moral responsibility. As is well known, according to some philosophers, Robert Paul Wolff in particular,[8] freely sacrificing autonomy is tantamount to failing intentionally to meet a fundamental moral obligation. Such a view is, of course, at heart Kantian: "Man . . . is subject only to his own, yet universal, legislation, and . . . is only bound to act in accordance with his own will, which is, however, designed by nature to be a will giving universal laws."[9]

The principle of autonomy is the cornerstone of the Kantian concept of the kingdom of ends. Kant likely, and Wolff without doubt, would regard the Millian delegate doctrine as heteronomous and, hence, as an affront to the moral dignity of the legislators.

I do not want to rehearse the familiar Kantian (or Wolffian) arguments for the moral necessity of autonomy. Pressed too hard, as Wolff does, they can appear to erode the very basis of government itself. In anarchy, representation is not a concern. Wolff's insistence that all "political obedience is heteronomy of the will" is too extravagant an indictment upon which to attack Mill. It has just not been shown that autonomy and authority are exclusive notions. Even Wolff recognizes that in a direct or perfect democracy in which a single negative vote constitutes a veto, autonomy and political authority would be compatible.[10] That particular system, however, is an artificial construct set up as but a straw man for Wolff's anarchistic arguments and is certainly not of interest here. It is clear that the delegate-legislator is supposed to be heteronomously obedient to the will of the electorate. He is expected to follow the instructions of the majority of his constituents, to regard his own judgment and will as secondary to that of his electors, and, hence, to preserve popular democracy. Having noted that, I do not, however, wish to pursue the difficulties in pressing the autonomy obligation against the delegate theory. It is too much of a double-edged sword to be effective.

V

Burke had occasion to express his theory of representation in his famous speech to the electors of Bristol on November 3, 1774. Bristol was a popular constituency, not a rotten borough, and had a long tradition of instructing its representatives in Parliament. Henry Cruger, the other member elected that day, had preceded Burke to the podium and had assured the electors that he would, following custom, regard all of their instructions as authoritative over his votes. Burke began by clarifying an important distinction. He agreed that he would, in all cases, prefer the interests of the Bristol electors over his own interests. However, preference of interests is not to be confused with sacrificing judgment to instructions. "Your representative owes you, not his industry only, but his judgment; and he betrays, instead of serving you, if he sacrifices it to your opinion."[11] Underlying this distinction is Burke's most fundamental conception of government as a matter of judgment rather than of will. Justice, for Burke, is a substantive, not a procedural, issue. Amicable resolution of a clash of wills is no guarantee of the moral defensibility of the political actions undertaken.

The authoritative instructions view directs the legislator to ignore his or her own convictions, judgments, and dictates of conscience when they are not identical to the opinions of the constituents. Such a doctrine robs the legislator of his autonomy in the very enterprise in which he most needs to exercise rational skills. The process of representative legislation is a deliberative process, a matter "of reason and judgment" that proceeds by discussion and decision-making. Burke argues: "What sort of reason is that in which the determination precedes the discussion, in which one set of men deliberate and another decide?"[12] Burke's comments draw attention to an often ignored though basic difference between the delegate and trustee theory. As we suggested above, the delegate theory assumes that government is primarily, if not solely, a matter of will and interests, while the trustee theory presupposes that successful and morally justifiable government must be a matter of judgment and wisdom. If Burke is right in his analysis of government, if there is truth to be found in political or moral-politico matters, then moral wisdom and what may be called, after Hilary Putnam, moral skill are the virtues of good governmental service.[13] To rob the government official of his exercise of judgment is not only to offend his dignity, it is to disservice the governed as well as to allow opinion to supplant reasoned decision-making concerning the morally acceptable political means and ends. If government is solely to be a matter of battering out compromises among conflicting interests and wills, then the delegate theory is the more attractive of the two, for the will of the people is therein of primary interest, with the legislative process conceived as the distillery of the general will on all political matters. I shall not here enter again into the dispute about whether or not moral issues, and hence most political issues, are resolvable on substantive rather than procedural grounds. As I have written elsewhere,[14] I think that by and large they are. It does, however, seem to me to follow that if moral resolutions of political matters are to be found, if there are morally right answers even in hard cases, then we are morally obligated to discover them. Therefore, the dispute on representation reduces to a question of the moral justification of that principle of popular democracy that may be characterized as the denial that morally correct governmental decisions are to be preferred to others that just happen to be reached by democratic means. I cannot see how such a denial can be morally justified.

Perhaps it should be noted in passing that Burke, in a Parliamentary speech, argued against a bill that would have actualized the Millian solution by making elections more frequent.[15] The electors' opinions are, he often allowed, to be given frequent and serious consideration; they are to be regarded as data to be shifted and computed in decision-making. But frequent elections, contrary to the Millian expectation, Burke maintained, will not necessarily combat legislative corruption. Also, Burke slyly pointed out, there is no denying that the electors are themselves corruptible. They are easily confused or seduced by politicians to misinterpret their own interests. (One imagines that Burke would have been particularly smug had he been a witness to the American presidential elections of the sixties and seventies.)

VI

As I suggested earlier, some might regard the principle of autonomy as providing the strongest argument against the delegate theory. Yet there is another way to consider the issue that also conveniently sidesteps Kantian commitments while focusing on the legislator and not on a theory of government, a way that concentrates on some of our basic convictions about the relationship between intentionality and accountability. Although the determination of intentionality is a factual issue, a generally accepted precept of morality is that a person can be held accountable for only and for all of that person's intentional acts.[16] One is morally responsible, we may say, only for those aspects of one's behavior for which there are true descriptions of what one did that says one did those things intentionally. William Wollaston nicely captures this principle when he writes:

> That act, which may be denominated morally good or evil, must be the act of a being capable of distinguishing, choosing, and acting for himself: or more briefly, of an intelligent and free agent. Because in proper speaking no act at all can be ascribed to that which is not endued with these capacities.[17]

Consider whether the votes of a delegate-legislator are properly ascribed as acts of that person. Two features of intentionality are crucial. Although intentionality clearly is a causal notion, it is an intensional one. It, therefore, does not mark off a class of events.

Furthermore, attributions of intentionality, in regard to any event, are referentially or semantically opaque with respect to other possible true descriptions of the same event. The fact that on one description of an event an action was intentional does not entail that on every other description it was also intentional. To use an example borrowed from Donald Davidson: We can correctly say that Hamlet intentionally killed the person hiding behind the arras in his mother's room, but it would be incorrect to say that he intentionally killed Polonius, even though Polonius, as it happened, was the person hiding behind the arras. It was not Hamlet's intention to kill Polonius. He thought he was dispatching the king. The event may be properly described by saying that "Hamlet killed Polonius," and also by saying that "Hamlet intentionally killed the person hiding behind the arras." But it would be false to say that "Hamlet intended to kill Polonius."[18] The referential opacity of intentionality ascriptions comes clearly into play if we apply the delegate theory to legislative voting.

Assuming that a particular legislator, call him L, is a Millian delegate of his constituents and that he cast a "nay" vote on a tax reform bill, the following should be true descriptions of what occurred:

L's body moved in some way (he pushed the "nay" button, or said "nay," or raised his hand, etc.).

L intended to push the "nay" button, or say "nay," or etc.

L's intention, however, was *not* (or at least was *not necessarily*) to vote against the tax reform bill.

L's intention was to represent the opinion of the majority of his constituents on this matter.

Hence:

L intentionally pushed the "nay" button;

L intentionally registered the opinion of his constituents; *but*

L did not intentionally vote against the tax reform bill.

L's intention is not to vote against tax reform; it is to register faithfully the opinion of his constituents even though to do so he must intentionally press the "nay" button.

If we apply the accountability (or responsibility) rule previously discussed, we should say that the legislator can be held morally responsible or accountable only for those aspects of the event of his pushing the "nay" button, redescribed in such a way that they make true sentences that say he did those things intentionally. Wollaston again captures this point:

> For that, which . . . has not the opportunity or the liberty of choosing for itself, and acting accordingly from an internal principle, acts . . . under a necessity *ab extra*.[19]

And he adds:

> But that, which acts thus, is in reality only an instrument in the hand of something which imposes the necessity, and cannot properly be said *to act*, but *to be acted*. The act must be the act of an agent: therefore not of his instrument. A being under the abovementioned inabilities, as to the morality of its acts, . . . can be but a machine (in our case a voting machine PAF): to which no language or philosophy ever ascribed . . . *mores*.[20]

The semantic opacity of intentionality ascriptions should shield the delegate from moral responsibility for the other aspects of the event when, for example, it is redescribed as a vote against tax reform. What L did intentionally was to register the vote of his electors. He may not at all share their views, and, even if he does, his delegatory act is not properly described as intentionally voting against tax reform. The delegate ought then only to be held responsible for the perfect translation of the poll of his constituency into a registered response on the question before the assembly. It seems rather straightforward, but of course it is not. Even though we seem to be able to drive in an intentionality wedge between different descriptions of the delegate's actions, the gap created is forced closed by application of other aspects of the common notion of accountability.

VII

The simple accountability rule utilized above is *too* simple. It captures many but not all of our intuitions about the relationship between intentionality and accountability. As a matter of fact, we at times hold people morally responsible for some of the unintended aspects of their actions, or the unintended effects they produce. We generally, for example, hold people accountable for acts of negligence, and that is because we regard most episodes of negligence as collaterally or obliquely intended. Hence, it is often maintained that if a person is relatively certain that if he does something an untoward event will occur, and even if he did not directly intend to bring about that result, if he still performs the causally efficacious antecedent act and the event does occur, he is said to have collaterally or obliquely intended that untoward outcome and so, *ceteris paribus*, can be held morally accountable for it. If our legislator L, the delegate, is relatively certain that if he votes as instructed by his constituents the result will be the passage of a measure that cannot be morally justified, that will have seriously untoward effects, and if he still votes as instructed, he can be said to have obliquely intended that result. And so, he may be held morally responsible for its occurrence. But doing so violates the principles that underly the delegate theory, for it implies that if L is relatively certain that voting as instructed will have untoward results, and if he votes as instructed, he can be held morally accountable for them and therefore should not vote as instructed. Furthermore, it suggests that the legislator ought to investigate the probable results of his casting a yea or nay vote on any particular issue regardless of the poll of his constituents. If L does investigate the probable outcome, he likely knows more of the situation than his electors and, hence, should rightly be regarded as more responsible than his constituents because he is clearly negligent (if not outrightly wicked) should he follow instructions and vote in a way that will likely be productive of unjust results. If, on the other hand, L steadfastly avoids investigating the probable results of his votes, he would be regarded as, at best, thoughtless and, more likely, as negligent for acting out of self-imposed ignorance. Expansion of accountability via collateral or oblique intention would seem to capture the delegate, even if it is true that he did not directly intend, for example, to defeat the tax reform measure when he pressed the "nay" button.

It may, however, be argued, along lines suggested by Mackie,[21] that the delegate-legislator ought not to be held accountable for the untoward outcome of his voting as instructed but only for his negligence in not voting in a different way when he was relatively certain those results would occur. This kind of argument may be quite persuasive when it is made in the case of dangerous or drunken driving that causes death. Negligent driving, whether or not causing death, is that for which one probably should be held responsible rather than the unintended causing of a death; otherwise, as Mackie writes: "mere chance may make a great difference in the treatment of two people who are equally negligent, . . . but it just happens that someone gets in the way of one but not of the other."[22] The negligence of the delegate-legislator, however, is not so easily divorced from the untoward outcome of his voting as instructed when he knows that doing so will probably have those effects, for the negligence of the delegate-legislator is built into that concept of representation. Not to allow oneself to be negligent, to let one's knowledge or well-founded belief that voting as instructed will have a morally unacceptable outcome affect one's pushing of the voting buttons is not to be a delegate.

VIII

The gap that was necessary to protect the moral status of the delegate-legislator is also closed by yet another common revision of the straight intentionality-accountability equation. The delegate conception of representation is, in effect, a kind of two-agent performance. It is not an action in which the represented is present in the act of representation except, of course, in some wholly symbolic way. Actually it is better to think of the action of the representative as provoked or caused or stimulated by the action(s) of the represented and thereby as a two-person performance. (The delegate is like the corporate agent whose actions are stimulated by corporate executive actions and who is therefore but an extension of the corporation.) Of course, the majority of the constituents are not a single person, but they may be treated as an aggregated collective or sum-individual whose collective action conjoined with that of the legislator constitutes the delegate vote. In a perfect delegate system, one might imagine that the two-agent performance will be such that the delegate's action is always a rather automatic and hence perfectly predictable response to the constituents' action. Normally we would regard the responsibility for the delegate's action—for example, voting against the tax reform bill—to fall back on the sum-individual, that is, the electorate, by reason of collateral or oblique intention of second effects. However, we also recognize in matters of agency that if the second agent, the delegate, should have or did know that the outcome would be morally unacceptable, and if he could have done something other than what he did that would have had a morally acceptable outcome, then he must share the responsibility; indeed, he may be held primarily accountable for the event caused. The only catch with this sort of analysis, one that may at first appeal to the delegate theorist, is that, as Mackie suggests,[23] historically the more automatic the response of the second agent, the more the responsibility is to be referred back to the first agent. However, this will not really help the delegate theorist, for if he wants to argue that the legislator ought to commit himself to automatically respond to the instructions of the majority of his constituents, he cannot assume that automatism is the case. And, insofar as the legislator does have the choice of voting as instructed or voting according to his own lights, no matter what the theorist tells him he should do, accountability should be shared or even fall more upon the legislator than upon his constituency. Of course, we need only remind ourselves that the more automatic the representative's actions become, the less of a moral agent he becomes, the more of an instrument, the more of a means only to the ends of others. (And it might well be asked whether willfully enslaving oneself can ever be morally justified.)

IX

A crucial mistake often invades would-be Burkean accounts of the trustee legislator and appears to strengthen defenses of the delegate theory: it is that of failing to distinguish between what may be called legislative style and legislative focus. Burke talks in his speech to the Bristol electors (and elsewhere) as if the trustee must always focus his legislative activity upon the interests of the society at large and away from his borough. He told them:

> Parliament is a *deliberative assembly* of *one* nation, with one interest, that of the whole—where not local purposes, not local prejudices, ought to guide, but the general good. . . . You choose a member, indeed; but when

you have chosen him he is not a member of Bristol, but he is a member of *Parliament*.[24]

Burkean trusteeship, however, is not incompatible with an almost exclusive district focus. And the local district is not the only focus that may compete for the attention of the trustee. The interests of ethnic or racial groups that comprise only a minority of the persons in a district may sometimes be legitimately regarded by legislators as their primary focus. The real issue that underlies the confusion of style with focus hides in the Burkean concept of representation itself. It is usually assumed by political theorists that the representative must represent some persons or group of persons or the legislator is not representing at all. (Some would say that that is contained in the very notion of representation.)[25] But that assumption is dependent upon the theory of government as a clash of wills rather than as an attempt to make and carry out judgments about the good and just for society (the will/wisdom dispute mentioned earlier).

Burke, who takes the side of wisdom over will, nonetheless recognizes that "representative" would be a misnomer unless the legislator represented something. In so far as legislators do not (or ought not) uncritically adopt the opinions of their constituents or any other people *per se*, Burke argues that they are to be seen as representing interests. By "interests" he means abstracted types of human endeavor—the farming interests, the mercantile interests, the banking interests, and so forth. Hence, he argues that representation crisscrosses boroughs. And he thereby scandalizes modern popular democrats by talking about virtual as opposed to actual representation. The idea is that, for example, the interests of the blacks of Birmingham, Alabama, may be virtually represented by a senator from Michigan though not actually represented by him. Virtual representation, of course, as Hanna Pitkin observed,[26] has the virtue of always, tautologically, being good representation. If the senator does virtually represent the interests of blacks then he indeed represents those interests. If he does not represent those interests, he does not virtually represent them either. Actual representation may vary in quality as concerns the interests of the majority of people in the district. But here the distinction between focus and style is to be most clearly drawn. Focus is a substantive question, style is not, and, for Burke, representation is a matter of substance, of content. It ought to be the representation of what Pitkin calls "unattached interests,"[27] not people. The interests represented by the legislator constitute his focus, and insofar as representing such interests does not compromise the autonomy of the legislator by making him subservient to the will of others, no question of style is involved. The argument that the trustee theory is no theory of representation must define representation in terms of wills, wishes, and opinions, in terms of people; and that is the real bone of contention.

X

The Burkean conception of government by judgment can only be successful if the powers of legislation are in the hands of those best suited to make well-reasoned and morally justifiable decisions. To the casual reader of Burke, it may appear odd to find that many contemporary legislators embrace the Burkean conception of representation. *The Official Guidebook for Ohio Legislators*, for example, quotes Burke's Bristol speech with approval and adds that:

> The pressures of the legislative arena, the need for rapid decisions, the difficulties the legislator is likely to encounter when sampling the views of his constituents, and the technicalities associated with proposals he must consider, require him to rely extensively on his own perception of the merits of the matter under consideration.[28]

The practical concerns aside, the adoption of a Burkean position by proclaimed democrats is difficult to reconcile. After all, Burke's representation doctrine, as is well known, is but a corollary to his championing of a natural aristocracy as the only way to ensure good government.

The natural aristocracy doctrine is clearly consistent with the commitment to the autonomy of the legislator, and, for Burke, the wisdom necessary to legislate could only reside in the traditional landed aristocracy of his time.[29] But, if the natural aristocracy doctrine, as Burke understood it, is necessarily entailed by trusteeship, then we might have to put aside the earlier arguments endorsing it against the delegate theory. For surely, elitism, especially as defined in terms of inherited wealth, is morally suspect. Even Rawls, however, has shown that trusteeship need not be unjust.[30] Of course, we must forego the commitment to a ruling elite of the leisure class despite Burke's eloquence when describing its virtues. That does not, however, mean that we should not insist that legislative offices be placed in the hands of those in the society who have superior political wisdom, decision-making abilities, and practical and moral reasoning capacities rather than in the hands of those whose only claim on the office is their popularity with the masses.[31]

Trusteeship in itself does not deny the principle of fair opportunity, but if the trustee is to be a good legislator, on the Burkean ideal, then that principle will be denied. Wisdom and judgmental ability are not characteristics of all persons. Hence, some people will be excluded from legislative positions if those characteristics are treated as qualifications for office. Even when all persons of like ability, regardless of social rank, are included in the class of potential trustees, the principle of fair opportunity is denied. As Rawls points out, however:

> To be consistent with the priority of fair opportunity over the difference principle it is not enough to argue . . . that the whole of society including the least favored benefit. . . . We must also claim that the attempt to eliminate these inequalities would so interfere with the social system and the operations of the economy that in the long run anyway the opportunities of the disadvantaged would be even more limited.[32]

Burke, of course, argues only that the natural aristocracy benefits the whole of society. But he could have argued, within Rawls' framework, that the relevant condition is also met. Again, however, the argument must be based on the more fundamental commitment to the wisdom over the will conception of legislative government. Defense of that commitment is a task for another time.

Notes

1. John Locke, *Two Treatises of Government* (1690): *Second Treatise*, ch. 13, sec. 149.
2. *Ibid.*
3. *Ibid.*
4. James Mill, *An Essay on Government* (1820).
5. *Ibid.*, sec. 7.
6. *Ibid.*

7. *Ibid.*, sec. 8.

8. Robert Paul Wolff, *In Defense of Anarchism* (New York: Harper and Row, 1970). See also Wolff's "On Violence," *Journal of Philosophy* 56, no. 19 (Oct. 2, 1969): 601–16.

9. Immanuel Kant, *Foundations of the Metaphysics of Morals,* trans. Lewis W. Beck (Indianapolis: Bobbs-Merrill, 1969), sec. 2.

10. Wolff, *In Defense of Anarchism,* p. 22.

11. Edmund Burke, *Works,* (Boston: Little, Brown, 1865), vol. 2, p. 95.

12. *Ibid.*, pp. 95–96.

13. See Hilary Putnam, *Meaning and the Moral Sciences* (London: Routledge and Kegan Paul, 1978), especially lectures 5 and 6 and part 2.

14. *Ethics in Government:* (Englewood Cliffs, N.J.: Prentice-Hall, 1981). See also my *The Scope of Morality* (Minneapolis: University of Minnesota Press, 1979).

15. Burke, *Works,* vol. 7, pp. 71–87.

16. See my *The Scope of Morality,* ch. 1, and J. L. Mackie, *Ethics: Inventing Right and Wrong* (Hammondsworth: Penguin Books, 1977), p. 208. Mackie refers to this as the straight rule of responsibility.

17. William Wollaston, *The Religion of Nature Delineated* (1724), sec. 1.

18. Donald Davidson, "Agency," in *Agent, Action, and Reason,* ed. R. Binkley, R. Bronaugh, and A. Marras (Toronto: University of Toronto Press, 1971) pp. 3–25.

19. Wollaston, *Religion of Nature Delineated,* sec. 1.

20. *Ibid.*

21. Mackie, *Ethics,* pp. 208–15. He is not, however, interested in the representation question.

22. *Ibid.*, pp. 211–12.

23. *Ibid.*, p. 164.

24. Burke, *Works,* vol. 11, p. 96.

25. See Hanna F. Pitkin, *The Concept of Representation* (Berkeley: University of California Press, 1967).

26. *Ibid.*, pp. 175–76.

27. *Ibid.*, chap. 8.

28. Ohio Legislative Service Commission, *A Guidebook for Ohio Legislators* (Columbus, Ohio: The Commission, 1970), p. 72.

29. Edmund Burke, *An Appeal from the New to the Old Whigs* (1791).

30. John Rawls, *A Theory of Justice* (Cambridge: Harvard University Press, 1971), pp. 300–301.

31. An appeal of this sort has recently been made by Edmund Beard in "Conflict of Interest and Public Service," *Ethics, Free Enterprise, and Public Policy,* ed. R. de George and J. Pichler (Oxford: Oxford University Press, 1978), pp. 232–47.

32. Rawls, *Theory of Justice,* pp. 300–301.

GERALD C. MacCALLUM, JR.

2 The Extent to Which Legislators Should Serve Their Consciences or Their Constituents

Speaking for myself, the interest attaching to this topic emerges when we understand the word "or" in the above formulation as an exclusive "or," and we are on this understanding thus being asked to make a genuine and possibly a hard choice. On this understanding, we may put out of our minds any happy speculations about having it both ways. For example, we might otherwise have been attracted by the thought that many, if not most, legislators serve their consciences *by* serving their constituents. But having excluded this possibility from the cases we are considering, we must think very carefully about the conditions of conflict among the two options. We are viewing ourselves as being asked to consider situations in which a legislator cannot, on the same occasion and in every respect, both serve conscience and serve constituents. Either the legislator may serve each on each of these occasions, but less than completely, and that because the other is being served at least partially; or there is a series of situations on some of which conscience is being served to the exclusion of serving constituents, while on others the constituents are being served to the exclusion of serving conscience.

In the above formulation of the topic, the word "should" need not be understood as having only moral import. But it probably ought to be understood to have at least some moral import, and that is the

I should like to thank Susan Feagin, my wife, for considerable substantive as well as logistic help with this paper.

23

understanding that most interests me. I shall consequently, after an initial discussion of the difficulty of coming up with good examples of what we are talking about, organize my discussion of the topic around two questions: Have legislators a moral obligation to serve their consciences? And have legislators a moral obligation to serve their constituents?

I. Finding Examples

One of my colleagues from whom I have learned a great deal stresses the value in philosophy of working through cases of what one is discussing as substantial as one can find or imagine. I have tried to do that here. But I have not been able to find or imagine any substantial worthy, clear, and unequivocal cases. Perhaps that is mostly because I have set three limitations upon any possible worthy examples. I believe that these limitations are reasonable, and I am willing to defend them.

The first limitation is that the presence of a conflict between service to conscience and service to constituents is in the perception and judgment of the legislator. It is easy to imagine that *I* may perceive a conflict between *your* efforts to serve *your* conscience and service to *your* constituents. For example, I may perceive that your refusal to support legislation permitting abortion or contraception is an effort to serve your conscience at the cost of substantial service to your constituents. It may then be possible and significant for me to discuss where the priorities should be placed between our tolerance and support of your efforts to serve your conscience and your probable duty to serve your constituents. But this discussion may not touch you at all because it is a discussion of a matter that you do not yet find relevant. You do not find it relevant because you are unconvinced that any sacrifice of genuine and long-range service to your constituents is involved. The discussion that might touch you is a discussion of that issue.

I should like here to engage in a discussion that *legislators* find relevant, and the limitation above contributes to this end. The aim, therefore, will be to address legislators asking the question, "What shall I do?" rather than address persons examining the behavior of legislators and asking "What shall we do about them?"

When we look closely at the matter from this perspective, we may see that a great deal depends upon how the apparent conflict arises. The appearance of a conflict surely is a time for careful examination, but what seems clearest after examination? That a particular course of action is contrary to the legislator's conscience or that it will serve his or her constituents? If what seems clearest is that it will do one of these things, but not so clearly the other—a situation probably most common—then sharp questioning will and probably should be given by the legislator to whether it will do the other at all. (I do not, however, mean to suggest that what seems clearest does not need examination.) If what seems clearest is that the action is contrary to his or her conscience, then what the legislator will and should more sharply question than had been the case previously is whether the action will, in fact, serve the constituents, and contrariwise if the service of the action to constituents seems clearest. What is happening here is that a special burden of more careful questioning is being placed in one direction or the other because of the situation. There is nothing extraordinary or untoward about this. We do not like to make sacrifices and, when we have come to believe that they are imminent, we press especially hard on that portion of our conclusion that seems most dubious. The fact that an action is clearly contrary to their carefully formed consciences (see below) is taken by our legislators to be reason to doubt whether the action will genuinely, and in the long run, benefit their constituents. Contrariwise, legislators tend to take the fact that an action will clearly and genuinely serve their constituents to be reason to doubt whether that action *is* contrary to a carefully formed and informed conscience. In the end, I should think that as objective third parties we should not be offended if our legislators go with what seems clearest to them after all this questioning.

It is a matter of relative clarities. The clarities, however, may be equal. It is certainly not impossible that there actually be a conflict, and the legislators should take this possibility seriously. It is merely that I have been unable to come up with substantial actual or imagined cases where this is clearly so, where it is plausibly equally clear to legislators that a particular act will both serve constituents and be contrary to their own carefully formed consciences. Our discussion will probably provide some such cases.[1]

The second limitation is that the service to the constituents be "in the long run" and "on the whole." My intention is to exclude cases in which the service to constituents is admittedly only "in part" or "in some respect," and is also admittedly not "on the whole" or "in the long run." I wish to exclude these latter cases because they are resolvable simply in terms of what service to constituents amounts to and whether we should prefer long-run service and service on the whole to short-run and partial service that is neither of the former. It may be the case that there are conflicts between service to a legislator's conscience and partial service to constituents that is only short-run or "in some respect." But these cases raise no conflict irresolvable within terms solely of what services to constituents are preferable. If we want to reach the difficulties peculiar to our topic, we will therefore not pause to consider these cases. For example, we will not pause to consider a case where the public demands the dropping of an atomic bomb on some foreign territory, and where the legislator for one reason or another finds that support of this project is contrary to conscience, but is *also* quite willing to agree that dropping the bomb would be contrary to the long-range interests of the public. (Parenthetically, we should note that the long-range interests of the public do not include their interest in such things as salvation in the hereafter. Because of the separation of church and state in the American political tradition, such considerations are, for at least American legislators, beyond the bounds of legitimate consideration.)

The third limitation is that the conscience to which service is being contemplated belongs to a person who admits, at least on this occasion, the relevance of concern for whether the conscience is correct and is being correctly understood. This limitation will be discussed more fully below where we consider whether legislators have a moral obligation to serve conscience. For the present, we should note that it does not mean that the legislator must *in fact* inquire into the correctness of his or her conscience, though it does demand that the relevance of such inquiries be admitted. One wonders how else in modern times service to "conscience" can be given any moral force at all. We do not have moral grounds for giving any consideration at all to a legislator allegedly trying to serve conscience who will give no consideration whatever to any challenges to whether that conscience is correctly informed. Note, it is not being claimed that the legislator must *defend* the conscience at all, let alone defend it to our or anybody else's satisfaction. The legislator may have feelings of the appropriate sort for which he or she cannot articulate reasons. The limitation is only that he or she should be willing to admit as relevant and, let us say, listen to at least some conceivable arguments or evidence to the effect that the conscience might be mistaken or misunderstood. He or she need not be willing to listen to any and every purported argument or piece of evidence that comes along, but he or she cannot refuse to listen to any conceivable argument or evidence. Substantial cases where this limitation is not observed are easy to imagine. For example, a legislator unwilling to consider any inquiry into the possible rightness or wrongness of his or her conscience and treating the conscience as something of which he or she is an unfortunate and helpless victim would be able to claim that support of desegregation would be contrary to that conscience while freely admitting that desegregation would be a service to the public because desegregation would be both just and politically astute. We should, however, note that it is precisely the treatment of conscience as something of which he or she is a helpless victim that frees the legislator to make the latter admission easily and clearly. If it were not for the "helpless victim" posture, I do not see that the latter admission could come either clearly or easily.

In sum, I have placed three limitations on examples, each with what I think to be good reason. First, the conflict between service to conscience and service to constituents must be in the view of the legislator because I am trying to address the legislator's problems. Second, the imagined service to constituents must be "on the whole" and "in the long run" because the conflict we seek must be clear and hard and thus not resolvable by appeal to the concept of genuine service to constituents alone. Third, the conscience appealed to must be one whose rightness or wrongness the conscience-holder believes to be relevant to the resolution of the conflict because without this limitation, the appeal to conscience can have no moral force.

II. Have Legislators a Moral Obligation to Serve Conscience?

Appeals to conscience, as just suggested, have often served as argument-stoppers. They have been used by persons who do not wish to defend their positions any further. We have tolerated such appeals in the past perhaps because they have found shelter under a tradition of religious toleration in a history of religious conflict. Religion itself is often a matter of conscience. Secularly, the leading idea is that, as we came ultimately to believe about religion, conscience is something private and highly personal. But toleration of argument-stopping appeals to conscience has been a mistake, and this can be shown if one reflects briefly on what conscience *is*.

Conscience has, in recent years, been denigrated with respect to its moral importance by being "psychologized." The psychologizing of conscience has underwritten attacks on the moral force of conscience by presenting conscience as merely a residue of one's personal psychological history. These attacks have been answered most persuasively, in my opinion, by viewing conscience as considered and responsible judgment of the moral qualities of one's acts, either retrospectively or prospectively. The persuasiveness of this view is supported by two considerations: First, attempts to sort out phenomenologically the promptings of conscience from internal twitches, whims, compulsions, prejudices, and hang-ups, and so forth, fix upon, rightly I believe, as one of the distinguishing marks of the promptings of conscience, a willingness not only to attach a certain importance to the views emerging from these promptings but also, connectedly, to recognize the relevance of inquiries into their rightness or wrongness. Second, when it comes to determining the *genuineness* of appeals to conscience (for they are often shelters for scoundrels or persons who are otherwise dissembling), a disinterest in what Hegel called "the test of truth" and a denial of its relevance are among the marks of non-genuineness.

If we adopt the understanding just offered, then our question becomes: Have legislators a moral obligation to act on their considered and responsible moral judgments, either retrospective or prospective? With this understanding of what we are inquiring into, we may avoid worries both about the moral force of conscience and about whether the authentic voice of conscience is being heard. But we will not avoid worries about erroneous or over-scrupulous consciences. The former have been sources of worry at least since the time of Aquinas, and we have worried about the latter at least since seventeenth-century England.

Something may seem to hang here on how one understands "serve conscience." If one understands this expression as mandating merely acting in accord with the dictates or "verdicts" of conscience (insofar as they point to the appropriateness of doing something in particular), there is still clearly a problem. If, however, one understands this expression as mandating action from some conception of what will benefit conscience, then the persistence of a problem may not seem so clear.

Have legislators a moral obligation to do as erroneous or over-scrupulous consciences may direct? In one respect, certainly not. Such consciences, though by hypothesis embodiments of considered and responsible efforts to determine the moral quality of actions either prospectively or retrospectively, are mistaken. The conclusions arrived at are wrong. Thus, if certain behavior is judged to be obligatory by such consciences, it may indeed be obligatory, but no thanks to the judgment that it is so. The judgment is *whether* the behavior is obligatory; it does not *make* the behavior obligatory.

In another respect, the situation is somewhat more complicated. Consider again what conscience is. We have considered it to be, whether erroneous or over-scrupulous or neither, a considered and responsible effort to determine something. In our tradition, we have achieved two rather nice things by giving such efforts some moral weight (note that I say *some* moral weight). First, we have given social support to such efforts. We have encouraged persons to take them seriously and to honor them. We do not thereby render them decisive, but we do not leave the judgment-makers dangling either. The efforts are not regarded as irrelevant in such a way that they can make no difference whatever if the judgment-maker gets the matter wrong. Second, we have relieved ourselves of the sticky problem of determining who are to be the authoritative second-guessers to the judgment-makers. Our hypotheses are that the judgments have been considered and responsible. If they are nevertheless wrong, then this will normally mean that the issue is somewhat complicated, and an issue on which persons will differ. This does not mean that no one will be right or wrong on the issue, but it does mean that its resolution may very well pose significant political problems, and that the moral autonomy of each of us will be somewhat endangered by the setting up of public authorities whose decisions on such matters will be final and authoritative. We thus, to preserve what moral and political autonomy we can, give moral as well as political weight to conscience. We show this by the way we treat people who, in our opinion, get it wrong. We let them off the hook both politically and morally where we feel we can, and we mitigate whatever penalties normally attach to what they did when the behavior is not conscience-directed.

Our first realization throughout should be that the persons whose consciences these are are not convinced that the consciences are mistaken. A question often raised in this connection is whether the persons have taken sufficient precautions to assure that the consciences are correct. Concerning this question, it would be popular and easy to say that many persons who have such consciences have not cared. As we have already noticed, it seems that they regard their consciences as private and personal things, and do not suppose that, so long as other people are not held to them, it matters. But this position is deficient on grounds already suggested as well as on one further ground in the instant case. Remembering that the persons being considered here are legislators presumably engaged in recognizably public business, the allegation that what is being considered is a purely private and personal affair is implausible. It thus is clear that these persons should, if they do not already, care about whether their consciences may be erroneous or over-scrupulous.

But it is also clear that their caring will not guarantee success, and we are then still left with the question of what we are to say and do. It depends upon what *they* are led to do. In terms of the overall problem posed by our topic, if they find that the directives of their consciences outweigh what are, in our view, their other moral obligations—for example, their obligations to constituents (see below)—they are to be congratulated for the effort they have taken, and the moral strength they may have shown in pursuing the dictates of their consciences, but they are not thereby to be allowed unhindered progress toward the achievement of their intended goals. As with civil disobedience, these are awkward positions for one to maintain simultaneously. The issue of whether they *can* be maintained simultaneously may require extended discussion. I believe they can.

An important question here is: What hindrances may be placed in the legislator's way? For it is a matter of no small importance to think what preventive or obstructive behavior here would be permissible. May we indulge in punishing the legislators, or merely in voting them out of office when we next have the opportunity to do so in cases where their conduct has been offensive to us in this way? The latter measure, that is, voting them out of office when we next have an opportunity to do so, may be understood occasionally as a form of punishment, but it is clearly to be distinguished from genuinely punishing them—putting the legislators in prison, for example, or fining them. No impartial person would object merely to voting them out of office. But, as already remarked, the question of punishing them raises issues similar to those raised by civil disobedience, and we may expect substantial disagreements to arise in these cases. As with civil disobedience, questions of motivation and intention bear some weight but do not settle the problem.

Concerning consciences that are neither erroneous nor over-scrupulous, I take it that there is no great problem. If such consciences determine that something is morally obligatory, then it *is* morally obligatory. But it is not morally obligatory because the conscience has determined it to be so. Rather, the conscience has determined it to be morally obligatory because it *is* morally obligatory. Note that we are not here talking about whether the moral obligation in question does or does not outweigh any possible obligation to serve constituents. We are talking only about the effects of conscience upon moral obligation.

III. Have Legislators a Moral Obligation to Serve Constituents?

The first thing to notice in examining whether legislators have a moral obligation to serve their constituents is that if legislators *believe* that they have such an obligation, then the conflict we are exploring will very likely be *within* conscience, rather than between conscience and something else. Such conflicts are, or should be (especially as conscience is characterized here), meat and potatoes to moral philosophers. They are nevertheless important here, and we shall touch on them. They give us, for one thing, an occasion to re-characterize the conflict in question. If it is to be treated as a conflict within conscience, then it might be best regarded as a conflict between some vision of moral obligations to constituents, and some vision of whatever moral obligation(s) one has that cannot be filled simultaneously with meeting the obligations to constituents. It is a matter of weighing the obligations on either side, something that must be done on a case-by-case basis.

Our overall topic, in the present formulation, has embedded in it certain presumptions concerning political arrangements. It is important to bring these to view so that we are certain to be aware of them and of their effects upon the way we treat the topic. The first appears in the use of the word "constituent." The relationships of legislators to the people subject to their legislation are various. When the people subject to this legislation are called "constituents," something rather special is being suggested. An open tyrant would not call citizens "constituents," except perhaps ironically. Constituents are thought of not only as persons subject to the legislation, but as persons for whose sake the legislation is made, and even more than this. The relationship being suggested is one in which the persons subject to the legislation are being in some way served by the legislators, and even *represented* by them. The concept of representation thus comes into play, and, as is commonly known, this is a complex matter. It is not so well understood as it might be, and there is room for much elasticity in our notions of what it involves. For the present, we need merely note that we can all imagine the relationships of legislators to subjects or citizens being different from this, and the fact that the relationship is to be one of representation is politically, socially, and morally significant, especially when one comes to consider the obligations of legislators.

Other things are embedded in our likely understanding of the problem. Because of our own political environment, we are perhaps quick to assume that the problem is formulated in a context involving more than one legislator. But it is quite possible, of course, to imagine a single legislator doing all the legislative work that is required or demanded. For example, consider Moses or Solon. The presence of more than one legislator raises the possibility that a legislator is assigned responsibility for representing fewer than the total number of persons for whom the legislation is being created—in short, that the legislator has as constituents a proper subclass of the total body of citizens subject to the legislation. Suppose that we have a collegiate legislature rather than a single legislator; the choice then is between supposing that each legislator represents each and every citizen of the whole community for which legislation is being created, and supposing that each legislator represents a proper subclass of the total body of the citizens. In the past we have not thought our way through this choice too well. If there are persons subject to the legislation who are not being represented by the legislator, then we have a moral problem (and a political problem) of somewhat different character than we would otherwise have. The question is whether the legislator legislates "over" persons whom he or she does not represent.

This is one aspect of larger problems about unborn generations of citizens and about non-citizens who may be affected by the legislation in question. The central trouble-making feature of these problems is whether a legislator serving his or her constituents will be a legislator serving fewer than all those persons for whom he or she legislates or who will feel the effects of that legislation. The legislator would not clearly be doing service to the latter though he or she may contingently achieve it in the sense of creating legislation that may benefit those other people though not intended for their sakes. No one expects legislators to legislate for the whole world or for all time. But we are discomfited by such matters from time to time.

The initial problem is obfuscated by the fact that legislators are, in our political environment, collegiate. Somehow, the confused and ill-thought-out idea prevails that if each person subject to the legislation is represented by someone among the legislators, then the resulting legislation can be, in every sense that we desire, for the sake of all persons subject to it. But there is no good reason to suppose that if each legislator faithfully executes the responsibility to serve his or her constituents, all the constituents individually or collectively will thereby have been served. This particular lack of clarity in our political tradition will emerge again as potentially important when we come to consider below the possibility that service to one's constituents will require behavior recognizably immoral.

Turn now to another presumption that may be operating undetectedly in our minds. Imagining our own political setting; we may suppose that the legislative work is being carried on in an environment also populated by a judiciary and an executive. These things, however, might be otherwise. It is conceivable either that the legislator performs also the functions we assign to executives and judiciaries, or that, as in some politically primitive societies, there are no distinct offices of these latter sorts. What we presume here will make a difference in our assignment of a range of legitimate tasks to the legislator, and will make a difference thus in the responsibilities that we assign to him or her. There may be limits on the way *legislators* may serve constituents. A legislator is perhaps not mandated to serve constituents in every way possible, but only in certain ways, presumed to follow from the status of being a legislator. Thus, for example, if one takes John Stuart Mill's view of the jobs of representatives, a view corresponding less well to the practices of American legislatures than to the practices of the British Parliament (but not thereby unnecessary to consider in connection with American institutions), then the way in which a legislator will seek to serve constituents is limited to controlling—that is to discussing, evaluating, and limiting—the making and executing of laws of the community with a view to the ways in which these laws do or do not express the interests of constituents. Such a person would not accurately be called a "legislator," but might nevertheless, in the profusion of theories of representation, come to be called so. Furthermore, in Mill's view the legislator is fit for this role primarily by virtue of his or her representative character, which in Mill's view means his or her status as a specimen or sample of what the constituents are like.

This view of the job of legislators has a profound effect upon our capacity to find the conflict we are seeking to understand. If legislators are to be representative of their constituents by virtue of being specimens or samples of those constituents, then the best way they can behave is by just "behaving naturally." That is to say it would be part of their appropriate behavior as representatives of their constituents to act on their consciences when their consciences directed them to do this or that. Presumably, as specimens or samples of constituents, they are to be considered together with their consciences as "representative." This means that their consciences and what these consciences may direct them to do are together part of what makes them samples or specimens. Thus they would be serving their constituents appropriately by giving expression to their consciences and the dictates of those consciences. Their special service to constituents would arise out of their status as specimens or samples of these constituents, and that status includes their having the consciences they have, with whatever directives those consciences provide. This is an illustration of the complications introduced to our topic by the varieties of theories of representation afloat in our political heritage. Obviously, our overall topic would have had little interest if Mill's were the only view of representation we take.

One further remark on "constituent." A constituent is a member, but not generally the only member, of a constituency. This fact, as Hanna Pitkin has pointed out, is of the utmost importance in understanding the concept of political representation. It means that political representation—unlike private representation, in which there is a relationship between a representative and a principal—cannot be understood as generating a responsibility discharged merely by the representative's doing what the person represented desires. In the case of public representation, the representative cannot even discharge his or her duty by doing what the majority of his or her constituents desires. The legislator must understand that even the members of any particular minority among the constituents must still be represented in the sense that their desires must be understood to be relevant and taken into consideration. What more is required is not easy to specify. Perhaps these people still have a hold on the representatives in the sense that they must somehow still be served. I can merely point to this problem, not resolve it.

Calling attention to the problem, however, usefully introduces the importance of close understanding of what it is to serve constituents. If serving one's constituents meant simply doing what they direct one to do, then the legislator probably would be called upon to do what he or she otherwise had a moral obligation not to do. But it seems more likely that serving one's constituents does not amount merely to following directives from them, but rather also, and sometimes conflictingly, to doing what will benefit them or further their interests, at least in the judgment of the legislator. In discussions of the matter, a dichotomy has often been posed between one of these construals and the other.

The latter construal is presented as dangerous because it threatens to disenfranchise the voter. It invites the legislator to ignore the voter's vote as indicating *directly* what should be done and to regard only some other conception, differently arrived at, of which actions would benefit or be to the interests of the voter. But the dichotomy providing a framework for the posing of this threat is an illusion.

Consider Tussman's caution that voters' directives to legislators cannot be so unequivocal and so clear that the legislators are called upon merely to follow the directives. Even where the voters speak loudly and clearly, which must be a rare thing indeed, they do not speak only once. That is, they want more than merely one thing and they tell the legislators about their wants for other things as well as for that on which they have spoken loudly and clearly. And the significance of their votes with respect to issues is most often highly indefinite. Thus, whatever directives they may be thought to deliver are at most, as Tussman says, like the sketches of a prospective house handed by the client of an architect to the architect. They merely suggest what is wanted, a suggestion that normally, even at its clearest, needs to be solidified and embodied by essentially creative work on the part of the architect. A legislator is given so many and such indefinite directions—possibly conflicting with each other— from the electorate (even considering only majorities), that substantial creative work remains to embody the accumulated directives in specific legislation. Of course, the legislation itself consists of a not purely unequivocal set of directions to administrators and administrative agencies. The latter also most often need to engage in considerable creative embodiment of directions given to them by legislatures. This problem surfaced abundantly in World War II, as well as in certain other crisis periods both before and after, where legislators sought to create, by means of broad legislative acts, merely some broad directions to administrators that were then supposed to be executed in a discretionary way by the latter. The question before the U.S. Supreme Court in this type of case is whether these directives are too broad to be valid pieces of legislation. This question has been raised in connection with legislation in diverse fields of law, for example, in criminal legislation. A common question there has been whether the legislatures have not tried to create something—for example, in vagrancy statutes—too broad to protect the constitutional rights of citizens.

So, it seems that with both legislators and administrators the sharp dichotomy between merely following the directions of those whose expressed wishes are supposed to be authoritative and doing something more creative that will serve the latter's interests and intentions is a false dichotomy. In receiving directives, legislators and administrators cannot normally avoid engaging in some considerable creative judgments concerning where the interests and intentions of voters and legislators (respectively) lie and how to further them. At the same time, they must be cautioned against forestalling the possibility that the "authorities" (voters or legislators) *can* make errors and should be permitted in accordance with our political ideology to make them. They must, in short, allow the "authorities" the right to risk making errors, and not forestall the exercise of this right by second-guessing.

It would be a mistake, I believe, to treat this overall problem on an issue-by-issue basis. Our legislators are said to be our representatives, and it is true that they bear the primary burden of representing us. But as Hanna Pitkin points out, they are acting in a governmental context of some complexity, and it must not be forgotten that the whole government is said to be a representative government. One implication of this fact is that other agencies of the government than the legislature bear some responsibility for the representativeness of representative government.

Also, legislators cannot deal with issues on an issue-by-issue basis, nor should we suppose that we can render a faithful account of their problems and challenges if we overlook that important fact about what they do. One result of considerations such as these just mentioned is to loosen the tightness of our fixed grasp upon the idea that legislators should always act in accordance with the wishes of their constituents when their constituents have specifiable wishes in connection with any particular matter. We should, as Pitkin suggests, ask only that the legislators be generally responsive to the wishes of their constituents in two senses: we should not normally expect them to act contrary to the wishes of the masses of their constituents when these wishes are easily knowable, and we may legitimately expect from them an account of their decisions when these decisions do appear to have been contrary to those easily knowable wishes, an account that explains how these decisions were arguably in the interests of the mass of their constituents.

The above view of what "service to constituents" amounts to, a view that currently prevails, offers many escape hatches from threatened conflict between service to constituents and service to conscience. To indicate the effects of the availability of those escape hatches, we need merely ask whether *you* believe that genuinely serving constituents' *long-range* interests or benefiting them "on the whole" can ever amount to carrying out, in their name, something that you believe to be immoral or unjust.

Plato would have answered a similar question with a resounding "no," but we need not. There are numerous conceptions of benefit and interests that are independent of moral considerations and thus may conceivably conflict with the latter. Thus, it is conceivable that attempts to serve one's constituents' interests, on this common view of what that must mean, may conflict with attempts to serve one's conscience. And this is even on the assumption that one's conscience is *not* outrageously erroneous or over-scrupulous. Still, you can doubtless sense the enormous strength of the tendency to suppose otherwise.

The likelihood of a clear conflict arising depends, as suggested earlier in this discussion, in part upon whom we identify as the legislator's constituents. If the legislator is, for example, serving an exclusive and wealthy suburb, and *only* the persons in that suburb are his or her constituents, then we may expect that serving them *may* amount to forwarding their interests by behavior that would be knowingly unfair to other persons in the general community for which the legislation is being adopted. You might test the situation by imagining yourself to be a constituent-resident of this legislator's district and telling this person to follow the dictates of his or her conscience whenever a conflict between those dictates and serving your interests appears to arise. It might be easy for you to imagine such a conflict if you were considering only your short-range and partial interests. But what about your long-range interests and your interests "on the whole"? Will you readily admit that a conflict between both serving the latter interests and serving your legislator's considered and responsible conscience can occur? An unequivocal answer to this question is essential to understanding the nature of the problem we are trying to confront.

In thinking about one further aspect of the question heading this section we might consider whether the status of a legislator-with-constituents carries with it a moral obligation to serve constituents at all. One could imagine such an obligation absent on grounds other than the ground that the service was immoral. Except possibly for the immorality of the service, however, the assumption that legislators have such an obligation is commonly made without question and, I believe, rightly so. One may, however, have assumed the status of legislator unwillingly, involuntarily, or inadvertently, and in that case the addition of moral obligations onto one's agenda may be unclear or nonexistent. This would be highly unusual and would require supposing rather bizarre circumstances to make it plausible. Nevertheless, the existence of the obligation we are discussing may still seem somewhat less than perfectly clear because, for example, apart from one's involuntary or inadvertent assumption of the status of legislator, the *regime* of law and government under which the legislator is working may not be totally acceptable. Indeed, it may be unacceptable in any of several ways. Legislators are normally only *part* of systems of law and government. The question of whether to cooperate with *that* regime of law or government, or *that* political system or scheme, may have no particularly clear answer. The regime may be or have become terribly unjust or disturbingly so. The formulation of the overall question given us may invite the bypassing of issues such as these, or seem to do so. For the question is not whether to serve the regime but whether to serve one's constituents. The problem then becomes whether serving one's constituents *simpliciter* can lead to immoral behavior, as certainly one imagines that serving a political system, scheme, government, or law or serving constituents *within* and in terms of such a system, and so forth could do.

IV. Conclusion

Supposing that constituent interests could, in the considered opinion of a legislator, be benefited in the "long run" and "on the whole" by behavior sharply and clearly contrary to the considered and responsible conscience of the legislator, I think we should say that the legislator has no moral obligation to serve the constituents by trying to benefit them in this way. Legislators are responsible for doing many things besides considering and voting on legislation. Thus, the appropriate course of action for a legislator to take in this circumstance is not immediately clear. That course cannot be determined without considering the alternatives and those will vary with the activities in question. Sometimes a simple abstinence will be enough. Sometimes resignation will seem called for. Various alternatives may take personal strength and sacrifice, as well as sacrifice of opportunities to do further good. There may be a need to balance considerations of some delicacy here, and there is nothing automatic about it, nothing that can be settled by clear and helpful rules beforehand. What seems to be clear on these occasions is that we would not want our legislators to continue serving their constituents only at the price of their personal integrity. That is why we certainly must continue to offer outlets at least as drastic as protest and resignation. We should not demand of persons who are legislators that they continue to serve the public no matter what.

We must, of course, be perceptive concerning the stakes, and ingenious concerning the availability and costs of various alternatives. In evaluating the stakes, I suggest the following scales of evaluation: first, the relative weight of reasons on behalf of saying that either conscience or constituents are being served; second, the relative importance to conscience of the service to it, and to constituents of the service to them; third, the relative weights of the obligations to serve, respectively, conscience and constituents. I have not said anything helpful here about the last two scales or about interscale weighings, but the discussion is already too long. How one engages in these weighings is undeniably important, but is merely among the important matters that remain to be treated in connection with this topic.

Note

1. It did. The three cases brought forward shared the following characteristics: (a) there were victims of the immorality, (b) these victims were either foreign or non-citizen resident native populations, (c) they were helpless then and later to retaliate, and (d) they had no friends willing to retaliate then or later.

LISA H. NEWTON

3 Representation: The Duties of a Peculiar Station

The burden of this chapter is that the legislative representative in a large-scale pluralistic democracy labors under certain limitations—fundamentally moral limitations—that restrict the kinds of concerns that may figure in his decisions. The question is not so much, Where does my duty to my constitutents leave off and my duty to myself begin? as it is, What kinds of concern may I address without threatening either my constituents' integrity or my own? The answer I come up with will probably please neither supporters of participatory democracy nor supporters of moral idealism in government. Along the way, I hope to indicate the continuing usefulness of the notion of "role morality," Bradley's quaint "my station and its duties," in determining moral duty.

I

Recent years' concentration in the fields of applied ethics have given me an incurable preference for concreteness. I shall feel much better with an example, even a hypothetical example, to refer back to. Let us assume the following:

You are a congressional representative from a rural district in the Midwest. (I never use the East for my examples; I keep getting into personalities. And California is too unpredictable.) You are, by all ordinary criteria, an honest and conscientious person: you are not susceptible to simple bribery, and you honestly want to do what is right, whatever that may turn out to be, in the job of "representing" your constituents. A legislative choice is presently before you: a

41

surprising and substantial budgetary surplus has emerged from a computational error made by the Department of Agriculture, the only restriction on the use of this money being that it must be spent in rural districts, yours included. Three pieces of legislation to spend the money have been submitted: a bill to reinforce defense and retaliatory capabilities of intercontinental ballistic missile (ICBM) installations in rural areas; a bill to remit the surplus to the citizens as credits on farm machinery; and a bill to expand the collections of rural libraries and extend library outreach activities into their communities. Assume for simplicity's sake that the money must be spent in one lump: one, all of one, and only one of these proposals can be adopted. Your problem: to discern the proposal that, all things considered, you ought to vote for. Now, with the example in place, I feel free to take on the theoretical structure for its analysis and solution.

II

Aristotle reminds us that the three objects that are "lovable" (*philetos*)—sources of attraction of all human inclinations, friends as well as votes—are the Good, the Pleasurable, and the Useful.[1] The contemporary translation of these attractions would, plausibly, identify the attraction of the Good with the voice of conscience, inclining us toward objects or actions by reason of their moral worth or conformity with moral principle; the attraction of the Pleasurable with preference or taste, likes and dislikes that have no more than personal gratification as their justification; and the attraction of the Useful with material interest, an objectively measurable increase in physical goods or the means thereto. As a member of Congress, you might feel inclined to vote for any proposal on grounds of your conscience, your interest, or your mere preference. (Historical note: as my modification of Aristotle's order illustrates, our Puritan fathers have taught us to value material substance more, and the lure of pleasure less, than did the ancients; we shall decline more slowly than Rome, but much less enjoyably.)

Suppose for the moment that the proposals do in fact, on first impression, draw you, for different reasons, in different directions:

The library proposal immediately captures your imagination—here, at last, is a chance to translate your life-long passion for books into effective public action. The vision of revitalized libraries and programs to make reading accessible and attractive to the members of their communities, all over your district and beyond, throughout the region, is well-nigh irresistible. There is no doubt that this legislation would be the greatest source of Pleasure for you.

On second thought, it strikes you that maybe you had actually better resist that inclination, for your own best interests. Books have never had a large constituency among the rich and the powerful. The friends you need in Congress are the "hawk" types, who are always in favor of spending on military hardware, no matter where or why. In return for your support for the ICBM proposal, they might very well work, and very effectively, for projects that will benefit your district enormously. A new military base in your district is possible; lucrative small contracts to your small but ambitious industries—and to top it off, your constituents, who are typically supportive of the military for patriotic reasons, will automatically approve of your stand. From the point of view of your own re-election, your future power and influence in Congress, and your post-congressional employment—military industry is a lucrative employer for good hawks—your best move, in pursuit of what is personally useful, would be to align yourself with the pro-military bloc right now.

On third thought, you have qualms about both these courses. Do you really have a right to follow your personal tastes or interests in this matter? Wouldn't your constituents expect to be taken into account—as something more than the source of re-elections? Do you have a duty to serve your constituents here rather than following the course you personally would choose? *If* you do, which of these proposals is such that your vote for it would discharge that duty?

We may take on those questions one at a time. First, under what conditions do you have a perfect duty to represent your constituents (that is, they have a right to complain of misrepresentation if you fail), and under what conditions is that duty imperfect and ambiguous, allowing you discretion for the exercise of which you should not be held answerable to the electorate? Here we may distinguish among several degrees, or "levels," of the obligation to represent. At the highest level of obligation, where the duty to represent is virtually absolute, there are your specific campaign pledges. Whatever you directly promised your constituents, provided that the acts in question are legal and physically possible, you have a strict obligation to do: you promised, you were elected in reliance on the promise, and now you must perform. At the lowest level of obligation are those issues that played no part in your campaign, nor could play any legitimate part, for only by the most remote and tenuous links do they affect your constituents at all (the regulation of the East Coast hatpin trade; phased federal taxation for certain retired executives now residing abroad but planning to return within five years or less, and so forth). At this level, your constituents ask only that you vote your common sense—or vote what you like, just as any one of them would do. Where your constituents have no interest in the outcome, you are free to follow whatever inclination moves you.

Intermediate levels of obligation fall between those above. Found in these intermediate levels are all issues where the constituents are clearly affected, to a greater or lesser extent, but where no *specific* commitment was made prior to taking office (commitments to "Bring pride back to Putnam County" don't count). This area, of course, is the greater part of your job; most issues fall here, and the issues before you at the moment are clearly included. Your qualms of conscience were entirely correct: you are under an obligation to set your preference *per se* and your interests pure and simple to one side; the "right" course may very well coincide with one of those you would choose—the chances are two out of three, at this point—but no decision will be legitimate that does not proceed from your perception of your duty to your constituents.

Very well then, what *is* that duty? The representative's duty to his constituents, whether or not that duty is seen as absolute, is often indifferently expressed as "to do what his constituents want him to do," or "to serve the interests of his constituency," or "to do what is good for his constituents." Following Aristotle, we discern, in these three formulations, three totally different duties, which may very well not coincide with each other. Your constituents, like you, have preferences or "wants," material interests, and moral directions. Finding out what these inclinations are, and distinguishing among them, is very much part of your job. And it is no simple one. Presumably, you can distinguish among your own inclinations by reflective introspection—at least I hope you can, by this time, tell a whim from a moral imperative—but your constituents' communications do not permit that kind of discernment. Further, your duty is to serve all your constituents, so you must balance, compromise, and find common denominators and simple external tests to reach a set of priorities that you can call "the consensus of my constituents."

Most likely you will begin with your constituent's interests, since these can be objectively measured. Whatever increases the total wealth of your constituents, in accordance with a formula for (relatively) fair distribution of that wealth, is good; whatever decreases it is bad. You might then move on to your constituents (moral) "good." This dimension is much more difficult to figure out; you have a wide assortment of religious institutions and other groups oriented to moral guidance in your district, and you may not favor one or some of these at the expense of others; such favoritism would be political suicide (not to mention illegal). It is hopeless, then, to identify "the good for the constituents" with the collective voices of their consciences. But there are some notions of "good" that side-step the vagaries of individual conscience by focusing on the necessary preconditions for any person to become moral. To become a conscientious or "autonomous" person, one must, obviously, be alive and in decent health; one must, as Kohlberg points out, have achieved a certain level of rationality;[2] one must, as Pritchard points out, have the capacity for, and develop, a certain level of sympathy for other people.[3] The means to health, to education, to broadening one's knowledge of other people and deepening one's sensitivity to them, are universally means to the moral life. If you would serve your constituents' consciences, then, you should support all measures to create and maintain facilities for the advancement of health and education.

Your constituents' "preferences" include every inclination they manifest other than those included in the two categories above. Preferences include every desire other than the desire for money or for what money will buy, every tendency other than taking care of their health and extending their education. Naturally this conclusion is not satisfying, certainly not to the constituent. For it means that as far as *you* are concerned, his most profound moral convictions, reached in his maturity and informed by his own cultural heritage, are of no more consequence than his preference for strawberry ice cream. He may write you about his convictions more than about his ice cream, thus demonstrating a greater intensity of preference, but you have no right to grant his peculiar moral beliefs more intrinsic weight than any taste. This is the consequence of cultural pluralism, America's pride and joy and the bane of every sincere crusader: we can live with each other's differences only if we are willing to regard each other's moral codes, not as serious threats to the Right and the Good that we believe in, but as mere culturally conditioned preferences. And to survive, and view other cultures' moral codes in that way, we must consent to have our own convictions so regarded in the public forum. There is a way that constituents may employ to translate their moral convictions into public action, namely by exacting a campaign pledge to further them (see below); but absent the specific contractual obligation created by this method, you as representative may not accord them any more weight than other strongly held opinions. This emphatically does not mean you ought not to take your constituents' preferences into account at all. Other things being equal, you ought to do what your constituents would prefer you to do; preferences are determined by "opinion polls," and that is why so many congressmen send such polls back to their districts at regular intervals.

To determine what you ought to vote for in this case, then, you have three criteria by which to measure benefits to your constituents: if the measure brings about the preservation and advancement of health, knowledge, or sensitivity, it will serve the constituents' *good*; if the measure will increase wealth or goods in their possession, now or in the future, it will serve the constituents' *interest*; if a majority of the constituents would respond (on a questionnaire sent out from your office) with support for a certain measure, that measure will serve the constituents' *preference*. Of course, any two, or all three, criteria might coincidentally indicate the same measure as most beneficial. Such is not your luck in this case. Only the bill to expand the rural libraries will serve their good, as defined. Only the bill to buy them farm machinery will significantly advance their interests. And since you just got back the results of the latest poll, you know exactly what your constituency's preference is: if they had their way, they would vote for the bombs. Your three criteria therefore indicate three different courses of action. Which one takes priority?

How do you answer such a question? You might, if your training is philosophical, look for the answer first in democratic theory, hoping to find some accepted statement of the proper relationship between the legislative representative and his constituents. This approach, while surely illuminating, is not likely to be conclusive. Some theorists have argued that the representative is simply the one sent to vote as his constituents would vote, if only they could all be there and fit into the one building and participate in the voting. The ideal, on this theory, is direct democracy; representative democracy is adopted only on practical necessity; and the representative is to vote as his constituents want him to vote, that is, according to their preferences. Yet another school would have the representative vote on behalf of the interests that are peculiar to the region of the country in which his constituents reside. This geographical representation is justified by the likelihood that the diverse economic interests of the various regions of the country will all be counted in the legislative process. But it has also been argued that the representative's first duty is to the good of the nation as a whole, and that he must, on occasion, set aside his constituents' preferences and postpone their interests to achieve the solution that will be best for the nation in the long run. These three views of the nature of representative democracy are not really incompatible, it may be noted, especially where a bicameral legislature permits a partial division of labor separating out the third task from the other two. But a disagreement on emphasis is certainly present: "democratic theory" is divided right along the lines of your problem, and will not tell you how to vote on spending the surplus.

Another approach to determining your duty as representative holds more promise of success. The nature of the job itself holds a clue to its moral content. A job is a role, defined for these purposes as a "cluster of rights and duties with some sort of social function."[4] Inspired by Hegel and by a vision of society as organism that few today would follow, F. H. Bradley once elevated the role and its duties to the highest criterion of moral excellence.[5] Role morality cannot, outside such a vision, be viewed as the whole of the moral life (to be fair, Bradley admitted that); but it remains, as Norman Bowie has pointed out,[6] a solid starting point for the analysis of duties. Duties and roles correlate; if one is known, it determines the other. If neither one is surely known, as in your present dilemma, and if the alternative duties seem to be morally equal, as we presuppose they do in your present dilemma, perhaps a look at the roles entailed by each of the duties will help decide the matter.

The three alternative roles for the representative entailed by the

48 / Lisa H. Newton

various schools of democratic theory can be briefly designated as servant, agent, and leader. The servant is under a duty to the master to do what the master wants, within only broad legal and moral limits. The entire relationship, not to mention the entire humorous literature of master and servant, turn on the implicit understanding that the servant has no right to evaluate, and therefore must never question openly, the master's expressed desires. The servant's mind, his ability to understand and act autonomously in a novel situation, has no legitimate function in his role. This is the role entailed for you as representative by the theory that makes constituent preferences the major source of your duties. When you simply translate your constituents' preference for military hardware into your support and vote, without an independent effort to evaluate the choices and decide which course would be best for them, you act as their servant. (Obviously if you've thought this far in the argument, you've renounced that possibility. Incidentally, if you do vote for the ICBMs in order to carry out your constituents' wishes, there is no reason why you should not proceed to cash in on the political advantages therefrom.)

A second possible role is that of agent, one who is "acting for" another, in protecting and furthering his interests. The agent has much more freedom than the servant; what exactly he is to do in any given situation is not determined in advance, but is to be decided by him according to the (possibly changing) situation. The agent can proceed without supervision because material interests are relatively permanent and objectively determinable; they do not vary with the client's (or constituent's) whim, and the agent, especially if professionally prepared for such work, can find out what they are as well as, or better than, those he represents. He can even openly disagree with his clients and legitimately assert the superiority of his judgment to theirs without threat to a relationship in which his duty ultimately is to them and not vice versa—as long as there is clear agreement that it is the clients' material interest that is the object of all the agent's action. This agent role is the one you adopt when you decide that it is your duty to vote for the farm machinery credits, which will put a substantial amount of money in your constituents' pockets in the near future, rather than the rockets they would like or the libraries that might do them more good in the long run.

The third possible role is that of leader. The leader of any collectivity conceives of his role as determining what is genuinely best for his group, to promote not only their material welfare but also their moral character and their spiritual growth. As the leader sees it, the reason that the group has placed him in a position of leadership is that it trusts him to make the decisions that will benefit the group. His leadership position gives him access to information that the other members of the group cannot possibly have, so he really does know, a lot better than they do, what is good for them. And as people cannot really be divided up into "interests," "beliefs," "attitudes," "virtues," and whatever other psychological entities there may be, it makes no sense at all to tell him to watch out for some parts of the members— say, interests—and let other parts alone. He sees his duty as owed to the whole person in the long run. This leader role is entailed for you as congressional representative on that theory of democracy that bids you consider the whole good of your constituents, and act according to your conscience alone in deciding what to do to promote that good. (The constituents' check on such a representative is frequent election.) As their superior in judgment, you can see, as perhaps they cannot, that the educational advantages of the bill to expand rural libraries will, at length, outweigh the merely material satisfactions that would be derived from the farm machinery, or the irrational pleasure that would be derived from seeing more engines of destruction installed in the region.

These three roles, then, each entailing its own set of duties and privileges, are available to you. Your duty will be chosen, from among the choices presented, by the role you pick. And here is where the worth of the analysis shows itself: Put aside a few personal prejudices, like a perfect horror of bombs, and I see nothing to choose from, morally, among the three bills up for your consideration. But, insofar as you are motivated to choose one or the other by different conceptions of your role as representative, the moral dimension of the vote becomes evident, for these three roles are not at all morally equivalent.

The principle of "respect for persons," ordinarily accepted in our recent tradition as the first and most fundamental touchstone of moral evaluation, entails at least this: that an institution fails to be morally good if it systematically discounts the moral agency of any competent adult. A social role, which is a social institution subject to that principle, then fails to be morally good if it systematically discounts the moral agency of the role occupant or of those who stand to him as role legitimators—in this case, of the representative or of his constituents. The role of legislative representative can not be morally good if it has no room for the moral agency of the legislator, as the servant conception of the role would entail, or no room for the moral capacity of the constituents, as the leader conception would have it. Only the agent conception, where constituents and representative are considered on a plane of equality, incorporates respect for all the persons involved: the representative is not bound by the current desires and opinions of the constituency, but is free, and required, ultimately, to make his own determinations on where his constituents' interests lie and how they may best be served. The constituents, on the other hand, are not bound by the legislators' conception of what is "good" for them, what style of life they should choose for themselves. On the contrary, their representative is held to be totally incompetent to pronounce judgment on the lives they have chosen; his only job is to protect and advance the material goods and other interests they have acquired in the course of living out their choices. He is in charge of their means, not their ends.

Theoretical indications that the agency theory of representation is superior to alternatives are borne out by experience with officeholders who have held different conceptions. I had intended to stay away from specific examples from recent history in this essay, but two cases I can think of are simply too close to the point to pass up. I had the dubious privilege some years back, of residing in the congressional district "served" by the late Adam Clayton Powell. "Serve" was his word: "I am your servant" concluded all his campaign letters. His claim was that he did only what the people of his district wanted him to do, and he was telling the truth; the public spectacle he made of himself did satisfy the pride of his poverty-stricken constituency, and the repeatedly discovered dishonesty by which he enriched himself was shrugged off by people who had never personally profited very much from honesty. The majority of voting constituents that he needed every two years was easy enough to arrange for by short impressive displays of crusading zeal for some project they liked; for the rest, he spent no time whatsoever on the affairs of his district. His ability to serve his constituents' uneducated preferences made it entirely unnecessary for him to consider real benefits for them and bred in him, as representative, the cynical contempt that servants develop for stupid masters in nineteenth-century novels. The other example that comes to mind as an illustration of the leader type is, of course, former President Nixon; but one, whose comparison of the American people to "the child in the family" raised hackles (and turned stomachs) the length and breadth of our profession. In this case, we see the awesome extent of the cynical possibilities of the role: if the American people are incompetent minors, they can be lied to (to protect them), they can be manipulated (for their own good), and, if a higher ideal beckons, the laws they have (foolishly) agreed upon can be safely ignored. The assumed greater wisdom and wider vision of the "leader" grants a moral superiority that justifies any violation of merely legal rights. In both those cases, the legislator's conception of the role he played led to contempt for the electorate and systematic dishonesty, a curious convergence of results from dissimilar origins.

The agent role, then, the role of moral and political equal assigned to advance material interests, is the appropriate role of the legislative representative. Your problem in the particular case before you is solved: you should support and vote for the bill to return the surplus to the farmers as credits on farm machinery. And several general questions are answered for you, should you be the type to worry about general questions. For example:

Should a legislative representative (as it is often put) do what his constituents want him to do or what his conscience tells him to do? Answer: he has no right to do either. What his constituents want (their preference) may be irrational, ill-informed, or inconsistent with their interests. A minor task of the legislator is to teach his constituents what course of action, given the current world situation, is, in fact, in accord with their interests; he may put his staff to work on this aspect of his job. And what "his conscience" tells him to do has no bearing on the office he has accepted. His conscience *ought* to tell him to carry out the duties of his office; for the rest, he can serve his conscience on his own time. If the fulfillment of his office is inconsistent with the directives of his conscience, he should resign.[7]

How may a legislator with profound convictions of conscience in one area (say, against all military spending) legitimately represent his constituents in that area? (Suppose a large military base in your district would really help unemployment, but you have to vote for the military appropriation in order to get it.) Answer: By making it absolutely clear to all constituents beforehand that no matter what, you will not vote for military spending. Then, when they cast their ballots for you or for your opponent, they know the risk they are taking.

How may a constituency that shares a strong preference, or profound moral conviction, make it effective in the public realm? (Ecological, school prayer, and pro-life issues would fall into this category.) Answer: Exact a specific campaign pledge from the candidate prior to the election to introduce a certain bill, or support certain types of bills, if elected. There is, after all, no reason why voters cannot vote their tastes and consciences as well as their crass material interests. Voters may vote for a candidate for any reason they like; they are not responsible to anyone else for that vote. Only the elected representative, who *is* responsible to others for his actions, is limited in the kinds of concerns he may deal with in the area of his responsibility. So the voters are perfectly free to vote for a candidate who promises, for example, to oppose Medicaid funding for abortions, even when they can see perfectly well that that opposition, if successful, is going to cost the district a lot of money. And once pledged to the opposition as a candidate, the legislator is then perfectly free to carry on that opposition even though he can see it is flatly contrary to his constituents' material interests—as a matter of fact, he is obliged to. Once pledged, failure to carry out the promise is simple betrayal.

The second and third questions are structurally identical. Each asks, how can the political dialogue, the debate among the representatives, include the voice of conscience, when a pluralistic system denies its validity? The answer to each is to settle these questions by contract prior to the assumption of the role of the representative. In the former case, the constituents contract for a pacifist; in the latter, the legislator contracts to support the desired bill; and the moral obligation of the contractor is very different from the moral obligation of the representative.

Some remarks by way of conclusion: The problem of representation is unique to the peculiar situation of large-scale democracy.

Small-scale or "participatory" democracy, where each citizen takes part in the political dialogue, the debate that eventuates in public commitment and action, works on entirely different principles. In participatory democracy each citizen is encouraged to refine his conscience in public discussion, to vote his conscience when the question is put, and to act on conscience in the carrying out of public decisions. The existence of the public is, in fact, the source of conscience. But the Rousseauian analysis of small democracies is not appropriate for the large ones (for which Rousseau specifically refused to take responsibility), and discussion of its virtues must be postponed. In large democracies, as the founding fathers realized, we must be protected from our governors, not from our passions—hence the limitation on the representatives.

Notes

1. Aristotle, *Nicomachean Ethics,* vol. 8, 11556, 15–20.
2. Lawrence Kohlberg, "Stages of Moral Development as a Basis for Moral Education," in C. M. Beck et al., eds., *Moral Education: Interdisciplinary Approaches* (New York: Paulist-Newman Press, 1972), *passim.*
3. Michael S. Pritchard, "Responsibility, Understanding and Psychopathology, *Monist* 58 (Oct. 1974): 630–45.
4. R. S. Downie, *Rules and Values* (London: Methuen, 1971), p. 128.
5. Francis H. Bradley, *Ethical Studies* (1876), essay 5. (Indianapolis: Bobbs, 1951).
6. Bowie, "Role Morality and Business Ethics" (unpublished manuscript).
7. The way the question appeared on communications from this conference, viz. "the extent to which a legislator should serve his/her conscience or his/her constituents," is ambiguous—are we to *assume* a democracy, a system of representation. For those "constituents" could be like a bishop's "flock," simply "those he has been assigned to care for," not "those who elected him and have therefore the right to expect representation from him," and that would change the answer. And if we do assume representative democracy, the answer to the question is that only the constituents have a right to his service, analytically on the notion of "representation." And if that service is inconsistent with conscience, he must overrule conscience or resign, removing himself from the category "representative." The question must be rephrased as *how* to serve the constituents, and that is the question I have addressed.

JAMES O. GRUNEBAUM

4 What Ought the Representative Represent?

The question "What ought the representative represent?" has been answered by three different kinds of theories. First, the delegate or mandate theory is that the representative ought to represent what is wanted by those whom he represents. Second, the trustee or independence theory is that the representative ought to represent what is in the interest of those whom he represents. Third, what we can call an eclectic theory of representation is that the representative, in some circumstances, ought to represent the wants and, in others, the interests of those whom he represents.

The first two theories depend on oversimplified assumptions about the relationship between what is wanted and what is beneficial, or in a person's interest. The delegate theory assumes a logical relation in which what a person wants defines what is in his interest, while the trustee theory assumes only a contingent relation where wants and interests may vary independently of one another. Eclectic theories, by and large, rather than attempting to discover the relation between wants and interests, have laid down only vague, general guidelines that amount to little more than *ad hoc* procedures for representing wants or interests.

These three answers are complete. While there might be a fourth— that the representative ought to represent the rights and liberties of his constituents—there is no reason to establish this additional category. For the purposes of representation, the concepts of interest and well-being are broad enough to contain the protection of rights and liberty. In most circumstances it is not in anyone's interest to have his liberty restricted or his rights ignored. Moreover, an examination of attempts to prescribe the limits of liberty (as opposed to license) or to prescribe inviolable civil rights (as opposed to defeasible claims) shows that the interest or welfare of the constituents is the basis of the argument.

What follows is a rationally justified principle for choosing when the representative ought to represent the wants and when he ought to represent the interests of those whom he represents. The principle is formulated to serve both the representative in deciding what he ought to represent and the represented in evaluating the effectiveness of those who represent them.

The argument consists of three steps. The first is an examination of the delegate and trustee theories to see how their assumptions about the relation between the concepts of want and interest lead to an overly one-sided picture of what ought to be represented. The second step is the justification of the principle for choosing when the wants and when the interests of the represented ought to be promoted. Comment on the proof is postponed until that point. The third step is an application of the principle that offers a decision procedure that the representative can use when he must choose between representing wants or interests, and that the represented can also use to decide how well he or she is represented.

A final point before beginning: No attempt will be made to analyze what it is for someone to be a representative of someone else. The task involves explicating in what specific sense one person can stand for, stand up for, or make present another person. The normative conclusion about what the representative ought to represent will be consistent with many specifications of the senses of "represent." Besides, such metaethical or linguistic considerations are too involved to be dealt with here.[1] Needless to say, all have a good idea of who are representatives—members of Congress, city councilmen, faculty senators, union leaders, trade lobbyists, spokesmen for interest groups, and so forth.

The Delegate and the Trustee Theories

The delegate theory's answer, that the representative ought to represent the wants of those whom he represents, is too vague as it stands to offer the representative or anyone else a principle by which to judge his actions as a representative. However, no distortion will result if the delegate theory is understood to imply that if n members of a representative's constituency want x then the representative is under an obligation to promote x, where n is a majority of the constituents or where n is less than a majority and the majority neither wants x nor wants not x. Here it is assumed there is no reason why a representative cannot promote what a minority wants so long as the majority is indifferent, that what constitutes a member of the constituency can be defined,[2] and that the obligation the representative is under is a role obligation that may be overridden by a moral obligation, for example, to protect his family, and more importantly, the obligation to refuse to promote immorality, even if a majority of his constituents want it, since it is a well-established moral principle that everyone has an obligation to forbear from what is immoral.

Within the context of the delegate theory, it is in principle easy for the representative to decide what to promote. For any given decision where he is officially called upon to act, he need only know the number of constituents who favor, the number who oppose, and the number who are indifferent, to each alternative. He need not consider the intensity of the members' wants, if some sort of political equality is assumed, or if the intensity of wants may be a morally irrelevant accident.[3]

In practice, of course, the representative's decision is far more complex. Since whatever people want, they want it under some particular description; his constituents may want something under one description and not want it under another. For example, they may not want Bill xyz, "proposed by that scoundrel representative A," even though Bill xyz is the "Noise Abatement Act" they do want. In addition, the representative must contend with individuals and groups who, at the time when the decision must be made, either do not express or have not yet formed any opinion one way or the other. Here the representative may have to guess what they want. The representative's task is also more difficult, some say impossible, if there are three or more alternatives, since preference rankings of the constituents as a whole may be intransitive; there may be no best, that is, most preferred, alternative.[4]

Finally, the delegate theory implies that a representative may actively promote a project the majority of his constituents do not want (desire) if that project is an indispensable means to some goal they do want. The delegate theory permits the representative the use of expert or technical judgment where the judgment is limited to selecting the best means of goal realization. The assumption here is that everyone wants the best (not to be confused with the most efficient) means to achieve the goals they want. Only to this extent is a representative allowed to act independently of the constituency.

Arguments in support of the delegate theory of representation are both teleological and deontological. The teleological arguments attempt to justify the theory by claiming that adherence to the delegate theory will maximize the constituents' welfare or interest. One popular version depends on the logical claim that the particular things constituents want wholly define what is in their interest.[5] So the interests of the constituents can only be promoted by giving them what they want. If members of a constituency want quiet unbroken by the sounds of supersonic jet liners landing and taking off, the representative ought to promote noise control legislation since it is in his constituents' interest, by definition, because they want quiet.[6] If this analysis were correct, the delegate theory would promote the interests of the constituents by promoting only the ends they want.

A second form the teleological argument takes is an empirical claim that adherence to the delegate theory maximizes welfare because, as a matter of fact, what people want is the most accurate index of what is in their interest. The argument would depend on a well-supported empirical generalization that there is a high correlation between what people want and what is truly in their interest. One might go so far as Mill, who tries to explain the correlation on the grounds that each person knows his own situation more fully than it is possible for others to know it.

The deontological arguments in defense of the delegate theory emphasize the political equality shared by all people, or the universal right of liberty. Since political equality denies any inherent superiority, the delegate theorist could argue that the only justification for one person having political authority over another is that the latter consents to it, or that citizens have an obligation to obey only laws to which they consent; that is, representatives only support laws that the constituents want. On this assumption, then, only a delegate theory of representation would be consistent with the grounds of political obligation.

None of the above arguments is sufficient to establish the truth of the delegate theory. The first teleological argument depends on the false assumption that what people want logically defines what is in their interest. People (even the best of us) frequently want things that are against their interest. An extreme case is the alcoholic who wants to be intoxicated, more perhaps than he wants anything else, even though being constantly intoxicated is not in his, or anyone's interest. Less extreme cases also occur such as the case of those who continue to smoke cigarettes.

The second teleological argument fares little better. There is scanty evidence that a high correlation exists between what people want and what is in their interest. Consider as an example the felt needs of a community. This argument assumes a high correlation between the felt needs and the real needs; but as even a casual observation of aid to education in this country will show, there is little correlation at all. Even assuming that each individual is well informed about his own state of affairs, a not wholly realistic assumption, he may lack the wisdom, prudence, or experience necessary to make correct judgments about his interests. And even if this were not sufficient to invalidate the argument, the fact that it requires an independent criterion of what is in a person's interest makes the correlation with what people want superfluous. In order to establish the empirical correlation between what people want and what is in their interest, it is obvious one needs to know what is in their interest. However, given such knowledge, a representative can promote his constituents' interests without depending on information about what they want. This, in essence, is the trustee theory to which we now turn.[7]

The trustee theory, that the representative ought to represent the interests of those whom he represents, also needs to be made more precise if it is to be of any use in evaluating the actions of the representative. Again, no distortion will result if the trustee theory is understood to imply that if x is in the interest of n members of the representative's constituency, then the representative is under an obligation to promote x, where n is a majority of the constituents or where n less than a majority and x does not affect the interests of the majority. Again, we are assuming that the members of the constituency can be identified, that the obligation is a role obligation, and that there is no reason why a minority's interest cannot be promoted if the majority is not affected.

Central to the argument in support of the trustee theory is the notion that government must promote the interest of those whom it governs. Consent of the governed might, at best, be a necessary condition, but it is not sufficient to justify government since, as Hume points out, people may consent to government out of fear, out of custom, or out of religious commitment, none of which confer moral legitimacy. What the advocates of the trustee theory insist upon is that the advancement of one's interest is the reason why one should consent to be governed. It follows, therefore, that the representative is remiss in his duty if he fails to promote the interests of his constituents. Most importantly, the theory maintains that each person is not the logically authoritative judge of what is in his interest, and that the representative is justified in acting independently of what his constituents want where his actions promote their interests. In contrast to the delegate theory, the trustee theory permits the judgment of experts with respect to both the means to and the goals of government action, since wise and prudent men and women may be in a better position to determine what will benefit the people than are the people themselves.

The obvious difficulty that the trustee theory must contend with is that no criterion for determining what is in people's interest is available. If we abandon the logical definitional connection between wants and interests in order to account for the possibility of mistakes about one's interest, we will need a new criterion to replace it.

Such a criterion is developed in the following section. Before beginning that discussion, however, we must look at one more problem with the trustee theory. Recently, many philosophers and economists have expressed doubts about the meaningfulness of interpersonal comparisons of utility. And since a person's utility is equivalent to his interest, a representative who must make decisions about promoting the interests of his constituents may be an awkward situation where he is required to compare the utility functions of several constituents. The representative's situation is not hopeless. The criterion we develop permits him to make decisions without having to make such comparisons. If, however, devices are developed to measure interpersonal utility differences, they can be used quite consistently with our criterion.

Interest and Want

As we have seen, different assumptions about the relation between the concepts of interest and of want account for many of the differences in the delegate and trustee theories of representation. The former, in one version at least, assumes there is a logical relation between interest and want such that the things people want wholly define what is in their interest. The trustee theory assumes only a contingent relationship emphasizing the possibility of mistaken judgment about one's interest.

Neither assumption is wholly correct. While it is true that there are kinds of wants people have that do define what is in their interest, there is also an area of people's interest that is independent of the wants they have and that depends on the necessities of human existence. This latter area we will call the area of basic needs. We will argue that all men have a reason to want basic needs filled so long as they want anything at all. Basic needs will be independent of the particular things men want and will therefore explain how mistaken judgment of one's interest is possible. The other area of interest, complementary to the area of basic needs, is where what each man wants does define what is in his interest. This area of secondary wants contains those things men have a reason to want only because they want other particular things; and here mistakes in judgment of one's interest is impossible.

What is most interesting about basic needs is that their existence can be established from the assumption held by the delegate theory that would ostensibly deny their existence. The assumption of the delegate theory, it will be recalled, is that what people want defines their interest, or that something is in a person's interest if, and only if, it increases his opportunity to get what he wants.[8] Thus, if someone wants to be a concert pianist—and a necessary means of becoming one is to practice five hours a day—then practicing five hours a day is in his interest. He has a reason to want to practice five hours a day because of what he wants to become. Unfortunately, this method of defining interest in terms of what people want implies that we must also judge that it is in a person's interest to imbibe eight hours a day at the local bar if he wants to be inebriated. Somehow we want to be justified in arguing that such behavior is not in the alcoholic's interest. We can do this as soon as we ask if there are any necessary conditions that must be fulfilled for it to be possible to want anything at all (and thus to get what one wants). Clearly such conditions exist and everyone has a reason to want them, whatever else he wants. Similarly, everyone has a reason against wanting anything that makes the satisfaction of these conditions impossible, since without them nothing at all could be wanted. Among the conditions for wanting anything at all to be possible are being alive and all that life presupposes: food, clothing, shelter, love, and so on. There may be cognitive conditions presupposed by an ability to want;[9] and there may be the need for self-respect if significant wanting is to occur.[10] The list is tentative; it may grow or be shortened, but what is important is that anything that can be determined to be a basic need is in a person's interest.

These necessary conditions of being able to want anything at all, or basic needs that everyone has a reason to want, provide the explanation of how mistaken judgment about one's interest is possible.[11] There are two ways a person can be mistaken about what is in his interest. The first way is to be mistaken about the means to his ends. This is a factual mistake that involves no special value judgments. If a person wants to lose weight, and if a necessary means of losing weight is to both exercise and restrict one's food intake, a person who wants to lose weight but does not exercise and restrict food intake will be making a mistake about what is in his interest. The mistake is about means only; the ends or purposes that the person wants in this case logically define his interest, that is, the irrationality of the goal, wanting to lose weight, is not questioned.

Both the mandate and the trustee theories admit that mistakes of this factual kind are possible. But what the mandate theory denies and the trustee theory asserts is that mistakes about interest are possible because a person wants some end or some goal that is not in his interest.

A theory that implies that a person's actual wants wholly define his interests cannot admit value mistakes about his goals or ends unless they are themselves means to some other higher-order end or goal. If a person's wants were to define his interests, then his wants cannot be against his interests. The concept of basic needs, however, shows how value mistakes are possible because basic needs can be used as a criterion to establish the irrationality of an agent's ends or goals. A person who wants an end or goal that conflicts with the satisfaction of his basic needs is mistaken about the value of his end or goal. Since a person has a reason to want the satisfaction of his basic needs whatever he happens to want, he has reasons against wanting what conflicts with basic need satisfaction. Thus, the concept of basic needs can be used to support the trustee theory. A representative might be justified in supporting a policy that his constituents do not want if the policy is necessary for satisfying his constituents' basic needs. The constituents, in this case, are mistaken about the value of what they want, and the representative is not acting arbitrarily because he has a truly objective principle by which he may justify his actions.

A corollary to the basic needs argument, if we may indulge in a brief digression, is that the definition of rationality as the ability to calculate the means to one's ends needs revision. The strategy used to show that basic needs are in a person's interest also shows there is a rationality criterion for ends. Wanting to shake one's little finger is more rational than wanting to destroy the world, since the latter want is inconsistent with the necessary means of its own fulfillment. It cannot be rational to want something and also to want what one knows will make impossible the fulfillment of that want, or any want whatsoever. Hence, we must say that being rational is the ability to calculate the means to those ends that are consistent with the ability to have any ends at all.

Secondary wants are those things people want that do not affect the satisfaction of their basic needs. Within this area what people want does define their interest, and mistakes about interest are impossible. Basic needs define the area of bare necessity. What is needed to satisfy them are nourishment, whether appetizing or not, shelter, which need not be aesthetically pleasing, and clothing, which may only consist of well-worn rags. But, since almost all human beings want more than this—food that pleases, living quarters that reflect their personality, and clothing that is attractive—secondary wants define this area of enriched interest. We can say that the ability to read is in a person's interest, not because it is a means to the satisfaction to his basic needs, which it is not, but because reading is a means to many other things he does want that are consistent with his basic needs. The same argument applies to food, clothing, and shelter. The name "secondary wants" should not mislead; the means to the satisfaction of secondary wants are in a person's interest and what conflicts with their satisfaction is against it. The two areas compliment each other. The area of basic needs includes the necessities of life and volition, while the area of secondary wants includes aspirations, aims, and achievements.[12]

We have offered a proof that a person has a reason to want the satisfaction of his basic needs whatever else he wants, and we have shown how they account for the possibility of mistaken judgment. To this extent, the trustee theory is correct since, where the representative promotes his constituents' basic needs, whether they want him to or not, he is acting in a manner they have a reason to want. The concept of basic needs also preserves what is of value in the delegate theory, since only what people want and what is necessary for their wanting function as criteria for what is in their interest. Also, the delegate theory can be shown true for the class of decisions where only the secondary wants of the constituents are involved.

A Decision Procedure

We are now in a position to develop a rational procedure for deciding when the wants and when the interests ought to be represented. No problem for the representative arises in cases where what the constituency wants corresponds to what is in their interests. The only cases that need discussion are those where the wants and the interests of the constituents conflict.

The general procedure the representative should follow is to promote the basic needs or interests of the members of his or her constituency, whatever the members actually want; but where the basic needs of the members are not in question, the representative ought to promote what they want, for their secondary wants define their interest. To show this procedure is rational, we will illustrate how it applies in one of the cases where wants and interests conflict.

Let us assume that some proposed government policy is in the interest of the members of a constituency and they do not want it. What is in their interest may be either a basic need or the means to some secondary want. If what is in their interest is a basic need, the representative ought to promote it even if the members do not want it. The representative ought to promote the policy that guarantees the satisfaction of basic needs even in the face of his constituency's opposition since his action will, by hypothesis, enable his constituents to satisfy their basic needs, which must be satisfied if the members are to have and to satisfy any wants at all. The representative can correctly argue that by promoting the policy he is acting as the members have a reason to want him to act, both if they knew that their basic needs were at stake and if they appreciated the significance of basic needs.

The fact that the constituents do not want the policy may be due to their not understanding that the policy is necessary to protect their basic needs, or they may fail to understand that the satisfaction of basic needs is necessary for the satisfaction of any of their other wants. The representative would be justified in supporting the policy because he has an objective criterion for showing that everyone has a reason to want the policy.

Suppose now that what is in the constituency's interest is a policy that will promote the secondary wants of the members and they do not want it. Here the situation is more complex. Since, by hypothesis, the policy will in fact promote what the members of the constituency want, it is important for the representative to discover why they do not want it. There are two possible reasons for this. The constituents may not want the policy because they are not aware that the policy will promote their secondary wants; or the constituents may not want the policy because it has additional consequences they do not want if the policy promotes their interests. If the policy is not wanted for the first reason, the course the representative should take is rather straightforward. He can act to promote the policy and at the same time apprise his constituency of the policy's value. Where their reasons are of the second kind, the representative must do further investigation. He must determine whether the members of his constituency want those of their secondary wants the policy promotes more than they do not want its other consequences. Suppose the policy in question is to give tax relief to certain manufacturers so that the community can maintain full employment. However, the tax relief and the increased manufacture will have the effect of raising traffic congestion in the streets since there will be less money for traffic control. The representative must ask whether his constituents want full employment more than they do not want the increased congestion. If the constituency does not want the congestion so strongly that in this case they are willing to sacrifice full employment, then the policy that would create full employment is not in their interest, and the representative ought actively to oppose it. But, if the members of his constituency object to the congestion less strongly than they desire full employment, the representative ought to promote the employment policy and override their wants, since the policy is in their interest as defined by their own most strongly felt secondary wants. Of course, what would be most in the constituency's interest would be to have what they want without the unwanted side effects; but that is another example.

I have been assuming that it is the same members of the constituency whose interests are affected and who also either want or do not want the policy. The role of the representative is not always so simple; therefore, it is necessary to discuss what the representative ought to represent when there are conflicts of interests, conflicts of wants, or conflicts between interests and wants. When the conflict is between the basic needs of one group and the secondary wants of another group within the constituency, it is tempting to say that the representative ought to represent the basic needs of any group no matter how small a minority the group happens to be. Succumbing to that temptation would be to oversimplify the role of the representative. To invest a large portion of available social resources to satisfy the basic needs of a small group might, in some circumstances, unjustifiably reduce the well-being of a substantive majority, and, therefore, I do not believe that a representative would always be correct in giving priority to basic needs over secondary wants. A representative who finds that certain policies adversely affect the basic needs of a small number of his constituents may have to weigh the effects to both the majority and the minority. Even though basic needs ought to be given priority, it would be absurd to claim that they ought to be given priority at all costs.

The possibility of conflict between interests and between interests and wants reveals the need for a moral principle or a principle of justice by which a representative can decide what to represent. Here a moral principle is needed to give the representative guidance. It might be argued on Kantian grounds that one could not will that the neglect of basic needs become a universal law since, as we have shown, such a will would be in conflict with itself. Similarly, it might be argued on universalizability grounds, that if a policy is most valuable to me because it satisfies my basic needs, and then if a policy satisfies another's basic needs, it must also be most valuable, unless there is a relevant difference between us. Merely resolving the debate between the mandate and the trusteeship theories of representation does not provide each representative with a complete decision-making procedure, but only a partial one.

What action should the representative take where the satisfaction of basic needs of a large part of the constituency conflicts with the satisfaction of another large part? Where situations arise in which the constituency, or the nation as a whole for that matter, is so constituted that the survival of a large number of citizens is incompatible with the survival of some other large group, then the basis both of government and of representation break down because both are predicated on the possibility of reconciling clashes of interest. Where there are wholesale conflicts of basic needs, reconciliation would seem to be impossible. About the only possible action the representative could take would be to advocate a policy in which the interests of his constituents had a fair or just chance of being advanced. At this point the limits of representation have been reached.

The decision procedure offered for the representative to use in his decisions, and the represented to use to evaluate the representative's actions, falls under the eclectic theory answer to the question, What ought the representative represent? We have shown that the representative sometimes ought to represent the interest of his constituents even against their wishes and that sometimes he ought to represent what they want. The decision procedure avoids the flaw of typical eclectic theories since it is not in any way *ad hoc* but firmly grounded upon basic wants that all persons have a reason to want if they want anything else at all.

Notes

1. For an excellent discussion of this topic see Hanna F. Pitkin's book, *The Concept of Representation* (Berkeley: University of California Press, 1967). She also offers an example of an eclectic theory of what the representative ought to represent.

2. There has been a good deal of debate whether the representative ought to represent his own constituency or the nation as a whole, only the voters or all who reside in the geographical constituency, only those who voted for him or all the voters, etc. The question, Who ought the representative represent? is independent of the question, What ought he represent? Even if the first question could be satisfactorily answered, we would still have to ask whether he ought to represent the wants or the interests of those whom he represents.

3. Cf. John Rawls, *A Theory of Justice* (Cambridge: Harvard University Press, 1971), p. 238.

4. See A.K. Sen, *Collective Choice and Social Welfare* (San Francisco: Holden-Day, 1970), pp. 47–52.

5. For example, see Carl Cohen, *Democracy* (Athens: University of Georgia Press, 1971), p. 200, or Brian Barry, *Political Argument* (London: Routledge and Kegan Paul, 1965), p. 176.

6. The contrary is also true, that if they do not want quiet nights the representative is not under an obligation to promote noise control legislation.

7. Criticism of the deontological argument will follow almost immediately in our discussion of the justification for the trustee theory.

8. Here I am borrowing from Barry, *Political Argument.*

9. Cf. Anthony Kenny, *Action, Emotion, and Will* (London: Routledge and Kegan Paul, 1963) pp. 118–20.

10. Cf. Rawls, *Theory of Justice,* p. 440.

11. It should be clear we are not considering the possibility of error of judgment about the means to one's ends; since both sides recognize these are possible, no difficulty arises. The problem is how people can be mistaken about the ends they should value.

12. For another attempt at establishing a hierarchy of needs, see S.I. Benn and R.S. Peters, *Principles of Political Thought* (New York: Free Press, 1965), pp. 165–71.

5 Two Concepts of Democracy

To what extent should a representative serve his or her conscience as opposed to his or her constituents? This hoary question admits several different interpretations, but I shall address myself to the following traditional version of it: Should a representative vote in accordance with his or her constituents' actual preferences on a given issue, or should the representative vote *against* those preferences when he or she believes that compelling purposes would be better served by a contrary vote? These "other purposes" may be the interests of the constituents (as distinguished from what they want), the interests of the nation as a whole, the interests of mankind, or the ends of justice (for example, protection of the legitimate rights of some minority group).

How this question is to be answered depends on the perspective from which we view it. We can view it, in the first instance, from the perspective of a constitutional convention, and ask whether or not political institutions should be designed to minimize the extent to which representatives will vote against their constituents' expressed preferences. Such minimization can be accomplished by a variety of means: educational and socialization techniques may be employed to ensure that representatives are motivated to vote in accord with their constituents' wishes; the electoral system can be structured to guarantee that representatives vote against their constituents only on imminent peril of losing office; rules governing the decision processes in representative bodies can be designed to bind the representatives' votes to expressions of preferences obtained through popular referenda. Similar tools can be employed to secure the opposite effect of obtaining for the representatives greater freedom of judgment and scope for leadership. In deciding this question, no doubt attention

68

must be paid to the nature of the issue being voted on in a particular case; perhaps fundamental policy issues should be decided in accordance with the constituents' preferences, while issues concerning the application of these policies to technical areas may be left to the independent judgment of the representatives.

But we may view our question in the second instance from the perspective of an individual representative; given his or her concrete historical context, should a representative vote in accordance with his or her constituents' preferences or in accordance with some contrary compelling purpose? In this chapter I will focus on the question from this second perspective. I shall argue that to answer it we must distinguish between two different conceptions of democracy, and that on one of these conceptions, arguably the most important, democratic considerations themselves do not compel the representative to vote in accordance with his or her constituents' preferences.

I

Before addressing ourselves to the question from this second perspective, let us review briefly the kinds of considerations that have been offered on either side of the question. Standard treatments of this issue typically fail to distinguish between the two perspectives I have described, but the arguments advanced tend to be ones more relevant to the question as viewed from the constitutional convention stance. Rehearsal of these arguments provides background for approaching our target, namely the question as viewed from the stance of the individual representative.

On the side of allowing the representative not to be bound by his or her constituents' preferences, it is most commonly said that the people as a whole lack the information and intelligence to make wise decisions on most questions of public policy, whereas their elected representatives possess these attributes in sufficient degree to assure the adoption of policies consonant with the true public good. It is also argued that the people as a whole lack the requisite motivations to determine public questions adequately: the people are largely indifferent to political issues, and may lack the patriotism and love of justice that characterize their representatives. It is further claimed that a system that allows great latitude to the judgment of representatives is more efficient, since, for example, the information necessary to make informed decisions need only be conveyed to a small body of persons. In line with this, it is pointed out that deliberation, discussion, and political compromise are only possible within small groups, but that the goods gained by such methods are utterly lost if the representatives who form such a group must vote in accordance with the preferences of their constituents, who did not benefit from these discussions. It is also argued that on many issues no majority view exists, since the constituents are so ill informed and apathetic; hence, it is impossible for the representative to be guided by his or her constituents' preferences. And it is sometimes suggested that the people have an obligation to further the national interest or the ends of justice, and that if they fail in this obligation, it is the duty of their representatives to act for them.

On the side of restraining the representatives to vote in accordance with their constituents' preferences, it is argued that the electorate as a whole embodies greater wisdom than any single person and, hence, that the representatives should be bound by their declared will on an issue. Some theorists identify satisfaction of preferences with happiness and, for this reason, identify satisfaction of the majority's preferences with the greatest happiness for the group. Thus on utilitarian grounds they advocate voting in accordance with the majority. It is further maintained that voting against the preferences of the constituents leads to popular frustration and eventually to civil discord. But the primary justification advanced in favor of representatives' voting in accord with their constituents' preferences is that their doing so brings their political system, on this occasion, closer to the ideal of pure democracy, in which the people themselves regulate their own affairs.

II

With this debate as a backdrop, let us now turn to the question of what an individual representative should do in an actual case when faced with the dilemma of having to vote in accord with his or her constituents' preferences or against them in favor of some independent value. In one sense, the answer to this question is simple: a representative confronted with this choice must do whatever is best overall. What is best overall is a matter of numerous considerations, or values, that may be at stake in the concrete situation. Some of these are short term: the representative's own political commitments and obligations as they impinge on this vote, his or her ability to influence future decisions by willingness to engage in vote-trading on this issue, his or her prospects for re-election as they are affected by this vote. Others are longer-term or more fundamental values: the effect on the welfare of the representative's district, the effect on individual rights, the effect on the welfare of the nation, and so forth. Of course, it is a difficult matter to balance all these considerations against each other when they conflict, but that is not our present concern.

Our present concern is this: Among the various values that may be at stake in such a vote, is there in addition, as many writers have claimed, an intrinsic democratic value that may be realized by the representative's voting in accordance with his or her constituents' preferences? Does such a vote indeed bring the political system, at least on this occasion, closer to the ideal of pure democracy? And, if so, what weight should be ascribed to this value when it conflicts with the other values just described?

To answer this question, we need a definition of democracy. Such definitions are legion, but I shall avail myself of one deriving from a formulation by David Braybrooke and say that democracy is a form of government in which collective preferences determine policy.[1] Although this definition closely resembles many others, it has the virtue of carrying on its face an ambiguity, hitherto largely unnoticed or ignored, that other accounts contain in a more concealed fashion. This ambiguity arises from the word "determine." On one interpretation of this term, the definition must be understood as follows: democracy is a form of government in which policy *accords with*—or agrees with—collective preference. The idea here is that public policies are always the ones that the collectivity desires, however that happy result may be brought about. (Of course there are deep problems in specifying what the collectivity desires, but these may be side-stepped in our discussion.) We may call a system of government that satisfies this definition an *accordance democracy*. On the second interpretation of "determine," the root definition may be understood as follows: democracy is a form of government in which policy is *controlled by* collective preferences. The idea here is that the people's preferences play a controlling or causal role in the selection of policies. (For our purposes, we may assume that such a process always results in policies that accord with their preferences.) A government that satisfies this definition may be called a *control democracy*.

An example will help to clarify the difference between these two concepts of democracy. Imagine a dictator who comes to power by purely military means. Once in power, he feels an obligation to follow the wishes of his new subjects, and so decides every question of policy in accordance with what the people (or a majority of them) prefer. Eventually the people cease resenting his usurpation of power and even prefer his government to any other. However, he retains control of the militia, and the people have no means of deposing him or guaranteeing that he continues to act in accordance with their wishes. Such a government would count as an accordance democracy, but not a control democracy, since actual control of policy decisions is in the hands of the dictator, not the hands of the people. This example may be far-fetched, but historical examples of governments at least claiming to approach such an accordance democracy are available. For example, in certain colonial regimes in Africa, legislators were appointed by the colonial power to "represent" the interests of the native population; such legislators were obligated, in principle, to follow the preferences (or at least the interests) of the native population in issues that came before the government. Certain one-party systems may be seen in the same light: the party comes to power by largely military means and subsequently proposes legislative candidates to the people, whose only option is to ratify these candidates. The elected representative then is supposed to decide on matters of policy by reference to the preferences or interests of his or her "constituents."[2]

It is my impression that most citizens of Western-style democracies would reject the benevolent dictator, the colonial regime, and the one-party system as not being truly democratic, even in theory. Of course, such systems are highly vulnerable to abuses that quickly make them failures as even accordance democracies. But I suspect most people would say that, even if such systems work, they do not count as genuine democracies. If this suspicion is accurate, then it suggests that the core notion of democracy that citizens in Western-style democracies employ is closer to what I have called control democracy—the idea that the people control what policies shall be made, not just that the policies adopted agree with their preferences in the matter. Of course, the fact (if it is a fact) that control democracy is the dominant conception does not mean that control democracies are better forms of government than accordance democracies. But for the moment, let us put aside the question of which of these two forms of government is the better and employ the control conception of democracy to answer our initial question: whether or not there is an intrinsic democratic value to be achieved by a representative who votes in accordance with his or her constituents' preferences on an issue.

III

To simplify our task, let us consider a clean case—the sort that never arises in real life, but that philosophers have the privilege of inventing. The case is one in which no other value (besides the putative democratic value) is at stake: no matter how the representative votes, his or her subsequent political influence will not be affected, his or her re-election will not be affected, local interests will not be affected, civil rights will not be affected, the national interest will not be affected, and so forth. Moreover, the representative holds the tie-breaking vote in this case—how he or she votes determines the outcome of the issue. The population in the country outside the representative's district is evenly divided about the issue at hand. But a majority of the representative's constituents prefer that the issue pass. The representative believes all this.

Let us grant, for the sake of argument, that it is indeed an intrinsic value that the political system be brought closer (on any particular occasion) to the ideal of pure democracy—one which outweighs all other values and all other combinations of values. Other theorists would regard this democratic value merely as one that must be weighed in the balance against others and that must sometimes give way to more important considerations. I personally am inclined towards this second position. For example, if a representative's constituents favor a certain segregationist measure, I believe considerations of justice require him or her, nevertheless, to vote against this measure, even though doing so will forfeit the intrinsic value of rendering the social decision more democratic that would be realized by the representative's voting in accord with his or her constituents' sentiments.[3] But given the way our clean case is structured, so that the value of a democratic decision does not conflict with any other, we may answer our immediate question without resolving how weighty the intrinsic value of democratic decision-making is.

Our immediate question is this: In the clean case, if the representative votes in accordance with the constituents' preferences on the issue, does he or she thereby bring the system closer to the ideal of pure democracy—that is, does he or she realize, in this vote, the intrinsic value of democratic decision-making? If the answer to this question is "yes," then clearly the representative ought to vote in accordance with his or her constituents' preferences, since we have stipulated that no other values are at stake in the case and we have agreed for the sake of argument that bringing the system closer to pure democracy is indeed a value.

If our ideal of pure democracy is an accordance democracy, then the answer to this question is obviously "yes," since a positive vote by the representative would ensure that the policy at hand accords with the preferences of the majority of the people.[4] But we have accepted, at least provisionally, the ideal of a control democracy. And on this conception, it appears that the answer to our question is "no." At least, it appears that if the representative votes positively on the issue merely because he or she believes that democratic considerations obligate him or her to do so, then the vote itself fails to bring the political system closer to pure democracy. For if the representative votes merely out of a feeling of moral obligation to do so, the constituents do not control, through the representative's vote, the policy decision, any more than the people in the benevolent dictatorship control, through the dictator's acts, the policies of their country. The acts of both the representative and the dictator are freely willed. They might easily have chosen to do otherwise, at no peril to themselves. The fact that they chose to do as the people desire does not show that the people themselves controlled the decisions. In view of this, the representative cannot realize the intrinsic value of democratic decision-making through a positive vote, and we must conclude that this value provides him or her with no reason to vote in accordance with his or her constituents' preferences.

Now imagine a case, exactly like the one just described, except that the representative will lose his or her office if he or she does not vote in accord with the constituents' wishes. This prospect is sufficiently unwelcome to motivate the representative to vote as the constituents wish. Such a vote is coerced by the constituents, and through it they control the resulting policy decision. In this case, a vote with the constituents does bring the system closer to an ideal democracy. Thus, there are two reasons the representative ought to vote with the constituents: to save his or her seat, and to engage in democratic decision-making. The second of these values, so to speak, rides piggyback on the first; it would not exist unless the first were sufficient to motivate the representative to vote that way even without the second.

Real cases, of course, will involve situations in which any number of values are at stake in the representative's vote. Without examining all the possibilities in detail, we can draw the following general conclusion. When the prospect of sanctions from the constituents—if the representative fails to vote in accord with their preferences—is *sufficient* to motivate him or her to vote with them, or is a *necessary part* of considerations that are sufficient to so motivate the representative, then the intrinsic value of democratic decision-making is realized in that vote. However, this value only arises because the representative is already sufficiently motivated to vote this way by independent considerations. When the prospect of sanctions from the electorate does not motivate the representative, then a vote in accord with the constituents' preferences does not realize the intrinsic value of democratic decision-making. In short, when a representative is trying to decide how to vote, he or she need not consider whether a given vote would enhance democracy, since, even if it would, this fact cannot tip the balance in favor of voting that way.[5]

IV

At this point an objection might be raised. Suppose, in the first case just described, the representative believes there is a moral obligation to vote as the constituents wish. After eliciting their preferences, the representative votes accordingly. Clearly, in such a case, the constituents' preferences caused the representative's vote and the ensueing policy decision. In view of this, how can it be said that there is a significant difference between this case and the one in which the constituents cause the representative's vote by threatening to remove him or her from office? In both cases the constituents cause the ultimate vote, and it appears we must say, as well, that they control it—and, hence, that the value of democratic decision-making is equally realized in both cases, contrary to the conclusion just drawn.

I believe this objection rests on a mistake. To see this, let us return to our definition of democracy as "a form of government in which collective preferences control policy." This definition implicitly contrasts democracy with forms of government in which the preferences of some person or group distinct from the collectivity control policy. Or more accurately, since many groups may have a hand in controlling policy, it implies that whether or not a government is democratic depends on which group has greater control over policy decisions—the collectivity or some subset of it. Thus, to determine whether or not the policy decisions in the cases just described are truly democratic in the control sense, we must know whether the constituents or the representative has greater control over the decision in question. The issue is not whether the constituents cause the ultimate decision, but whether they—as opposed to someone else—control it.

How do we decide who has greater control, or greater power, over a given policy decision? Here it is helpful to introduce an analysis of power proposed by Alvin Goldman in a paper entitled "Toward a Theory of Social Power."[6] Goldman proposes a definition of *comparative power* that incorporates Weber's and Mill's characterizations of power as the ability to get one's way despite resistance.[7] In an initial definition, the power of two individuals is compared with respect to an issue, E, that has only two possible outcomes, e and $-e$:

S$_1$ has more power than S$_2$ with respect to issue E if and only if:
(1) if S$_1$ wanted outcome e and if S$_2$ wanted outcome $-e$, then e would occur; and
(2) if S$_1$ wanted outcome $-e$ and if S$_2$ wanted outcome e, then $-e$ would occur.[8]

In this definition, the wants in question are assumed to be wants "on the whole" or "overall." Thus, if there are two individuals, Smith and Jones, who are each trying to control whether a door will be open or shut, the 250-pound Jones has greater power with respect to this issue than does the 90-pound weakling Smith, since, whichever outcome Jones wants, he will get it despite any resistance from Smith. If the "individuals" in question are groups, the counterfactuals in the definition require that each member of the group want the outcome in question. Therefore, if a group of ten burly people and a group of five skinny people are trying to control whether the door will be open or shut, the first group has more power, since, if each of its members wanted the door to be open (or shut), their will would prevail over the combined wills of the members of the smaller group.

As Goldman notes, this initial analysis is not sufficient. To see this, consider what would be said in a version of the Jones and Smith case in which Smith, the 90-pound weakling, credibly threatens to fire Jones unless Jones lets Smith have her way. Jones cares more about his job than about the door, and so lets Smith win the argument. Intuitively, we want to say in this version of the case that Smith has greater power than Jones over the issue of whether the door will be open or shut. However, the above analysis implies that Jones still has greater power, since it is still true that, if Jones wanted *overall* to open the door when Smith wanted to shut it, Jones would prevail. The analysis must be amended to account for the fact that which person will win in any situation depends on the *cost* to each of them of securing the outcome he or she desires, and the *degree* of desire each has for the outcome in question. In our second case, it is very costly for Jones to balk Smith's will, and, since he cares relatively little about the door, he gives in. Thus, when these factors appropriately are taken into account, Smith has the greater power with respect to this issue.

Since the intuitive point is clear enough, I will not attempt to specify precisely how these factors should play a role in defining comparative power. Let us now return to the question of which group—the constituents or the representative—has the greater power with respect to a particular policy decision.

Our analysis of comparative power now enables us to see that there is a significant difference between the case in which the representative feels obligated to do as his or her constituents wish, and so votes in accordance with their preferences, and the case in which the representative wants to keep his or her seat, and so votes in accordance with the constituents' preferences in order to retain it. In the first case, the representative has greater power with respect to the policy issue, since, however the representative wanted to vote, he or she could do so without hindrance from any opposing preferences of the constituents. But in the second case, the constituents have greater power with respect to the policy issue, since, if their will were opposed to that of the representative on which way to vote, their will would prevail, given the sanction they are in a position to wield. Their threat to remove the representative from office gives them greater power in this issue, just as Smith's threat to fire Jones gave her greater power in the issue of the door. Thus, the mere fact that the collectivity's preferences cause the representative's vote in both cases does not show that the collectivity controls the policy decision in both cases. To find out if the collectivity controls, we must ask whether the collectivity as opposed to anyone else controls. On our analysis of comparative power, in the first case the representative, as opposed to the collectivity, controls, while in the second case, the collectivity, as opposed to the representative, controls. Hence, the second case but not the first counts as a true case of democratic decision-making, in which the people rather than some subgroup (here the representative) control the policy decision. Our initial distinction between these two cases was correct.

V

I have argued that we must recognize two concepts of democracy: accordance democracy, in which policies accord with the people's preferences, and control democracy, in which policies not only accord with but are actively controlled by the people's preferences. A representative who votes in accord with the people's preferences necessarily brings his or her system closer to the ideal of an accord democracy. But a representative who votes in accord with popular preferences does not bring his or her system closer to the ideal of control democracy unless that vote is independently motivated by regard for sanctions the people would deploy if a different vote had been cast. The fact that a vote would bring the system closer to control democracy cannot tip the balance of practical reasoning in favor of casting that vote, since the balance must already have been tipped.

But let us now return to the previously deferred question of which of these two forms of democracy is superior. This question primarily has importance from the perspective of a constitutional convention. If we are designing our government, may we assume that everything valuable about democracy can be achieved by a mere accordance democracy, or is there some additional value that can be achieved by a control democracy? If some additional value is achievable, then the convention will want to design a system in which representatives are constrained to vote with their constituents, not just by moral compunctions, but by threat of sanctions wielded by the constituents or by binding regulations. Obviously, a control democracy has incalculable instrumental value: an accordance democracy that is not a control democracy is an all too easy target for abuses. Uncontrolled benevolent dictators turn into tyrannical despots; colonial legislators classically ignored or misunderstood the interests of the native groups they were supposed to advance; and one-party states standardly run roughshod over the welfare of their people. An accordance democracy is easily converted into no sort of democracy at all, and, of course, the people's actually having control over policy decisions may be the best way of preventing this from happening. This means, among other things, that it may be empirically unrealistic to speak of an accordance democracy that is not also a control democracy. But we are interested here not just in the instrumental value of control democracy but in the question of whether or not a control democracy has greater intrinsic value than accord democracy.

One way to approach this question is to survey the traditional arguments that have purported to show that democracy is superior to alternative forms of government. Some of these arguments may apply only to control democracies, or may apply better to control democracies.

Justifications for democracy tend to fall into two categories. One school of thought, exemplified by Bentham and James Mill, stresses the results or benefits to be gained from democracy.[9] Members of this school argue that in a democracy, as opposed to such alternative forms of government as oligarchies, the people will suffer less, they will be treated in a more equal fashion, more of their liberties and general civil rights will be preserved, and so forth. This argument seems to assume that in a democracy the people will get what they want, as opposed to what some leader misguidedly wants for them, or what some despot wants for himself. And it is assumed that the people do not want to suffer, to have their liberties constrained, and so on. Whatever we may think of the success of this argument, it is clear that it does not differentiate between accordance and control democracies. The guiding premise is that a democracy results in policies that accord with the people's preferences, and this is true in both kinds of democracy with which we are concerned. Such an argument cannot be used to show that a control democracy is superior (or inferior) to an accordance democracy.

A second school of thought, exemplified by John Stuart Mill and Rousseau, stresses not so much the benefits of democracy as the benefits of the democratic decision-making process.[10] Adherents of this view claim that when people participate in decisions affecting their lives, the participatory process itself, quite apart from the policies ultimately decided upon, provides significant benefits. For example, it is argued that political participation induces people to develop ties with others in the community, to identify more closely with each other, to appreciate the viewpoint of other persons, to become better informed about the issues of the day, to accept community decisions more readily, and so forth. Clearly, there is reason to think that if such benefits do arise, they will arise in a control democracy, where the people are actively engaged in decision-making and in the supervision of their representatives. But it is not impossible for such benefits to arise as well in an accordance democracy that is not a control democracy. For example, in the benevolent dictator case, if the people know that the dictator takes their preferences seriously and always adopts policies that accord with them, it is reasonable to think they will inform themselves about the issues of the day on which decisions must be made, join political debating societies, create forums for public discussion, and in other ways achieve the enhanced sense of community usually associated with control democracies. However, it seems to be a plausible empirical generalization that the benefits of participation are more strongly associated with control democracy than with mere accordance democracy.

This may be reason enough to induce a constitutional convention to adopt a control democracy rather than a mere accordance democracy (assuming that this arises as a practical choice, which, as we noted before, may not happen). But I suspect that the difference between these two forms of government runs deeper than anything we can grasp by focusing on the kinds of effects just cited. It seems to me that the contrast between these two forms of democracy can be illuminated by comparing it with another contrast, now deeply entrenched in philosophical mythology—the contrast between the life of an ordinary person and the life of a "brain in a vat." The brain in the vat is simply a detached brain, nourished by chemicals in its vat, and electronically stimulated by attendant scientists in such a way that it seems to the brain that it is living a normal human life. It can even be arranged that the life the brain appears to lead is spectacularly successful, pleasurable, and rewarding: perhaps the brain thinks that it participates in continuous orgies, or is the first person to conquer Mt. Everest, or discovers the cure for cancer, or has twelve children, all of whom are marvelous human beings and Nobel laureates to boot—whatever we like. When people are asked whether they would prefer living an ordinary life such as they can realistically expect to lead, or being a brain in a vat who lives a seemingly marvelous life (and who is never apprised of the true state of affairs), reactions differ. Some people choose the life of the brain in a vat. But in my experience the majority prefer the ordinary life. Such a life contains a full measure of suffering and anxiety—but it also contains a few, perhaps minor, but genuine accomplishments and worthwhile experiences. And a person who prefers this ordinary life evidently prefers the reality of being his high school's second-best violinist to the illusion of being a Jascha Heifitz, when actually he has never done anything more significant than tremble in his nutrient bath.

One can have a similar attitude toward political life: one can prefer controlling one's life and the decisions that affect it to living under a government whose policies accord with one's wishes but whose strings are controlled by someone else. Such a preference for a control over a mere accordance democracy may be almost metaphysical, but I suspect in many people it is deep and genuine nonetheless.

Notes

1. David Braybrooke, *Three Tests for Democracy* (New York: Random House, 1968), p. 149. Braybrooke himself does not put this forward as a *definition* of democracy. Of course there are numerous problems with this definition that are not germane to our enquiry.

2. These cases are described in Stanley I. Benn, "Democracy," *The Encyclopedia of Philosophy* (1967), vol. 2, p. 339.

3. It might be argued that, in the case of an American representative, the Constitution requires this vote, and since the Constitution is itself supported by the people, the vote is not contrary to democracy. But it is clear that the representative's own constituents do not support at least this provision of the Constitution.

4. Whether or not such a vote enhances democracy is a much more difficult question in a case where the vote does not actually affect which policy is selected, or where the preferences of the representative's constituents are opposed to those of the majority in the country as a whole. I shall not attempt to deal with this problem.

5. In a given case, the representative's self-interest in being re-elected might not qualify as a moral consideration in favor of the vote. If this interest nevertheless leads the representative to cast a vote with the constituents' preferences, then by so doing he or she brings the system closer to ideal democracy. Thus there is at least one moral value in favor of this vote, even if there are no others, and in a sense this tips the *moral* argument in favor of the vote. But the moral argument only comes into existence when the representative has *already decided* on *other* (self-interested) grounds to vote this way.

6. Alvin I. Goldman, "Toward a Theory of Social Power," *Philosophical Studies* 23 (1972): 221–68. For a further development of this theory, see Alvin I. Goldman, "On the Measurement of Power," *The Journal of Philosophy* 71 (May 2, 1974): 231–51.

7. Goldman, "Toward a Theory of Social Power," p. 246; Max Weber, *The Theory of Social and Economic Organization* (New York: Oxford University Press, 1947), p. 152; and C. Wright Mills, *The Power Elite* (New York: Oxford University Press, 1959), p. 9.

8. Goldman, "Toward a Theory of Social Power," p. 244.

9. James Mill, *Essay on Government* (Cambridge: Cambridge University Press, 1937); Jeremy Bentham, *Works,* ed. J. Bowring (Edinburgh: W. Tait, 1843). See discussion in Barry Holden, *The Nature of Democracy* (New York: Barnes and Noble, 1974). ch. 8.

10. John Stuart Mill, *Considerations on Representative Government* (Oxford: Oxford University Press, 1946), and J. J. Rousseau, *Political Writings of Jean Jacques Rousseau,* ed. C. E. Vaughan (Cambridge: Cambridge University Press, 1915). For discussion see Carole Pateman, *Participation and Democratic Theory* (Cambridge: Cambridge University Press, 1970), ch. 2.

ELIZABETH L. BEARDSLEY

6 Legislators and the Morality of Their Constituents

I

Somewhat neglected by philosophers is the general question whether the morality of its citizens is an appropriate area of concern for a government.[1] In this chapter I shall deal with this general question only as it relates to the activity of legislators. I shall consider, first, whether it is possible (conceptually) for a legislator to strengthen the morality of his or her constituents. I shall then consider the question whether, if this is possible, it is justifiable, and on what grounds. The discussion of these two questions, particularly of the second, will be shown to provide the answer to a third question: to what extent the attempt by a legislator to strengthen the morality of his/her constituents counts as serving the legislator's conscience and to what extent it counts as serving constituents' interests.

But first I must explain what I shall mean by "strengthening the morality" of an individual. To explicate what it means to "have a morality" I adopt Frankena's account:

X has a morality, or a moral AG (Action Guide), only if it includes judgments, rules, principles, ideals, etc., which concern the relations of an individual (e.g., X) to others . . . (and) involve or call for consideration of the effects of his actions on others (not necessarily all others), not from the point of view of his own interests or aesthetic enjoyments, but from their own point of view.[2]

By the expression "Y strengthens the morality of X" I shall mean "Y strengthens in X the disposition to consider 'the effects of his actions on others . . . from their own point of view.'" I shall call this the "fundamental moral disposition" (FMD).

83

I have argued elsewhere[3] that the mere fact that Y is *other* than X poses no conceptual barrier to saying that Y can strengthen the morality of X. Here we must consider whether a legislator *qua* legislator (L_1) can strengthen the morality (FMD) of a constituent (C_1). If L_1 is to accomplish this, it must be either by the giving of reasons to C_1 why he should consider the effects of his actions on others, or by the providing of conditions that will make it easier for C_1 to do this. I shall call the former method "rational persuasion" and the latter "causal facilitation."

It may seem at first that L_1 cannot strengthen the FMD of C_1 by rational persuasion. L_1 can give C_1 self-regarding reasons for refraining from harming others, but these have nothing to do with the FMD of C_1. A recent statement compatible with this general line of thought runs as follows:

> The virtue of an act has to do with the principles and passions behind it. If we refrain from force and fraud, that is only virtuous if, at least, we do so out of a decent respect for the rights of others, and not solely from fear of retribution. If the officers of the state were to do nothing but offer retribution as an incentive for refraining from violating the rights of others, they would not be concerned with whether we refrain because we are moved by decent motives—they simply would want to make us refrain. They would not aim to make us more virtuous.[4]

But to identify the law, even the criminal law, with a set of prohibitions backed by coercive sanctions is unacceptable. It is to disregard what has been aptly called the "expressive function of punishment."[5] In selecting certain conduct for criminalization, a legal system makes a statement that ranges beyond an appeal to self-interest. Nor is it only philosophers and legal theorists who have acknowledged this point. Noteworthy here is a statement by Justice Macklin Fleming. Having defined crimes as "intentional invasions of primary personal rights," Fleming goes on to assert that "by imposing sanctions on the criminal we seek to teach potential criminals the lesson that this particular crime did not pay, that crime is poor policy, and that crime is morally wrong."[6] Fleming here captures the multifaceted nature of a system of criminal law and recognizes the ability of this governmental institution to meet the test of other-regarding motivation, which rules out only an exclusive appeal to self-regarding consideration.

Let us consider a little more closely how the use of coercive sanctions is a form of rational persuasion, though not exclusively through its appeal to self-interest. The criminal law vividly shows how strongly society reprobates certain harms to others. By bringing to bear on certain conduct the entire apparatus of the criminal law (formidable if not always majestic), society expresses in the strongest possible terms the judgment that such conduct is wrong. But if C_1 learns from all this only that his community regards harming others as wrong, without going on to see that it *is* wrong in that it violates the rights of others, he has not progressed far toward becoming morally good.[7] Still, he has taken an initial step.

It seems clear, then, that the criminal law affords one means by which government can strengthen the morality of individuals. Understood in the way just described, legislation here becomes a mechanism that strengthens the morality of C_1 by teaching him something—that is, by a kind of rational persuasion.[8]

I turn now to the question whether, and if so how, L_1 can strengthen the FMD of C_1 by causal facilitation. Here it is natural to think, first, of factors that might weaken the FMD in C_1. Economic insecurity and anxiety about health problems come readily to mind. An individual whose thoughts are free from nagging worry about material well-being or health is psychologically more able to consider others when he acts, as is an individual who has satisfying human bonds.

Legislators can do much to insure that the minimal needs of constituents are met and to strengthen certain patterns of social organization (for example, families and communities). Such legislative measures can strengthen the FMD of constituents.

II

Our next question concerns the justifiability of the legislator's attempting to strengthen the morality of a constituent. Some may be tempted to remark that the answer is too obvious to make the question worth asking.

In the *Politics,* according to a leading expositor, Aristotle recognizes that "the good life of the state exists only in the good lives of its citizens" and "speaks as if the state were merely ancillary to the moral life of the individual."[9] Centuries later, a political theorist is said to defend the thesis that "the goal of politics is autonomy or moral agency."[10] If the purpose of government is to produce individuals of high moral caliber, then it is obvious that L_1 should strengthen the morality of C_1. But such a theory of "the purpose of government" is far from persuasive. It appears to invite legislating a certain treatment of C_2 and C_3 on the ground that this would strengthen the morality of C_1. This would be to treat C_2 and C_3 as means to the moral improvement of C_1, which would be morally objectionable.

But plainly if a legislator is justified in strengthening the morality of C_1, the justification must claim that this is in the interest of C_1 or that it is in the interest of others, say C_2 and C_3. Let us consider briefly whether either justification meets critical scrutiny. Much depends here on whether it is argued that his or her morality is instrumentally valuable for C_1 (as enabling him or her to secure other goods) or as intrinsically valuable for C_1. Consider first the assumption that C_1's morality is instrumentally valuable to him or her—that is, that to be morally stronger will help C_1 to further his or her own (nonmoral) interests. To use this rationale in seeking to persuade someone to improve his or her FMD is, as we have seen, conceptually impossible. The question is whether L_1 can have in his or her own rationale a reason that he or she must keep secret from C_1. Such a situation is familiar to us: parents often have reasons *for* persuading children to do or be something that are not the reasons they use *in* persuading the children. There is nothing contradictory or even hypocritical in the parents' behavior; but there is something very patronizing. At least, we should call it "patronizing" in a relation between adults, of which the relation of L_1 to C_1 is presumably an instance.

I therefore reject the justification that L_1 should foster the moral development of C_1 on the ground that his or her own moral development is instrumentally good for C_1. Let us consider now the other assumption—that his or her own moral development is intrinsically good for C_1.

Those who have, as I do, a strong antipaternalist bias, will here be on their guard. Paternalism has been defined as the restriction of an individual's liberty for his own good.[11] Since the coercion of C_1 was ruled out above as a possible means of strengthening his or her morality, paternalism in this sense is not in question. We are considering the justifiability of L_1's strengthening the morality of C_1 only by rational persuasion or causal facilitation. Such procedures may not be paternalistic, but they are patronizing.

This is because it is one thing for Y to try to help X secure a good for X at X's request, and quite another thing for Y to try to secure a good for X without X's request, however good the good may be. The latter procedure is initiated by a significant decision concerning X's life not taken by X. I believe that this way of treating X, if X is an adult, is patronizing. It is a mild form of a failure to respect autonomy. There is a moral spectrum here, with the treatment of X as a mere means at one end of the spectrum, paternalistic treatment next, and patronizing treatment next. These are morally objectionable in very different degrees, but I think it is important to recognize the common thread running through them.[12]

To justify strengthening the morality of C_1 on the ground that this will be valuable for C_1, either instrumentally or intrinsically, is open to serious question. This justification is, as I have argued, either conceptually impossible or patronizing. What can be said about the thesis that L_1 is justified in fostering the moral development of C_1 on the ground that this will be valuable for others?

This justification can be formulated so that it rests on a much stronger moral foundation. The thesis that C_2 and C_3 have rights (justified claims) to security in their persons and property is relatively unproblematic, as is the thesis that legislators have an obligation to protect these rights. Since morality in C_1 will assist in this protection, it is reasonable to argue that L_1 should strengthen the morality of C_1.

But this justification needs to be clarified in certain respects. First, it does not imply that other methods of protecting the rights of C_2 and C_3 are ruled out for L_1.[13] Second, it must not be understood as failing to respect the autonomy of C_1. Those who would argue that to strengthen the morality of C_1 on the ground that this will be in the interest of C_2 and C_3 is to treat C_1 as a means only have failed to grasp what is involved in strengthening someone's morality. If this project is conceptualized in the way proposed above, we may say that L_1 is morally justified in carrying it out.

Thus, whereas L_1 is not justified in treating C_2 and C_3 in a certain fashion on the ground that this would strengthen the morality of C_1, for L_1 to strengthen the morality of C_1 on the ground that this protects certain interests of C_2 and C_3 is justified. To put the matter in another way, we may say that C_2 and C_3 have a right to security but that C_1 does not have a right to the strengthening of his/her morality.[14]

III

If the arguments of the preceding section are sound, it is clear that for L_1 to attempt to strengthen the morality of C_1 cannot be construed either as serving L_1's conscience or as serving L_1's constituents. Since L_1 has no direct obligation to improve the morality of a constituent, to do so cannot be dictated by his/her conscience. But this is an oversimplification. Since L_1 does have an obligation to protect the rights of any constituent, and since this can sometimes be done only by strengthening the morality of other constituents, L_1 has an indirect obligation to strengthen the morality of C_1 generated by his or her direct obligation to C_2 or C_3. The direct obligation can be dictated by conscience, and fulfilling it can count as "serving L_1's conscience."

Similarly, to say that an attempt on the part of L_1 to strengthen the morality of C_1 is (or is not) an attempt to serve a constituent's interests is an oversimplification. It cannot serve the interests of C_1, though it can serve the interests of C_2 and C_3, who are equally constituents of L_1. Evidently, the dichotomy "serving a legislator's conscience or a constituent's interest" is ill adapted to foster an understanding of legislative activity in the enterprise of strengthening morality. But this enterprise does raise interesting philosophic questions of its own, as I have tried to show in this chapter.

Notes

1. I address the more general question in "Moral Development as an Objective of Government," in Gordon Schochet and Richard Wilson, eds., *Moral Development and Politics*. (New York: Praeger, 1980).
2. W. K. Frankena, "The Concept of Morality," in Gerald Wallace and A. B. H. Walker, eds., *The Definition of Morality* (London: Methuen, 1970), p. 156.
3. E. L. Beardsley, "Moral Development," in op. cit., Section I.
4. Lester H. Hunt, "Punishment, Revenge, and the Minimal Functions of the State," in Fred D. Miller, Jr., and Thomas Attig, eds., *Understanding Human Emotions* (Bowling Green, Ohio: Bowling Green State University

Press, 1979, p. 79. Note that Hunt sets forth this argument for consideration only.

5. Joel Feinberg, "The Expressive Function of Punishment," *Doing and Deserving* (Princeton: Princeton University Press, 1970), pp. 95–118. See also Henry M. Hart, Jr., "Criminal Punishment as Public Condemnation," in R. J. Garber and P. D. McAnany, eds., *Contemporary Punishment* (Notre Dame: University of Notre Dame Press, 1972), pp. 12–15.

6. Macklin Fleming, *Of Crime and Rights* (New York: Norton, 1978), p. 126. Emphasis added.

7. In a general form, this point is clearly stated by Kurt Baier, "Ethical Pluralism and Moral Education," in C. M. Beck *et al.,* eds., *Moral Education* (Toronto: Newman, 1971), pp. 94–95.

8. Constitutionalism can exert a notable moral force in strengthening the FMD. See David A. J. Richards, *The Moral Criticism of Law* (Encino, Calif.: Dickenson, 1977).

9. W. D. Ross, *Aristotle* (London: Methuen, 1956), p. 187.

10. This view is attributed to Andrew Levine by S. G. Salkever; see his review of Levine, "The Politics of Autonomy," *Political Theory* 5 (1977): 539.

11. Gerald Dworkin, "Paternalism," in Richard Wasserstrom, ed., *Morality and the Law* (Belmont, Calif.: Wadsworth, 1971), pp. 107–26.

12. I try to analyze this common thread in "Paternalism and Benevolence," in progress.

13. In thinking about this point I have benefited from Paul Tong's discussion of some of his unpublished work on Chinese legal concepts.

14. Here see Joel Feinberg, "Harm and Self-interest," in P. M. Hecker and Joseph Raz, eds., *Law, Morality and Society* (Oxford: Clarendon Press, 1977), pp. 285–308, especially for his discussion of "moral harms." I regret that this essay came to my attention only after my own paper had been completed.

Part II

The Proper Bounds of Government Regulation

In any analysis of ethical issues in government, one soon discerns that a complete analysis depends in part on successfully articulating a theory of the function of government. Plato and Aristotle surely had a point when they argued that there is a functional relation between the purpose of X and the goodness of X. Few debates generate more emotion than those that focus on the proper bounds of government regulation. If the intensity of the debate is to be lessened, one step should be an examination of the theoretical foundations that underlie the conflicting sides. In this section, three very distinct foundations are provided for determining just what the proper bounds of government regulation are.

Although agreeing that appeals to utility, polity, and individual rights set boundaries to government regulation, Lawrence Becker wishes to focus on the requirement of non-arbitrariness as the supreme principle for controlling government regulation. The requirement of non-arbitrariness is one of the four formal conditions of justice, the others being impartiality, certainty, and advance notice. The non-arbitrariness requirement stipulates that there be some acceptable purpose for the rule and that it be an acceptable means for achieving that purpose. Becker then argues that in cases of government regulation, all the other formal conditions of justice be subordinated to the requirement of non-arbitrariness.

Rex Martin considers the application of Rawlsian principles of justice to the problem of government regulation. When Professor Martin speaks of government regulation, he is referring to the regulation of the economic institutions of society. After sketching out the essential features of Rawls' theory, Professor Martin shows that the principle of the open and competitive market does not follow in any deductive way from the two principles. The principle of the market is justified by the notion of pure procedural justice so long as certain background conditions are realized. Moreover, Rawls' difference principle does not specify any rights to either shares of incomes or economic positions. Therefore, one can neither rationalize nor limit governmental intervention in these matters by reference to natural rights. Finally, ownership of the means to production must be viewed as resting on the collective asset idea and hence private ownership could be justified only if it encouraged the development and *use* of talents and abilities with the result that productivity is increased.

Eric Mack provides a libertarian critique of Martin's analysis. He challenges Martin's contention that Rawls' analysis of the market represents an application of the notion of pure procedural justice. If a practice is to be called *just,* the procedure itself must have some morally valuable feature. But Rawls' appeal to the market is based only on grounds of efficiency and there is nothing distinctively moral about that. In libertarian theory the appeal to the market is based on moral features—the market's compatibility with and protection of individual rights. By implication, whereas the libertarian evaluates government regulation of the market on moral grounds, Rawls and Martin are primarily concerned with considerations of efficiency.

LAWRENCE C. BECKER

7 The Proper Bounds of Government Regulation

My thesis is that government rule-making should be controlled by one complex principle—which I shall call the requirement of non-arbitrariness. Rule-making should not be the result of a disorganized attempt to juggle political expediency, social goals, individual rights, cost-effectiveness, certain formal constraints of justice on rule-making *per se,* and the requirements of our form of government. The operative word here is "disorganized" use of these considerations. I certainly do not say that they should be ignored. I only want to show that they are contained in, and made coherent by, the non-arbitrariness requirement. It is for that reason, and not because I think non-arbitrariness is some distinct super-principle, that I recommend exclusive reliance on it.

Like many sensible theses in political philosophy, this one also will turn out to be somewhat less interesting than it first appears. It can be trivialized by characterizing it as the simple claim that all laws should be justifiable. But ridicule is misplaced. In theory, the principles that are supposed to guide lawmaking in our pluralistic democracy are incoherent. They are produced by widely divergent lines of argument —running from the minimum state to maximal state extremes—and intersecting at just enough points to hang together. In practice, as anyone who reads government documents can see, laws are made with a dishearteningly narrow range of considerations. The value of a reconceptualization of the problem can therefore be considerable— especially if the new conception can both structure apparently competing principles at the level of theory and show how the practice of rule-making can be broadened to include them all.

I hope to persuade you that some of this can be achieved by focusing on the non-arbitrariness requirement. To do that, however, I shall first have to locate my remarks in the context of current theorizing about government regulation.

Other Approaches

It may already be evident that I construe the question of government regulation very broadly—as coextensive, in fact, with all government rule-making that has the force of law. All laws regulate conduct, whether they directly impose duties or grant entitlements, or whether they merely define offices and powers. Of course, it is possible to narrow the question by dealing only with "direct" regulation—that is, with what H. L. A. Hart calls primary or duty-imposing rules.[1] And it is possible to narrow the question even more drastically by confining oneself to government regulations—that is, to rules, having the force of law, issued by the executive branch and meant to help implement statutes, judicial decisions, provisions of the Constitution, or policies based on them.[2] Government *self*-regulation is sometimes also ignored. But in terms of the approach I shall take to the question, such restrictions are pointless.[3] Either the requirement of non-arbitrariness applies to all government rule-making in the same way, or it does not. If it does not, the fact will at least be revealed by the analysis. If it does (as I suspect is the case), then nothing is to be gained from dividing the question. So I shall construe the question of the proper bounds of government regulation as broadly as possible.

There are at least five strategies for fixing the proper boundaries. One is an appeal to social utility: Describe the regions of life in which government intervention would produce net disutility, and prohibit it in those areas. Find the areas in which government regulation is needed to maximize utility, and require it there. Economists and public policy theorists typically take this approach, and it has been given extensive technical development in the theory of public goods, public utilities, and the cost-benefit analysis of government regulation.[4]

Another strategy is developed from principles of polity: Identify the rules that would necessarily defeat or compromise the theory of governance, and prohibit them. Likewise, identify the places in which polity requires government controls, and insist on that. In a democracy, the areas that are especially sensitive to such considerations include the free flow of politically relevant education, ideas, and information (because a competent electorate is a necessity), and a good deal of administrative and judicial lawmaking (because it is in principle undemocratic). Other polities would have quite different concerns.[5]

A third strategy derives boundaries from individual rights: Decide what areas of personal liberty, privacy, and dignity may not be invaded, and then establish regulation to protect them; prohibit regulation that invades them. The Bill of Rights was designed in part to do this, and much of the recent legislation and litigation on privacy, freedom of information, abortion, euthanasia, sexual conduct, conscientious objection, and the like has taken this approach.[6]

All three of these strategies are well defined and much discussed. No proposal for defining the boundaries of regulation that ignored them could be called complete. I shall be concerned, however, with two rather ill-defined and little discussed strategies that I believe must also be a part of any comprehensive theory of government regulation. One has to do with satisfying the formal conditions of justice in rule-making. The other concerns the relation between the implementation of a rule and the moral character of the people involved. Each of these approaches yields the thesis that I mentioned at the outset: that rule-making should be controlled by the requirement of non-arbitrariness. I will begin by describing briefly some formal conditions of justice in rule-making.

Formal Conditions of Justice

There are competing theories of justice, and at the deepest level the competition is probably unresolvable. But all of the enduring, philosophically defensible theories of justice converge at important points. Murder, mayhem, theft, and negligence are always condemned. Kindness, helpfulness, honesty, and fidelity are always approved. Differences exist about whether something is to be required or only encouraged, forbidden or only frowned upon, enforced legally or only morally. But genuine differences over whether an act (under a given description) is on the side of good or on the side of evil are much rarer. (That is one reason the proper description of an act is so crucial. Describe it one way and everyone agrees that it is all right, another way and people are puzzled, still another and it is universally condemned. Moral disputes then take the form of arguing about the proper description of the act.)

In any case, I want to exploit one of these convergence points for the purpose of assessing government regulation. All of the standard theories of justice agree, I think, that the following formal conditions are necessary ingredients of a just rule. Utilitarians may treat them as mere rules of thumb and will typically have a much longer list. Social contract theorists may regard them as purely conventional. Natural law theorists may think of them as required by reason. But that there are at least these constraints on government rule-making is not in dispute. The constraints to which I refer may be called impartiality, certainty, non-arbitrariness, and advance notice. In jurisprudence these are sometimes found under the heading of natural justice.[7]

Impartiality

The requirement of impartiality has two aspects, which amount, respectively, to what I shall call the similar cases rule and a restriction on it. "Similar cases must be treated similarly" has been called the rule of justice, the generalization principle, formal justice, the universalization principle, and simply the similar cases rule.[8] It prohibits the singling out of individuals from the class to which a given rule applies. If an act is right or wrong for one person, it might be right or wrong for all who are similar in relevant respects. This is so because the basis for calling it right or wrong is bound to be some feature of a person's nature, or life, or circumstance, that is in principle shareable by others. And if that feature is sufficient to justify or condemn an act for that person, it is necessarily sufficient to do the same for others who share it—for all others who are "relevantly similar."

Of course, it is not easy to decide what counts as a relevant similarity. But the very centrality and difficulty of this question serve to shift attention in decision-making away from the peculiarities of individuals and toward an impersonal consideration of *types* of people and circumstances. Decisions must be justified in those terms, and we must be ready to make the same decision in all the similar cases.

Further, there is a crucial restriction on the similar cases rule as it applies to public life (that is, to the conduct of officials as officials— whether the "offices" involved be ones in government, private organizations, or social structures). Parents, employers, and judges all have this in common: they are not supposed to play favorites. Put another way, they are not permitted to count their purely personal preferences for or against individuals, or their purely personal gains or losses from a given situation, as "relevant similarities." A judge may not say: "I happen to dislike gun owners. I therefore systematically give harsher sentences to them than to others, but in doing so I am following the similar cases rule perfectly because I give the same treatment to all and only gun owners."[9] The same is true for the mayor who favors all and only friends, or the parent who favors all and only the "quiet" children. And the same holds for officials who decide cases so as to reap personal profit at the expense of the institution or organization they serve. In highly regularized institutions—such as the judiciary—we adopt the requirement of disinterested adjudication to help eliminate the use of personal preference.

These two things then (the similar cases rule and the restriction on it) define a condition of impartiality. I submit that it is imposed in some form, by all theories of justice, on all "official" rule-making.

Certainty

The requirement of certainty also has two aspects. One is that rules be (reasonably) determinable. "Acceptable clothing must be worn" is so vague that its meaning is largely indeterminable. Acceptable to whom? For what purposes? In what places? If enacted into law in this country, it would be rejected as unconstitutionally vague.[10] And such vagueness is said to be unjust—because, for example, it makes it impossible for people to know in advance what they are supposed to do. (See the discussion of advance notice below.) So the meaning of a rule must be reasonably determinable.

It must also be reasonably determinate—that is, it must decide cases. "Drive no more than 55 m.p.h." is clear enough, but it doesn't give the police any guidance about what to do with people who exceed the speed limit. Are they to be jailed? Or fined? Or only warned? Although policies and principles are expected to be somewhat indeterminate, legal or moral rules are expected to determine, more or less conclusively, the outcome of the cases to which they apply.[11] In fact, there is a tendency in practice, caused by the push for the other conditions described here, to make rules fully determinate—leaving no room for administrative discretion at all. I do not think that this is a requirement of justice, however, as I shall argue in a moment.

Non-arbitrariness

The third requirement of justice in rule-making is non-arbitrariness: both that there be some acceptable purpose for the rule and that it be an acceptable means for achieving that purpose. The standard of acceptability is justifiability in terms of one's theory of justice.[12] In our constitutional law, this gets translated into whether or not there is some legitimate (or even compelling) state interest behind the rule— some "intent" that is compatible with generally accepted views about the proper powers and concerns of government. If so, then the question becomes whether or not the rule is a reasonable means for achieving that legitimate state interest. Reasonability has to do with both causal efficacy and permissibility. The causal question is not "Is it the most effective or most efficient means to the end?" but rather "Will it work reasonably well and reasonably efficiently?" The permissibility question has to do with the rule's compatibility with other requirements of justice. Does the rule violate individual rights, for example? If one's purpose is to reduce motorcycle accidents (surely a legitimate one), a rule requiring motorcyclists to wear helmets is not a reasonable means to choose. It is arbitrary because it lacks causal efficacy. Shooting motorcyclists would be effective, but impermissible—arbitrarily ignoring other requirements of justice. But if the purpose of the helmet rule is to reduce the severity and frequency of head injuries (rather than accidents as such), the causal efficacy and permissibility questions look very different.[13]

Different theories of justice handle the non-arbitrariness requirement by different standards. Utilitarian theory requires optimific rules—the best achievable ends and the best useable means to those ends. Social contract theory adopts means and ends that are in some sense consensual. Natural rights theory defines permanent barriers immune from considerations of utility or convention. But the formal structure of the requirement remains the same for all theories: rules must have ends, and be means to those ends, that are justifiable in terms of the theory—that are in that sense non-arbitrary.

Advance Notice

The final requirement I shall mention (though I do not say that this completes an exhaustive list) is advance notice. Rules are said to be unjust to the extent that people penalized by them could not have known, beforehand, that such a rule existed, or applied to them, or would penalize them. We fail to get advance notice to the extent that the rule is not made public before the fact or, indeed, to the extent that the rule is invented after the fact and applied retroactively. The justification for this requirement need not detain us. Whether one's concern is for consensual arrangements, for fairness, or for social stability, the advance notice requirement obviously deserves its place alongside impartiality, certainty, and non-arbitrariness as a formal condition of justice in rule-making.

Formal Conditions on Government Regulation

I shall take it as given that every existing or proposed government rule has some purpose—that it is, in fact, an effort either to maximize utility, to carry out the principles of polity, to protect individual rights, or to do some combination of those things. It can therefore be evaluated, both for appropriateness and effectiveness, in terms of how well it fulfills its purpose(s). But it can also be evaluated in terms of how well it fulfills the formal conditions of justice in rule-making. As we shall see, the two sorts of evaluation overlap significantly—by way of the non-arbitrariness requirement.

The evaluation of rules in terms of the formal conditions is not entirely straightforward. There are two sorts of difficulties. First, there are the standard technical problems of interpretation: What counts as a relevant similarity for the purposes of the similar cases rule? How clear, or reasonable, or public, must a rule be? These are vexing issues, but every method of evaluation is plagued with comparable ones. (Even, perhaps especially, cost-benefit analysis. It is one of the wonders of modern rhetoric that problems of interpretation can be so successfully evaded when the analysis looks quantitative.) I shall not confront the problems of interpretation here. Instead I shall focus on another sort of difficulty—the one raised by the fact that, taken together, the requirements often seem to conflict with one another. When such conflicts occur, they must be resolved by setting priorities among the requirements. It is with the question of priorities that I shall be concerned.

Certainty and Impartiality

There appears to be considerable pressure on government rule-makers to compromise both the advance notice requirement and the non-arbitrariness requirement on behalf of certainty and impartiality.[14] In part, this is a product of current political and legal concerns—specifically, discrimination, corruption in government, and the regulation of industry. In part, it is the product of the apparent logical priority of this pair.

The Politics of the Priority

Discrimination (violative of Fourteenth Amendment guarantees) occurs when people are harmed by a violation of the similar cases rule, or by being subjected to unreasonable classifications as a means to some end, or when the end pursued (by way of a reasonable classification) is unjust.[15] Arguments against the most blatant instances of discrimination—for example, against racial and religious minorities and women—have traditionally been formulated as demands for equality—as claims that race, or religion, or sex, is not a "relevant difference." Further, once laws have been rewritten to specify equal treatment, regulations designed to contribute to enforcement quite naturally take the form of the similar case rule.[16] This aspect of the impartiality requirement thus becomes a central concern.

Its other aspect (the prohibition of favoritism and personal enrichment), along with one aspect of the certainty requirement, predominates in the reaction to political corruption. Bribery, kickbacks, nepotism, personal favors, and so on obviously violate the impartiality requirement, and a typical reaction to them is to "tighten up the rules"—that is, to try to increase the determinateness (certainty) of the rules so as to leave no room for discretion in their administration. The thought is that if there is no room for discretion, then at least it will be easy to identify violations of the impartiality requirement; there will be no room at all for arguments about "judgment calls."[17]

Finally, the regulation of industry quite naturally raises the similar cases rule and the certainty requirement to prominence. Wherever businesses can simply pass along the increased costs of safety or environmental regulations, or of product liability rules, they will necessarily be concerned, first and foremost, with not being put at a competitive disadvantage and with being able to determine exactly what the regulations require. Whether the regulations are arbitrary or not will be a secondary concern. Avoiding competitive disadvantage requires close attention to the similar cases rule: *all* the relevantly similar businesses must be subject to the costs imposed by the regulation. Being able to determine exactly what the regulations mean translates into a demand for certainty. So again these two conditions—impartiality and certainty—are the leading concerns.[18]

The Logic of the Priority

I do not mean to suggest, of course, that non-arbitrariness and advance notice are popularly thought to be unimportant. I only say that people seem willing to compromise them on behalf of the other two conditions. And there is more than political expediency or tradition behind this. Certainty is a necessary condition of advance notice: unless the meaning of the rule is clear, people cannot know in advance what is required of them—no matter how well the rule is publicized. Likewise, the similar cases rule is a necessary condition for non-arbitrariness: if there are no relevant similarities (or differences) among a group of people or cases, they cannot be treated similarly (or differently) without arbitrariness. But the reverse does not seem to be true: non-arbitrariness and advance notice are not apparently preconditions for impartiality and certainty. It is natural to treat the parasitic pair as subordinate when they come in conflict with the others.

More importantly, the non-arbitrariness requirement appears to be a source of disagreement in a way that the others are not. If theories of justice differ significantly at all on matters of substance (which they do), and if the citizens of our state hold differing theories of justice (which they do), then the formal requirement that all rules be justifiable in terms of *the* theory of justice seems to present insuperable problems. What theory do we use here? Or do we use them all and only adopt those rules on which all theories concur? That seems wholly impractical. Better to concentrate on the other formal conditions (since all theories do agree on them, at least), and make the necessary compromises with the non-arbitrariness requirement. A similar problem exists for the advance notice requirement. If the state had to make sure everyone were informed in advance of every rule adopted, very little could be accomplished in a large, complex, fast-moving, heterogeneous society. Better to water down the requirement by insisting only that the rules be available to people of "reasonable" intelligence who make "reasonable" efforts to become informed.[19] Likewise, if the prohibition on *ex post facto* legislation were taken seriously (the other part of the advance notice requirement), would not all judicial and administrative lawmaking be prohibited? And would not that make adjudication either impossible or unacceptably rigid?[20] Again, it seems natural to concentrate on the (apparently) less problematic pair of requirements—certainty and impartiality.

Some Undesirable Consequences

But there are some unfortunate consequences from doing so. The quest for certainty causes an enormous increase in the number of rules, for example. A statute is drafted, say to make federal money available to people who want to convert their home heating from conventional to solar systems. The grants are to cover 10 percent of the owners' costs. The agency charged with disbursing the funds (or perhaps the legislature itself) anticipates borderline disputes on all sorts of questions: What counts as a conventional system? What counts as a house? (A trailer? an apartment complex?) Who counts as an owner? (A management company representing the owners of a condominium?) And how are costs to be calculated? Rules are drafted to decide all these questions. But of course these new rules are themselves general—applying to "types" of people, or certain sorts of situations. And new borderline cases crop up immediately. (If "mobile homes" qualify because they are, after all, used as personal residences, must they be occupied to qualify? If not, then could retail sales lots apply under the new law? How about manufacturers?) To make the new rules determinate, still newer rules will have to be written to solve these borderline problems. And in principle, for any rule, some number of new rules will have to be written to make it fully determinate. The process of making rule R determinate with R_1, and R_1 determinate with R_2 . . . is a never-ending thing. In practice, one can only hope to call a halt to the process when the number or importance of the borderline problems is (by some standard) insignificant. But by what standard? Does not the requirement of certainty insist on a rule here, too? And if so, will not that rule also raise borderline problems that can only be solved by other rules? When will that new series be stopped? And by what rule? The push for certainty causes a fearsome and endless multiplication of rules.[21]

Further, the multiplication of rules for the sake of certainty can be self-defeating. At some point, rules become too numerous to be comprehensible. When that happens, a new sort of uncertainty is introduced, one which immediately defeats not only the certainty requirement, but the advance notice requirement as well. If the rules are too numerous to be comprehensible, *a fortiori* they cannot be comprehended in advance.[22] And an overabundance of rules also damages the non-arbitrariness requirement by increasing the likelihood of contradictory regulations.[23]

An obsession with impartiality starts a different line of undesirable consequences. Heroic efforts are sometimes employed to hide the fact that past decisions have been reversed: Since cases are never exactly alike, it takes only a little ingenuity to find a plausible way of distinguishing any given case from a clear line of precedents. Thus the illusion may be preserved that the similar cases rule is being followed when an accurate description would admit that the rule has been violated. And, of course, justice may require that the rule be violated when the precedent decisions were demonstrably wrong. Yet it is not merely a matter of candor at stake here. Every ill-conceived attempt to manufacture an *ad hoc* distinguishing principle condemns the next generation to even greater deceptions to save the similar cases rule. Legal history provides some fascinating examples. (See, for example, Edward Levi's account of the breakdown of the privity of contract rule, which took nearly a century.)[24]

Finally, there is the question of moral character. Rules are applied by people, for or against people, and there is much to be said for certainty and impartiality in the administration of the law. But when there is no longer significant room for administrative judgment (because the rules are so fully determinate that they do not permit it), then it is not surprising to hear the word bureaucrat used with contempt, to hear bureaucrats themselves complain of alienation and lack of self-esteem, and to find an increasing sense of impotence among all those who characteristically obey the rules.

Similarly, when strict adherence to the similar cases rule degenerates into rigidity or deceptive manipulation of precedent, and when the refusal to play favorites degenerates into a refusal to act at all out of sympathy or anger or human feeling, that is when impartiality becomes vicious—irrationality mixed with a chilling sort of impassive, impersonal conduct. It seems clear that an obsessive concern for impartiality can in fact produce these things, especially when combined with a similar overemphasis on the requirement of certainty.[25]

When such conditions become pervasive—when they become typical of one's encounters with government—they can force changes in moral character. The disposition to obey may be replaced by dispositions to defy, or manipulate, or evade. The disposition to act thoughtfully, to deliberate, to consider, may be replaced by passivity. Loyalty, courage, intelligence, and imagination may all be compromised.[26] And the virtues special to public life—namely the ability to balance all the elements of justice in action—may corrupt the areas of private life in which virtuous conduct consists in showing favor to one's family and friends, suspending the rules, acting spontaneously out of love, being generous and openhearted to people in need, and occasionally being purely arbitrary, impulsive, whimsical, and capricious.

I grant that this recital of woe is full of hyperbole and speculative social psychology. But I submit that symptoms of such a malaise, traceable in principle to an overemphasis on impartiality and certainty in government rule-making, are currently visible. Perhaps, like threats of disaster, they have always been visible. But that is no excuse for failing to treat them—if there is an acceptable remedy.

A Modest Proposal

At points like this, philosophers of the Aristotelian sort typically urge moderation in all things—to the relief of their colleagues and the disgust of nearly everyone else. I have evoked my share of those reactions. Here, however, I have an immoderate proposal to make. I suggest that in the case of government regulation, all the other formal conditions of justice in rule-making be subordinated to the requirement of non-arbitrariness.

The standard justificatory strategies are somewhat different. They insist that each rule have some justifiable purpose (for example, to be aimed at improving social utility, or at implementing polity or preserving rights), that it be cost-effective, that it not be self-defeating, and that it be written so as to follow the formal conditions of justice in rule-making. This approach has yielded the unfortunate overemphasis on certainty and impartiality that I described. And it creates the impression that once we have some reasonable goal in mind that requires a rule, we then have a long list of tests to meet (efficacy, cost-effectiveness, impartiality, certainty, and so forth). Meeting the tests often appears to be a matter of degree, and seems to require trading a little bit of one desirable thing for more of another. Compromise is inevitable. I think this misrepresents the essential coherence of the justificatory problem. To correct matters, I am proposing that we begin and end with one and only one condition—non-arbitrariness—and not compromise at all.

Justification

To see what this would mean, and what grounds there are for advocating it, consider again my characterization of the requirement: all theories of justice require that every rule have some acceptable purpose, and be an acceptable means to the achievement of that purpose. The standard of acceptability is justifiability in terms of the theory. Now it is obvious that in principle this must be the ultimate concern of every theory of justice, for if it is met, then every other requirement of the theory (for rule-making) will automatically be met also. (In fact, this is so obvious that it raises the suspicion that the analysis has been faulty all along in suggesting that non-arbitrariness was on a par with the other three formal conditions. Why not just say that there is one all-embracing condition—non-arbitrariness? This chapter could then be shortened magnificently. My answer is that the analysis was designed as much to help understand the practical problems of [justice in] rule-making as it was to reveal the theoretical structure of it. The practical problems are best understood, I think, through the set of competing formal conditions I have offered— assuming that one is permitted to lay aside for the moment considerations of social utility, political polity, and individual rights.) In any case it is clear that non-arbitrariness must have theoretical dominance—all conflicts among the requirements, proposed compromises, and so forth must be settled in terms of what theory can justify. No theory of justice can authorize compromises with what it justifies. Or rather, to the extent that it authorizes them, it is merely including, as a part of the theory of justice, a distinction between the ideal and the real—in Rawlsian language between full and partial compliance theory.

There is a sense, of course, in which the practical point of my proposal is certainly not a novel one. It is simply to force the question of justifiability into a controlling position—not only at the stage of legislative intent (where it typically resides), but also in the processes of rule-writing and implementation. As I understand them, writers who have taken other approaches to the question of the proper bounds of regulation have urged much the same thing, and for reasons that are matters of general agreement: First, government rule-making has grown at a furious pace over the last twenty years or so. Second, the body of local, state, and federal law is now so vast as to be virtually incomprehensible to anyone outside government, the legal profession, or specialized fields dealing with the law. Even then it is unlikely that one person will have anything approaching a comprehensive and detailed grasp of the law as a whole. Third, in part this is a consequence of the increasing size, complexity, and potential for self-destruction of our society. In part, too, it is a consequence of an ideological shift toward the welfare state. So, to some extent, the amount and type of government regulation is dictated by the size, structure, velocity, and direction of our social order. To recommend change in these aspects of regulation is really a covert way of recommending more fundamental social and political changes. Such discussions are better carried out in the context of the fundamental issues of social and political philosophy. Fourth, it is also true that a good deal of rule-making appears not to be tied to anything fundamental, but rather to be the product of special interest lobbying, momentary public enthusiasms, and the self-perpetuating —even accelerating—momentum of the regulatory process itself. This aspect of rule-making must be brought within bounds.

Now, as I say, whether one's concern is for social utility (or its myopic offspring, cost-benefit analysis), or for principles of polity, or for individual rights, one is likely to agree with the preceding four points and cast proposals for regulatory reform in terms of them. The natural consequence is to deflect questions of fundamental policy to other forums and simply to call for more care—more attention to justificatory argument—in the whole process. My proposal does the same thing. It does not disguise arguments for fundamental social and political change as attacks on the regulatory system. But it does, like the standard approaches, appeal for rational justification. Its virtues, I think, are that it sets this appeal in the context of one of the formal conditions (imposed by all defensible theories of justice) on government rule-making, and that it applies the same justificatory standard to all phases of the process—legislative intent, rule-writing, and enforcement.

But there is another sense in which my proposal is somewhat less banal. It holds that no matter how good its goal, no matter how efficacious in achieving that goal, no matter how cost-effective, or even-handed, or certain, or public, a rule is, if that rule cannot be drafted or administered without violating the non-arbitrariness requirement, it should not be imposed. If, for example, it is not administratively possible to isolate the cases in which the rule has an arbitrary impact from the ones in which it has its intended (justifiable) impact, then the rule should not be imposed. Classification schemes based on actuarial studies come to mind here. Of course, what counts as an arbitrary impact will depend on the theory of justice one uses. Social utility is much more willing to sacrifice individual welfare than is rights theory, for example. So insurance tables based solely on age may be permissible under one theory and not under another.

Philosophical Consequences

Two things make this result philosophically interesting. One is the apparently irreducible plurality of theories of justice. The other is its relation to the problems of moral character I mentioned earlier.

Plurality

If there are two or more equally defensible theories of justice (as I think there are), then we must either pick one and write only those rules it justifies, or we must somehow coordinate the requirements of all the defensible theories. If we pick one theory, we have the problem of how to pick it—and of how to justify enforcing the choice on people who oppose it. I think this is an insuperable problem, if it is in fact the case that the theories involved are equally defensible. But if we choose to coordinate the requirements of all the theories, we also have a difficult problem: whether to write only those rules justified by all the theories (thus being held hostage to the most minimal of the theories), or to opt for some principle of weighing that allows one or more of the theories to be compromised from time to time.

I have no space to deal with this problem here, but, as will be evident from my other writings, I would opt for a principle of weighting. For example, say the competing theories are some versions of utilitarianism, contractarianism, and natural rights theory. And say that a proposed rule is authorized by two of the theories but forbidden by the third. I would call the rule a justifiable one, unless it could be established that the opposing argument should be given greater weight than the others. This amounts to giving competing theories a rebuttable presumption of equal weight, and deciding conflicts (in the absence of a rebuttal) simply by aggregation. Ties would defeat proposed rules. I think that such a procedure is philosophically defensible, and it has a specious affinity with the democratic principles of polity under which we live—which helps to make it politically defensible as well.

Moral Character

The second reason that the dominance of the non-arbitrariness requirement is interesting is that such a policy seems likely to blunt the effects on moral character mentioned earlier. Again, I have time only to give a bare suggestion as to why this is so, but consider: The root of most of those difficulties lies in administrators being forbidden to make decisions that conform to their judgments of what justice requires. Instead, for the sake of impartiality, certainty, and advance notice, they are required to make decisions that merely conform to the rules. To the extent that theories of justice permit administrative discretion, then, this problem would be avoided. It is true that there are dangers in this, but it seems to me that, on balance, the dangers of not permitting it are greater.

The consequences of all this for the question of the proper bounds of government regulation are programmatic. The first item on the agenda is to decide what theory or theories of justice will be permitted to control rule-making. Next is the exploration of what the non-arbitrary use of theory will generate in the way of rules. And, finally, there is the question of how the results reached this way fit with results obtained from other approaches to the question: social utility, principles of polity, and individual rights.

Practical Consequences

How this proposal would work in practice is hard for me to assess. At a minimum, it would force policy analysts to develop and use a wider variety of standards than the cost-benefit concepts that now dominate official evaluations of government regulation. And I think such change would be welcomed by many. I recall, for example, some remarks made in 1976 by William Lilley III, then acting director of the Council on Wage and Price Stability.[27] In the course of a discussion of the inflationary impact of government regulation, he paused to mention what he apparently regarded as a novel distinction, which he attributed to a *Washington Post* editorial writer: namely, the difference between regulations imposed on one for the benefit of others and those imposed on one for one's own benefit. The editorial suggested that this should somehow be taken into account by government. Mr. Lilley promised to pursue this "interesting distinction," which of course is standard fare in theories of social justice. The point is that he welcomed it and obviously saw a use for it alongside standard cost-benefit analysis. Multiple standards of analysis, and a technique for coordinating the results, are politically useful in a democracy whose citizens hold diverse theories of justice.

Beyond that, I think it is probable that if the approach I have recommended were to replace the considerations that currently control regulation writing, there would be many fewer written. Once the goals themselves have been given, the driving force behind most rule-writing is a commitment to maximizing utility in the achievement of those goals. As evidence, one need only point to the generally accepted view, in government policy-making circles, that cost-benefit analysis is always *an* appropriate justificatory test to apply to a proposed rule, and usually *the* appropriate test.[28] The fact that many executive branch regulations appear to be written without such analysis, but rather with only a single-minded concern for implementing statutes, merely illustrates the bureaucratic separation of policy-making from regulation writing. The location of the justificatory test for rules in theories of justice generally, as expressed through the non-arbitrariness requirement, would have the salutary effect of closing the gap between policy-makers and rule-writers. And that alone would slow down the rate of rule-writing. (Juanita Kreps, for example, conceded that, as secretary of commerce, she could not justify taking the time to read "every word" of all of the regulations issued by her department.)[29] But it seems clear that if a proposed rule had not only to be tested for social utility, but to be tested by social contract and rights theory as well, we would have fewer rules. Whether we would also have the right ones is another question. No political procedural reform can guarantee good results. But it can improve chances. I think a change along the lines I have proposed would do that.

Notes

1. H. L. A. Hart, *The Concept of Law* (Oxford: Clarendon Press, 1961), ch. 5.
2. Congressional investigations of government regulations do this. See the documents cited below in notes 3, 18, and 22.
3. They are not pointless for other approaches. If one is concerned about the impact of rule-making on democratic polity, for example, there is obviously good reason for singling out judicial and administrative law-making.
4. For relevant literature on the theory of public goods, see the text and follow out the references in Jeffrey A. Hart and Peter F. Cowhey, "Theories of Public Goods Reexamined," *Western Political Quarterly* 30 (1977): 351–

62. Public utilities differ in that they do not necessarily provide public (i.e., non-partitionable) goods. They do, however, provide services or products that are "essential, bought continuously by many small consumers with urgent needs that are not postponable, and [have] no acceptable alternatives" (Douglas N. Jones, "Extension of the Social Control of Utilities," *Land Economics* 41 (1965): 297–302, at p. 298). When buyers are seriously disadvantaged with respect to the sellers of such goods and services, and other aspects of economic efficiency warrant social control, our legal system has typically been willing to declare the companies involved subject to extensive regulation. See the line of cases that includes *Munn* v. *Illinois* 94 U.S. 113 (1877), regulation of grain storage facilities; and *Nebbia* v. *New York* 291 U.S. 502 (1934), regulation of retail prices for milk. For readings on the cost-benefit analysis of regulation, a good place to start is with the report of the hearings on the cost of government regulation held by the Subcommittee on Economic Growth and Stabilization of the Joint Economic Committee, Congress of the United States, April 11 and 13, 1978 (Washington, D.C.: U.S. Government Printing Office, 1978).

5. For a rich selection of cases on the question of administrative discretion, see Louis L. Jaffe and Nathaniel L. Nathanson, eds., *Administrative Law* (3d ed.; Boston: Little, Brown, 1968), pp. 484–636. Also of interest is Kenneth Culp Davis, *Discretionary Justice* (Baton Rouge: Louisiana State University Press, 1969).

6. See Alan F. Westin, *Privacy and Freedom* (New York: Atheneum, 1970). Also the case of *Danforth, Attorney General of Missouri* v. *Planned Parenthood of Central Missouri,* 428 U.S. 52 (1976).

7. See text and references in P. J. Fitzgerald, *Salmond on Jurisprudence* (12th ed.; London: Sweet and Maxwell, 1966), p. 60 ff.

8. For some of the relevant literature, see Ch. Perelman, *Justice* (New York: Random House, 1967); Marcus G. Singer, *Generalization in Ethics* (New York: Alfred A. Knopf, 1961); R. M. Hare, *The Language of Morals* (Oxford: Clarendon Press, 1952); and Alan Gewirth, *Reason and Morality* (Chicago: University of Chicago Press, 1978).

9. For a cynical attempt to use this sort of approach, see the case that repudiated California's anti-miscegenation statute: *Perez* v. *Lippold,* 198 P 2d 17 (1948). There the Attorney General of California argued that the statute was not discriminatory because it treated whites and non-whites exactly alike: all the members of each group were forbidden to marry any of the members of the other.

10. See *People* v. *O'Gorman,* 8 N.E. 2nd 862 (1937).

11. Ronald Dworkin, "The Model of Rules," *University of Chicago Law Review* 35 (1967): 14.

12. Though this is a standard interpretation of what non-arbitrariness is, some writers persist in confusing it with conformity to a previously announced rule. And then because it is obvious that no government could properly decide every case by conformity to such a rule, a certain amount of "arbitrariness" (interpreted as "pure discretion") is regarded as inevitable—

even good. For an example of this posture, see Kenneth Culp Davis, *Discretionary Justice* (Baton Rouge: Louisiana State University Press, 1969), ch. 2.

13. For a summary of the relevant constitutional law, see Laurence H. Tribe, *American Constitutional Law* (Mineola, N.Y.: Foundation Press, 1978), ch. 10 and 16.

14. This is particularly true in the regulatory agencies. On the push for impartiality, see the texts and narrative of the saga of the FCC's licensing (and later reversal of same) of the Biscayne Television Corporation: Jaffe and Nathanson, *Administrative Law,* pp. 563–75.

15. Tribe, *American Constitutional Law,* ch. 10.

16. E.g., the Equal Rights Amendment. Some of the opposition comes from fear that the ERA will force people to ignore relevant differences.

17. I think here of the occasional push to replace "understandings" or "traditions" of ethical conduct with standards, and to replace standards with codes.

18. On the similar cases rule, see the concern about the differential impact of federal regulations on small business: e.g., "The Impact on Small Business Concerns of Government Regulations That Force Technological Change," a report prepared by Charleswater Associates, Inc., for the Small Business Administration, Sept. 1975 (Washington, D.C.: U.S. Government Printing Office, 1975). On certainty, see the testimony of Raymond V. Haysbert, Sr., pp. 60–71 of "The Cost of Government Regulation," *Hearings before the Subcommittee on Economic Growth and Stabilization of the Joint Economic Committee, Congress of the United States, April 11 and 13, 1978* (Washington, D.C.: U.S. Government Printing Office, 1978).

19. The Administrative Procedure Act, 5 U.S. Code §552 requires only publication in the *Federal Register* for the purposes of meeting advance notice. And §553 waters that down even further by stating broad exceptions to the rule that 30 days notice be given before the effective date of a regulation. See the intricate case of the *SEC* v. *Chenery Corp.,* 332 U.S. 194 (1947), in which the Court was willing to compromise advance notice—over a vigorous dissent by Justice Jackson.

20. The problem of retroactivity is a notorious one. For an overview, see the comment "Prospective Overruling and Retroactive Application in the Federal Courts," *Yale Law Journal* 71 (1962): 907, and Raoul Berger, "Retroactive Administrative Decisions," *University of Pennsylvania Law Review* 115 (1967): 371.

21. This is really too familiar a point to need documentation, but for the record, consider §504 of the Rehabilitation Act of 1973 (providing equal access to education for the handicapped).

22. See the testimony of William Lilley, III, acting director of the Council on Wage and Price Stability, on pp. 77–78 of "Inflationary Impacts of Government Regulations," *Hearing Before the Subcommittee on Economic Stabilization of the Committee on Banking, Currency and Housing, House of Representatives, Congress of the United States, December 17, 1976* (Washington, D.C.: U.S. Government Printing Office, 1976).

23. *Ibid.,* p. 77.

24. Edward H. Levi, *An Introduction to Legal Reasoning* (Chicago: University of Chicago Press, 1949), pp. 9–27. Also see the testimony of William Lilley, III, pp. 9–10.

25. For a vicarious experience of this sort, see Frederick Wiseman's documentary film "Welfare."

26. Hannah Arendt, *Eichmann in Jerusalem* (rev. ed.; New York: Penguin Books, 1977).

27. Testimony of William Lilley, III, pp. 7–8.

28. Hearing on "The Costs of Government Regulation," p. 38.

29. *Ibid.,* pp. 7–8.

REX MARTIN

8 Rawlsian Economic Justice and the Proper Bounds of Government Regulation

In this chapter I want to consider the application of Rawlsian principles of justice to the problem body of government regulation. I will concentrate, in particular, on Rawls' principle of economic justice and try to draw out its implications, as providing a rationale and as setting proper bounds, for governmental regulatory activity.

Such a study seems valuable not only for its intrinsic theoretical interest but also for the light it can shed on Rawls' theory, which is perhaps the dominant theory of justice today. Moreover, the applications of Rawls' theory in the economic sphere have not been as closely studied as other parts of his system, nor has Rawls drawn these applications together particularly well in his own writings. Finally, since the Rawlsian theory is congruent at many points with the reigning liberal orthodoxy on matters of economic regulation, an examination of the theory at this precise point constitutes a penetration into the systematic foundations of a scheme of regulations that appears to many to be makeshift, arbitrary, and lacking in secure or even serious intellectual and moral credentials.

The chapter consists of four parts. In the first I briefly set the stage for the subsequent argument by presenting what Rawls thinks the main principles of justice to be. Next I trace the main features in the application of his two principles, in particular the second (the one I am calling Rawls' principle of economic justice), to the "basic structure" of a society. In the third I explore an important asymmetry between the two principles on the topic of rights. And in the concluding section I attempt to bring out more clearly the exact bearing of the principle of economic justice and its application by considering Rawls' account of the contribution of individuals to the economy. I then attempt to use that account to tackle the issue of the ownership of productive property.

I

The *social* primary goods are the main concern in a theory of justice, for society determines their distribution.

> For simplicity, [Rawls says, let us] assume that the chief primary goods at the disposition of society are . . . liberties, powers and opportunities, income and wealth. [Later on he adds self-respect.] These [Rawls continues] are the social primary goods. Other primary goods such as health and vigor, intelligence and imagination, are natural goods; although their possession is influenced by the basic structure [of society] they are not so directly under its control.[1]

We can set the Rawlsian problem of justice, then, in the following terms. What we want to determine is the proper or just distribution of *social* primary goods. To do this we need a fair procedure (for there are no antecedent or independent standards for such a distribution). Accordingly, we create a hypothetical bargaining situation in which certain significant constraints operate: these constraints include those required to discount or bracket off all special, peculiarly personal, or circumstantial facts and biases; those constraints embedded in objective circumstances (such as relative scarcity) or in our psychological orientation (such as mutual disinterest in one another's life plans); and as well a number of other presumed constraints (such as that the principles agreed to are to be public, that they constitute the ultimate or foundational standard, that the principles are to be chosen once and for all, that they are to be chosen unanimously, and so on).[2]

As Rawls says, "The idea of the original position is to set up a fair procedure so that *any principles agreed to* will be just."[3] (And this is what he means, I think, by the phrase "justice as fairness.") In short, whatever principles emerge from the original position, they are the principles of justice for the organization of the basic structure of society.

His contention, then, is that under the constraints involved in the original position (constraints imposed in order to make for a fair and realistic bargaining situation) it would be reasonable to define two principles for the distribution of social primary goods and reasonable to rank these two principles (as a set or unified conception of justice) above alternative principles or sets of principles.[4]

The principles chosen would be, of course, the Rawlsian two principles, in the following order: (1) Liberties are to be arranged so as to achieve the most extensive set (or aggregate) of equal basic liberties. The liberties envisioned are liberties of the person (speech, conscience, association) and political liberties (right to vote, etc.). (2) Social and economic inequalities are to be arranged so that (*a*) they are structured by social roles and offices that are open to all under conditions of "fair equality of opportunity," and such inequalities in wealth, income, and position serve (*b*) to improve—ideally, to maximize—the life situation of the least advantaged group, subject to the proviso that enough foresight is exercised so that members of that group are no worse off in the foreseeable future than they are now.[5]

I will, in this chapter, simply ignore the proviso. Its object is to suggest a principle for just savings so as to avoid victimizing one generation of people in the interests of another. This involves, in its turn, the idea of some balance or ratio between consumption and savings, specifically, in the latter case, the idea of a continuing capital investment. For it is largely through the maintenance of a productive and a natural resources capacity that the proviso can be said to operate at all. And the presence of some such capacity we shall simply take for granted. Accordingly, I will focus attention on the second principle in what might be called its shorter or "contemporary persons" form: that is, economic inequalities are justified under conditions of "fair equality of opportunity" as long as these inequalities actually serve to improve the situation of the least-advantaged group.[6]

II

The two principles, as they emerge from the original position, are exceedingly abstract. Just as the primary goods belong to what Rawls calls a "thin" theory of the good,[7] so the two principles constitute a "thin" theory of justice. They require embodiment. Justice is, or should be, a virtue of society, specifically of its "basic structure." The object of the two principles is the design of the basic structure of a society. Included in that structure would be a society's political system and its economic system. Each of these in turn would be made up of a set of structural elements or institutions. We would require in the political sphere, for instance, a constitution, a form of government, modes of election, and, in the economic, some form(s) of ownership of the means of production, specific sectors for determining capital investments, devices to provide "public goods" and to deal with externalities, and so on.

The intuitive idea is that a just society conforms to the two principles by building them into its basic structure: institutions are set up that, when operating together, give results that tend to satisfy the two principles over time. These institutions, then, represent a set of middle principles standing between the two principles and the actual operation of a society. If the basic structure is sound, then the results (outcomes) or "states" of the whole social system will, over a period of time, be just. We can presume them just.

For Rawls the basic economic institution is a market system. That is, he wants a more or less open and competitive supply and demand market to provide the basis for many important investment decisions, for allocating resources, for pricing, for setting levels of demand and consumption and wage income, and so on.

Are we, then, to presume that market results are, over time, just? I think Rawls believes they are, but in a special sense of "just." He says, "if markets are reasonably competitive and open, the notion of pure procedural justice is a feasible one to follow. It seems more practicable than other traditional ideals, being explicitly framed to coordinate the multitude of possible criteria into one coherent and workable conception."[8]

The points in favor of a competitive market are: efficiency; practicality, especially as a simplifying and coordinating device; and fairness. This last point requires elaboration. A market is a fair way— a procedurally just one—of determining what is produced and so on, and of determining "legitimate claims, the honoring of which yields the resulting distribution."[9] What Rawls contends, then, is that there is no independent or self-standing criterion for *the* correct outcome in the distribution of goods (wealth and income). What we do, rather, is institute a procedure fair in itself, and the fairness of the procedure translates to the results. The outcome is fair (a particular distribution of goods) if the procedure by which it was reached (an open and competitive market) was itself fair. It is in this sense that a market can be said to be inherently just: it is a procedurally fair way to make allocations in the absence of an independent standard of what a *just* outcome would be at all the different points.[10]

Markets, though, pose three sorts of problems in Rawls' view. First, actual markets can tend over time, if left to their own devices, to become less open, less competitive. This means that their tendency is, or can be, away from fair outcomes (as the market "procedure" itself becomes less fair). Second, markets, as they tend away from those features that make them procedurally fair (in being open, competitive), tend to create larger and larger concentrations of wealth, both productive wealth and personal wealth.[11] These concentrations can actually threaten the higher order principles of justice (equal liberty and fair equality of opportunity). Finally, and most important, a market system even when it stays open and competitive does not, in a consistent way, serve the betterment of the prospects of the least-advantaged group.

This last point strikes me as crucial. The contention here is not that the open and competitive market does not, in some deductive way, follow from the two principles. This has already been admitted. The market is virtuous in a different sense—that of procedural fairness— and it is enough if the market, when just in that sense, is compatible with the two principles. But that is just the point: it is not. The market can violate, even when procedurally fair, the so-called difference principle. A competitive market cannot guarantee and does not necessarily deliver the compensating benefits for the less well-off that are required where differences in wealth and income are working to the advantage of the better off.

We do not conclude from this that inequalities should be ruled out (as unjust) but, rather, that the inequalities sponsored by the normal working of the market (and we assume that there will always be such inequalities) do not serve justice.[12]

The solution Rawls hits upon is to make the market the main economic institution and to include certain other features as additional background institutions that can be coordinated with the market. Among these he would include institutions designed to fulfill such goals as full employment, transfer or side payments for welfare purposes (payments to bring the income level of workers up to some social minimum as well as payments to provide income to the old, to the disabled, to dependent children), and the redistribution of corporate and personal income and family wealth through taxation.[13]

We simply build certain institutions into the market or its immediate context, set certain goals down side by side with market goals (that is, the market goals of efficiency, practicality of coordination, fair outcomes), and try to do justice by the whole mix. There are, of course, nonmarket costs that the market will have to bear; but then there are goals and benefits that the market cannot supply on its own.

We can look at these background institutions from two distinct perspectives. They are, in the first view, devices designed to alleviate the problems, or some of them, that arise when we consider the market and its tendencies in actual operation. The various devices used would have as their object the maintenance of a competitive market. Here policy aims such as antitrust regulation would clearly fit.[14] And since the notion of a competitive market as a fair procedure requires, as a precondition, that positions be open to all on a principle of fair equality of opportunity, there would have to be other devices, such as universal public education and programs against discrimination, in place and operating as well.[15] The second perspective is, of course, that afforded by the two principles of justice. Under this heading the background institutions are regarded as fulfilling policy aims that themselves follow from the two principles. For example, transfer payments can be regarded as that part of the unskilled worker's total income required by the difference principle (2b). And some devices, such as full employment or redistributive taxation, would likely come under *both* headings, that of maintaining an open and competitive market (and hence the values of the market) and that of maintaining the two principles of justice.

The background institutions check tendencies in the main institution that might over time take it away from its original seated disposition; they not only keep the main institution on track but also remedy its deficiencies, as regards justice. The result is that the "ongoing institutional processes are . . . constrained and the accumulated results of individual transactions continually corrected."[16]

The leading idea in Rawlsian distributive justice is to prevent those accumulations of wealth and power that would threaten equal liberty (Principle 1) or fair equality of opportunity (2a) or the procedural fairness inherent in an open and competitive market and at the same time to provide a level of benefit for the least-advantaged group so that their long-term expectations (that is, their basic situation as determined from the standpoint of a representative man) is more or less maximized: they are about as well off as could be arranged without cutting into the incentive and so on of the more productive groups, ultimately to the disadvantage of the least-well-off group itself.[17] As Rawls says, "The basic structure is just throughout when the advantages of the more fortunate promote the well-being of the least fortunate, that is, when a decrease in their advantages would make the least fortunate even worse off than they are. The basic structure is perfectly just when the prospects of the least fortunate are as great as they can be."[18]

The crucial point is that the basic institution (the market) and the surrounding or background institutions must *as a set* be compatible with the two principles and must, in their collective tendency, satisfy them. In this sense, then, they can *as a set* be described, loosely, as following from the two principles and, hence, as just.

III

Rawls' book has been widely acclaimed, in part as a "substantive contribution to the search for an adequate basis for a political philosophy of rights."[19] Yet it is worth noting that Rawls nowhere discusses rights as his main topic. His book contains, for example, no section devoted to rights,[20] no entry for "rights" or for "human rights" or for "moral rights" in its justly celebrated index (but there are three page citations under "natural rights"). It is, perhaps, not surprising then that incidental discussions in the literature have revealed a considerable variety of opinion about what Rawls has had to say on basic rights and their justification.

One point, though, is striking. There is an asymmetry in the way Rawls formulates his two principles of justice.

The first principle is usually stated by Rawls as itself identifying a right. For instance, in his standard statement of the two principles, the first is said to require that "each person is to have an equal right to the most extensive total system of liberties compatible with a similar system of liberty for all."[21] I would suggest, then, that the Rawlsian first principle states a basic moral right.

It also serves to govern the assignment of specific rights and duties by means of the basic structure.[22] Rawls thinks, for example, that the inclusion of a bill of rights within the constitution is one important way in which the first principle of justice could be institutionalized in a given society. So, the constitution (or some other feature of the basic structure) actually assigns determinate rights to individual persons; what the first principle does is "govern," or better *justify,* the business of assigning equal basic rights to individuals.[23]

The second principle, however, is not formulated by Rawls as a right. Rather, it is characteristically rendered in somewhat different terms: "Social and economic inequalities are to be arranged so that they are both: (*a*) to the greatest benefit of the least advantaged . . . and (*b*) attached to offices and positions open to all under conditions of fair equality of opportunity."[24]

It is not clear, though, exactly what this difference amounts to. For Rawls' conception of rights is, as I've indicated, opaque. I would suggest that a right for Rawls is an actual individual's legitimate expectation as to what he would receive in a just institutional distribution of social primary goods, where what is just is determined by the two principles.[25]

This reading gives us a reason for Rawls' inclination not to treat the *second* principle of justice as itself a basic moral right and not to regard the pattern of just distributions of wealth and social position as a pattern of rights. It is this: though specific liberties can be secured to any given individual (since all share in the basic liberties equally), specific economic or social standing cannot. In economic matters individuals float between an upper and a lower level (both determined by the difference principle, the principle that inequalities of wealth and social position must be arranged so that the prospects of the least-advantaged group are maximized). Thus no given individual has a legitimate expectation of receiving any particular distributive share and, hence, cannot be said to have a right to a particular share.

Even the minimum *level* established by the difference principle does not define the legitimate expectation of any given individual (not even those who form the group of the least advantaged); rather the expectation is that of a "representative" or ideal-type individual.[26] Accordingly, Rawls characteristically withholds the term "rights" in his discussion of the second principle and its applications. Rawls' approach here is markedly different from his handling of the first principle and its application.[27]

Now, if the difference principle does not specify rights to determinate shares of income or amounts of wealth or to particular social and economic positions ("offices") on the part of any given individual, then important consequences follow respecting the proper bounds of government regulation. We can neither rationalize nor limit governmental intervention in these matters by reference to natural rights. (Or, in Rawls' terminology, by reference to basic structure rights—excepting, of course, the higher order rights of equal liberty and fair equality of opportunity.) The individual has no legitimate expectations as to the exact share he would receive in a just institutional distribution of income or wealth or position. Hence he would not, for example, be able to regard himself as due, or entitled to, some precise share as the just reward for his economic contribution.[28] Nor could he claim, in the absence of some higher consideration grounded in equal liberty or fair equality of opportunity, that he was entitled to own some piece of property. Indeed insofar as the ownership of some thing is itself regarded simply as one's fair return on, say, the labor expended on it, there is no *right* to ownership under the difference principle. Correspondingly, one could not complain of taxation in principle, regarding it either as a deprivation of one's just deserts or as a form of forced labor.

Of course there is a place in Rawls' theory for economic rights of a sort: rights to determinate and particular shares of wealth or income, or to a given economic position on the part of assignable individuals. For example, workers in a certain industry, like steel or automobiles, might have a contract with firms there respecting such things as hourly wage rates, pension funds, and recognition of their union as sole bargaining agent, with the requirement that all the factory workers belong to the union. Indeed, as we follow a line of development away from the institutions of the basic structure, we would encounter a vast variety of subsidiary institutions and practices, of private associations and cooperative ventures. Expectations would attach to the operation of these subsidiary elements and, insofar as the institutions and practices in question were compatible with justice or loosely derivative from it, the expectations would be legitimate ones. Thus we can speak of subsidiary rights, as distinct from basic structure rights, of many kinds: rights under this contract or that, under particular organizational structures, and so on. In general Rawls encompasses these rights under the heading of fairness or fair play.[29] These are all institutional rights, some of them economic in character, justified primarily by their relationship to elements in the basic structure rather than directly by reference to the principles of justice themselves.

What I have argued, then, can be put more precisely: for Rawls there is no guaranteed provision of determinate and particular shares of wealth or income, no guaranteed provision of a given economic position attaching to assignable individuals (and certainly not to all individuals) in the basic structure of a society. Using the language of the previous paragraph, we can say that there are no basic structure rights under the difference principle. We could, however, say that if we "applied" the principle further, through the operation of institutions in the basic structure, we would come up with subsidiary rights, recognizably economic in nature, which are supported by that operation.

IV

Rawls' treatment of the economic contribution of individual persons is distinctive and completes the pattern of his basic analysis. Rawls apparently wants to discredit the claim that where the individual has contributed to the development of his own talents and abilities, he has earned or is owed as his desert a share of what he produces (contributes) through the employment of these talents. His point is, rather, that from the perspective of the original position it would be reasonable for persons to regard "the distribution of natural abilities as a collective asset" and to constitute society accordingly.[30] Thus, the idea that the talents and abilities of individuals are a collective asset is a moral ideal, an ideal of justice, and is meant to operate despite the actual distribution of natural and social endowment in a society and despite the actual contributions individuals make to improve this endowment.

Indeed, the peculiar point of the ideal is that one should (*morally* should) put the resources he is able to deploy towards benefiting all persons in a society and not just himself. Hence the claim that some person has contributed to the development of his own stock of natural talents is not incompatible with the idea of collective asset. So we have no reason, at least as given by Rawls' theory, to deny that an *actual* individual has contributed to the development of his own talents.

We are not able, then, to say that people deserve nothing because they have, personally, *done* nothing (which is what the idea amounts to, that all contribution to the development of an individual's talent is to be put on the natural and social endowment side of the ledger). But neither are we in a position to say that, when the individual has contributed to the development of his own natural talents, a presumption is created that he deserves a determinate share of what has consequently been produced, a share proportionate to the contribution made by his self-developed talents. The notion that an individual deserves something based simply on talents that he has, or on talents that he has developed, plays no role in Rawls' theory.[31]

Now, if Rawls does not depend on such notions as individual desert or individual rights in order to determine the just distribution of shares of income or of economic position to people, on what does he rely? One might say: on an open and competitive market. But a deeper answer would be: on the economic contribution of individual persons *through the market*. Here we must be rather more precise, to avoid misunderstanding.

The individual contributes to production and receives back a distributive share (of income, let us say). There is no one-to-one relationship mandated here, nor are background institutions installed so as to accomplish such a result. Thus, if we suppose an individual's contribution to production to be greater than average it does not necessarily follow that his received share will also be greater than average.

But the difference principle, as we have noted, does allow greater than average shares of income or wealth to be taken by individuals. The availability of such shares can encourage greater than average contributions to the stock of goods and services socially available. Those inequalities that we would regard as advantages probably conduce to entrepreneurial enterprise and to effective management. All in all then, Rawls believes, such inequalities seem to lead to greater economic efficiency and to make for a higher level—both qualitatively and quantitatively—of productivity in goods and services.[32] Just as we want liberties to be as extensive as possible, so we want wealth to be, consistent of course with those principles it would be reasonable to agree to *in the original position.* And where, in a rough way, greater shares do encourage greater contributions to production, then the ensuing inequality is justified—so long, that is, as the resultant increase in goods and services is distributed so as to improve the situation of the least-advantaged group.[33]

It also follows that where greater than average returns are often matched with greater than average contributions to production there will be an incentive for individuals to develop the relevant talents and abilities.[34] The individual here is not directly rewarded for the talent he is able to achieve; rather, he develops the talent in order to make a productive contribution, with the prospect that this contribution will be matched by a greater than average share. Not every participating individual will receive such a share; some will actually lose. And the amount of the gain (or loss) is not set exactly. For we cannot in justice gauge the fortunes of this person or that one (each known to us by a proper name). Rather, "it is the practice, or the system of practices, which is to be judged, and judged from a general point of view"; thus we consider the prospects "of a representative man holding the various offices and positions defined" by that system.[35]

Two of the main themes we have identified in this analysis so far are not explicitly found in the usual statement of the different principle; but they are there nonetheless—submerged, one might say—and the principle should be taken as including them. Thus, the augmented difference principle would read: in a given system, inequalities—that is, greater than average returns in income (or greater wealth or special offices)—are justified only if they (1) encourage contributions that (2) result in increased productivity in goods and services; and only if the operation of that system (3) serves to improve—or, ideally, to maximize—the life situation, as measured in income and wealth, of the least advantaged group.[36] The usual version of the difference principle, which gives us essentially only point (3), is a truncated one.

For it would seem, in the normal course of things, that the life situation both of the least-advantaged group and of the advantaged groups could not be improved unless there was an increase through productivity of the available supply of goods and services. And since Rawls regards the *use* of talents and abilities as the peculiar and indispensable contribution that individual persons make to economic production, such contribution must relevantly attach to the difference principle in any complete version.

Now that we have this expanded version available, let us use it to probe one of the most problematic issues Rawls raises: the ownership of the means of production. Rawls is conspicuous in defending a market system, consumer preference, free choice of occupation, and so on,[37] without a corresponding commitment to the private ownership of the means of production. The economic liberties are by and large absent from his principle of equal liberty: there is no right (or liberty) of private ownership and management, but equally there is no right (or liberty) of workers to participate in ownership and management.

Rawls defends a type of economic system as just, in principle; this system has historically included as an element, perhaps the basic element, the institution of private property. But Rawls is agnostic or diffident about this institution. We have in his theory, then, capitalism without private ownership—the question of ownership is deliberately left open. Rawls is seemingly as willing to allow social ownership as he is to allow private ownership of the means of production. His stance on this point contrasts, in an important way, I think, with what he is willing to say about the ownership of *personal* property.

Rawls' first principle of justice is not a general principle of liberty; it does not establish liberty in gross or in the abstract. Rather, it establishes a particular "list" of basic liberties; it identifies a specific set of liberties that are to be acknowledged as held equally by all.[38] These are, Rawls tells us, rights of citizenship and of the person: such things as the right to vote, freedom of speech and assembly, liberty of conscience, the right to own personal property, freedom from slavery and from arbitrary arrest and seizure, and so on.[39] They are standard *civil* liberties (or rights).

There is a certain coherence, though, to the items on the list. They are, every one of them, liberties of assignable persons; they can both be "individuated"[40] (parcelled out to individual persons) and be said to hold without qualification for all people. They are, then, liberties of persons (that is, of individuals viewed simply as persons) and they are justifiably on the list as liberties appropriate or essential to that status. Liberties that are not personal, that do not contribute to or are not required by individuals *as persons,* are excluded. Accordingly, the ownership of personal property is a specified liberty under the first principle, but the ownership of productive property is not.

The ownership of productive property is, I would suggest, an economic "office" and as such comes under the difference principle. Accordingly, we would have to turn to that principle, in its augmented form, to determine specifically how such offices, once they have been attained under conditions of fair equality of opportunity, are to be governed. Rawls' answer is that the institution of ownership within a particular industry, and presumably the size or amount of what can be so owned, is to be determined by what encourages contributions through management, investment decisions, innovation, and so on. We are speaking here, not of ownership in any technical sense (with the clipping of coupons and the taking of profits), but of contributions, through entrepreneurial and other skills, that result in increased social productivity in goods and services—subject, of course, to the usual proviso that the life situation of the least-advantaged class is thereby also improved. Since either private ownership or public, or some mix of the two, could satisfy this criterion within a given industry, or even within the economy overall, Rawls is agnostic on the question of private versus public, or of individual versus collective, ownership. What is important for him is the principle for determining which form of ownership is justified and the satisfaction of the relevant criteria by existing forms of ownership.

This matter is not treated abstractly in Rawls' theory. For the institution of ownership for productive purposes (whatever further detail such ownership might have) cannot be the basic economic institution. That status is reserved for the open and competitive market. Ownership, then, would be one of the economic background institutions within the basic structure of a society.[41] And the various elements in the institution of ownership (of the means of production) would be determined, then, not only by constraints imposed by the difference principle but also by the ability of ownership institutions to mesh with proper market goals (that is, goals of efficiency, practicality of coordination, fair outcomes) and with the operation of other economic background institutions, which have such diverse goals as full employment, antitrust regulation, and transfer payments to raise low-level incomes. The ownership of productive property, one might say, is the last brick in the basic structure of a society's economy.

Private ownership or, for that matter, public ownership, like greater than average income, would be justified only if it encouraged the development and use of talents and abilities, with the result that productivity in goods and services was increased. Institutions of ownership define ways of contributing to increased productivity and details of just ownership are to be determined, as any other economic contribution would be, by reference to the difference principle.

The picture that emerges is not simple. For ultimately the economic institutions of the basic structure of a society are a coordinated set that together with relevant political institutions in the basic structure must give results that satisfy the two principles of justice. Nonetheless the rationale for economic institutions and for governmental economic regulation has been sketched along fairly simple lines.

The market is the basic economic institution and governmental regulation is required both to keep the market open and competitive and to remedy deficiencies of the market, even when open and competitive, with respect to the difference principle, and as well to the higher-order considerations of fair equality of opportunity and equal basic liberty. The proper bounds of economic activity and of governmental economic regulation are principally set by the rationale for such activities in the first place. More specific bounds cannot be established except through the actual workings of the various institutions in the basic structure of a society. These institutions, as they interact, constrain one another and over time the proper content and bounds of government economic activity, and more generally of economic life, are set in finer detail.[42]

Notes

1. John Rawls, *A Theory of Justice* (Cambridge: Harvard University Press, 1971), p. 62; see also p. 303.

2. Rawls' own summary is given in *ibid.*, pp. 146–47.

3. *Ibid.*, p. 136 (italics added). In the next sentence he refers to this procedure as "pure procedural justice." See also pp. 84–88.

4. The point about ranking is found in *ibid.*, p. 18.

5. Rawls normally calls Principle 1 the Principle of Equal Liberty, Principle 2*a* the Principle of Fair Equality of Opportunity, and Principle 2*b* the Difference Principle.

6. See John Rawls, "The Basic Structure as Subject," in Alvin I. Goldman and Jaegwon Kim, eds., *Values and Morals* (Dordrecht, Holland: Reidel, 1978), pp. 58–59 and n. 11 on pp. 70–71; also *Theory of Justice*, pp. 284–303.

7. See *Theory of Justice*, p. 396.

8. *Ibid.*, p. 310.

9. Rawls, *Theory of Justice*, p. 88.

10. See John Rawls, "The Basic Structure as Subject," *American Philosophical Quarterly* 14 (1977): 163; "Basic Structure," in *Values and Morals*, p. 64; and *Theory of Justice*, pp. 270–74 and 304–10.

11. "[The] overall result of separate and independent transactions is away from and not towards background justice. We might say: in this case the invisible hand guides things in the wrong direction and favors an oligopolistic configuration of accumulations" (Rawls, "Basic Structure," in *Values and Morals*, p. 54; see also p. 66).

12. For Rawls, inequalities in wealth and position are probably inevitable; see John Rawls, "Distributive Justice," in Peter Laslett and W. G. Runciman, eds., *Philosophy, Politics, and Society* (3d ser.; Oxford: Blackwell, and Berkeley: University of California Press, 1967), pp. 67, 71; "Basic Structure," *American Philosophical Quarterly*, p. 160; and "Basic Structure," in *Values and Morals*, p. 56.

13. See *Theory of Justice*, pp. 274–78 esp.

14. See *Theory of Justice*, p. 276, and esp. Rawls, "Basic Structure," in *Values and Morals*, pp. 65–66.

15. See *Theory of Justice*, p. 275.

16. Rawls, "Basic Structure," *American Philosophical Quarterly*, p. 159. See this article and "Basic Structure," in *Values and Morals*, for elaboration of his theory of the basic structure.

17. Rawls tends to emphasize the incentive effect of inequalities: see Rawls, "Basic Structure," *American Philosophical Quarterly*, p. 160; "Justice as Fairness," *Philosophical Review* 67 (1958): 173; "Justice as Reciprocity," in S. Gorovitz, ed., *Utilitarianism [by] John Stuart Mill, with Critical Essays* (Indianapolis: Bobbs-Merrill, 1971), p. 251; and "Basic Structure," in *Values and Morals*, p. 56.

18. Rawls, "Distributive Justice," p. 66.

19. Barry Clark and Herbert Gintis, "Rawlsian Justice and Economic Systems," *Philosophy and Public Affairs* 7 (1978): 302–3.

20. I am indebted for this observation to Joel Feinberg, in conversation. Since the publication of *A Theory of Justice*, Rawls has written one article ("A Kantian Conception of Equality," *Cambridge Review*, Feb. 1975, pp. 94–

99) that bears on the topic of rights in an interesting, albeit somewhat indirect, way.

21. Rawls, *Theory of Justice*, p. 302; see also pp. 60 and 250.

22. *Ibid.*, pp. 54, 58, 84, 131.

23. See *ibid.*, p. 61, and the argument of ch. 4. A. I. Melden claims that Rawls has no place in his theory for moral rights (see Melden, *Rights and Persons* [Oxford: Blackwell, and Berkeley: University of California Press, 1977], pp. 89–90, 103, and esp. 112) and that the rights mentioned in the two principles of justice are actually *political* rights (see *ibid.*, pp. 108–10). Now, I would grant that the liberties *mentioned* or contemplated in the first principle are, by and large, political ones (as Rawls makes clear, in *Theory of Justice*, p. 61). It does not follow from this, however, that the first principle, the principle of equal basic liberties, is not itself a *moral* right. Indeed, since the first principle is formulated in the original position, as a principle for the design of the basic structure of a just society, it is prior to any society; it cannot, then, be regarded as a political right but rather as a prescription for political rights. And as a prescription it is moral, not political, in character; or so I have argued.

24. Rawls, *Theory of Justice*, p. 302; see also pp. 60 and 83.

25. See *ibid.*, p. 313.

26. See *Theory of Justice*, esp. chs. 2 and 5; also Rawls, "Justice as Reciprocity," pp. 247, 267. It is in this way that Rawls' idea of an *adequate minimum* (see *Theory of Justice*, p. 175) and of a *guarantee* (*Theory of Justice*, p. 169) should be taken.

27. It is possible that Rawls would want to treat the opportunities contemplated in 2*a* (the principle of fair equality of opportunity) as analogous to the liberties of the first principle. This seems reasonable in view of the importance attached, in the formulation of these principles, to equality (i.e., each individual is to have the specified liberties and opportunities equally). To allow for this possibility, I will restrict my point about the absence of rights in the second principle to point 2*b* (the difference principle).

28. See Rawls, "Basic Structure," in *Values and Morals*, pp. 59–62; also "Basic Structure," *American Philosophical Quarterly*, pp. 162–63.

29. See *Theory of Justice*, sec. 18, esp. p. 112; also Rawls, "Basic Structure," in *Values and Morals*, pp. 53–55.

30. The point and the phrase quoted are from *Theory of Justice*, p. 179. See also *Theory of Justice*, pp. 101–2, 104; and Rawls, "Distributive Justice," p. 68.

31. For Rawls is not willing to say that individuals *deserve* the natural talents they have or that they deserve them to the extent they have aided in their development. He does think, however, that we as individuals "have a right to our natural abilities" ("Basic Structure," in *Values and Morals*, p. 65; see also "Basic Structure," *American Philosophical Quarterly*, p. 164).This endorsement of the notion that individuals are *entitled* to their natural assets serves to bring Rawls closer to Robert Nozick and at the same time to

mitigate the force of much of Nozick's criticism (see Nozick, *Anarchy, State, and Utopia* [New York: Basic Books, 1974], pp. 213–31, esp. p. 225).

32. See Rawls, "Distributive Justice," p. 67 (but also p. 74. And see *Theory of Justice*, p. 78.

33. See *Theory of Justice*, pp. 101–2. In this regard the difference principle can be said to *specify* and to *establish* inequality (see *Theory of Justice*, p. 61).

34. Here inequalities are viewed as contributions to the costs of training and education (see *Theory of Justice*, pp. 102, 151, 315).

35. See Rawls, "Justice as Reciprocity," p. 247, for both quotations.

36. Norman Daniels claims (in "Meritocracy," in John Arthur and William H. Shaw, eds., *Justice and Economic Distribution* [Englewood Cliffs, N.J.: Prentice-Hall, 1978], pp. 171, 174) that Rawls is committed to a Productivity Principle according to which, in the filling of an economic office, "*overall* job performance is [to be] maximized" (p. 167; see pp. 166–68). This strikes me as a dubious reading, for two reasons. First, Rawls' concern is not with overall or macrolevel productivity but, rather, with microlevel productivity—the productivity of a particular office (or of particular holders within an office). Nor does Rawls require that productivity at this level be maximized. Second, any attempt to maximize *overall* productivity would lead in the direction of a command economy and away from features, such as free choice of occupation and noncentralized hiring, that Rawls would want to preserve.

37. See *Theory of Justice*, pp. 270–71, 310.

38. The interpretation of the first principle as specifying a list of basic liberties is made clearer, Rawls says, in revisions made for the German edition of *Theory of Justice* (*Eine Theorie der Gerechtigkeit* [Frankfurt: Surhkamp, 1975]).

39. *Theory of Justice*, p. 61.

40. The term is Dworkin's. (See Ronald Dworkin, *Taking Rights Seriously* [Cambridge: Harvard University Press, 1977], pp. 90–91.) For Dworkin a principle is individuated if it defines a class such that every member of the class is assigned the relevant benefit. In contrast, policies designed to attain collective goals—such as promoting the general welfare or maximizing the GNP—are concerned with aggregate benefit rather than with the benefits (or disbenefits) that accrue to particular individuals. A claim based on such policies will not amount to a right, even if the policy considerations invoked are very powerful, since it will lack the necessary individuated character.

41. See *Theory of Justice*, p. 265. Whether ownership of productive property should be private or public, Rawls says, is to a great extent a circumstantial matter (see *Theory of Justice*, pp. 273–74). I realize that, once the initial and inevitable decision is made to have private (or public or mixed) ownership, the institution chosen will have its effects on the subsequent operation of the economy, including effects on the returns in income to individual persons, so no evaluation of what results can be wholly free of such

effects, of the shadow cast by the institution of ownership and its more immediate implications (for investment, public goods, externalities, etc.). But at the same time there is no way to subject ownership institutions to evaluation, by reference to their contributory effects, without collecting such "colored" historical data. In any case the factor of "coloring" or bias will operate equally between public and private forms of ownership and is not therefore a ground for choosing between them.

42. During the spring semester, 1979, I served as Humanist in Residence in the University of Kansas School of Business (under a grant, on business and the humanities, to the school from the NEH). The present paper had its origin in public lectures I delivered then. A subsequent version was presented at the Center for the Study of Values at the University of Delaware, November 1979. I appreciate the helpful comments I received there and at other universities where I've read one version or another of the paper. The final draft was written at the Villa Serbelloni, Bellagio (Como), Italy. I want to thank Mr. Robert Celli, the staff, and the Rockefeller Foundation for the hospitality I enjoyed there.

The note on Dworkin (note 40) was taken from the paper I wrote with James W. Nickel, "Recent Work on the Concept of Rights," *American Philosophical Quarterly* 17 (1980): 165–80.

My views on Rawls have been sharpened by discussions with friends and colleagues, in particular, Joseph Pichler and Prakash Shenoy. Their help, that of John Rawls (on section III especially), and that of the University of Kansas General Research Fund are all gratefully acknowledged.

9 Rawlsian Economic Rights versus Pure Procedural Justice: A Comment on Martin

Rex Martin's essay, "Rawlsian Economic Justice and the Proper Bounds of Government Regulation," is a sympathetic exposition and expansion of certain Rawlsian themes. As such it shares with Rawls' own writings an assumption-laden vocabulary that those who, like myself, operate outside of the Rawlsian framework find misleading and even dangerous. Particularly disturbing to at least certain non-Rawlsians is the continual reification if not personification of aggregative notions such as "society," "the market," and "the economy." These reified entities often appear as the real agents whose roles and relationships are to be studied and prescribed for within the Rawlsian program. Thus we continually find talk about the contributions to "the economy," distributions determined by "society," goods that are "social" and that are "at the disposition of society," and so on. An essay about Rawls and his influence would have to challenge such talk and the assumptions it embodies. But that is not our task here. So while entering this caveat about the many fundamental assumptions shared by Rawls and Martin, I shall proceed to try to examine Martin's essay in its own terms.

There are, of course, a number of utterly uninteresting points that could be made about the positive implications for "economic regulation" of Rawls' views on justice. Given that Rawls, along with many others, favors a particular structure or profile for the holdings of economic goods among individuals—namely, that structure of holdings such that the most poorly endowed positions are as well endowed as they possibly can be—it is the easiest thing in the world to show that Rawls will favor taxes and subsidies for redistributive purposes. Similarly, Rawls believes that justice demands fair equality of opportunity and so it is no surprise that he favors a variety of compulsory state measures of the sort that are commonly thought to equalize opportunities. Finally, Rawls holds that justice demands equality of personal and political rights and on this basis he favors yet other bits of social engineering, for example, "public" (that is to say, involuntary) funding of political parties and, apparently, the prohibition of "private contributions."[1]

But none of this constitutes what would normally be understood as economic regulation. One can imagine someone who favored all of these and like measures and who could still, whatever his sins, correctly claim to be an advocate of economic laissez-faire. The only economic regulation mentioned in the course of Martin's paper— indeed the only governmental activity that would normally be classified as regulation—is anti-trust policy. Nothing is said about quotas, tariffs, zoning laws, building codes, wage and price controls, professional licensing, banking laws, blue laws, and so on—the very stuff of economic regulation. Yet surely this is what comes to mind when we are referred by Martin to "a scheme of regulations that appears to many to be makeshift, arbitrary, and lacking in secure or even serious intellectual and moral credentials."[2] What, then, is Martin's essay about?

Most generally, the paper seems to be about what fills the gap between Rawlsian abstract principles of justice, especially the Difference Principle, and real world Rawlsian judgments about the justice of this or that individual's economic position and specific bundle of goods. How can a theory that so abstracts from real people and so focuses upon macro phenomena speak to the justice of any particular person's economic fate? The question of what fills the gap is made interesting by two related facets of Rawls' view. The first is his insistence that the legitimacy of specific economic holdings is largely, if not entirely, a matter of pure procedural justice and that an important part of the relevant procedure is the operation of the "competitive and open market." The second is Rawls' recognition that the Difference Principle tells us almost nothing about whose holding of what will count as just. The Difference Principle only tells us how large the just holdings of the *representative* individual in a society's economically worst position would be.[3] It does not tell us either the size or the specific content of the just holdings of any actual individual thus represented. And not only does it fail to indicate anything about the size or the specific content of the just holdings of any other person, it says nothing about even the size of the just holdings of the society's other representative men. This illustrates a sense, which Rawls seeks to exploit, in which the Difference Principle is not allocative. It does not provide a chart of moral information by which public-spirited officials can allocate the "social goods" that are "at society's disposition."

We must discriminate here between two different gaps each of which has to be filled. First, there must be institutions that generate real world distributions of goods and services—and not only to the lowest members of society. Second, the particular holdings that are yielded to each individual by the favored institutions must be just. There is, then, both an institutional and a normative gap. The existence of the latter is brought out by Martin's discussion of the fact that, unlike Rawls' Principle of Equal Liberty, the Difference Principle cannot be construed as assigning rights. Rights to goods and services only appear in the context of ongoing, favored, economic institutions and activities. These Martin labels "subsidiary rights."[4]

My main contention in these remarks is that Rawls has no basis for his claim that pure procedural justice is an important element within his doctrine of economic justice. Martin errs in accepting this Rawlsian self-description. We shall take note of the role within Rawls' theory of what he takes to be a special kind of procedural justice. But it will be maintained that this is not any kind of genuine pure procedural justice.

According to Rawls himself:

> Pure procedural justice obtains when there is no independent criterion for the right result: instead there is a correct or fair procedure such that the outcome is likewise correct or fair, whatever it is, provided that the procedure has been properly followed.[5]

A paradigm of a pure procedural theory of justice in holdings is the historical entitlement doctrine advocated by Robert Nozick.[6] Recalling certain features of this kind of theory will allow us to highlight the difficulties in attaching the "pure procedural justice" label to Rawls' doctrine.

On the historical entitlement view a person is entitled to any particular object if he has come to possess that object by means of specified procedures. More specifically, a person is entitled to an object if he purposively acquires it from nature or creates it out of previously unowned material or if he acquires it through voluntary exchange or donation from another who has had title to it. Once having title to an object, an individual may reacquire it from those who have involuntarily deprived him of it. What a person possesses through the processes of just initial acquisition, just transfer, and just restitution is his by right. And whatever distributive profile among individual's holdings comes into existence by their respective engagement in these processes is a just distribution. The justice of the profile is itself a function of and is reducible to the independently ascertainable justice of the individual holdings.

Two important features of this type of doctrine need to be noted. The first is that what profile or pattern of holdings is just is entirely dependent upon how individuals have acted. Whether it is just that some individual possesses this or that particular object or possesses total holdings of this or that size or whether it is just that wealth or income in a given society displays this or that outline is determined by what specific individuals have chosen to do and what others have chosen to do with them. There is no process-independent measure of justice. Indeed, the only conceptually coherent strategy for achieving distributive justice is the procedural strategy of leaving people free to engage in the rights-respecting economic activities subsumed under the various principles of just acquisition.

The second feature associated with this theory is the availability of an account of *why* engaging in the specified procedures yields just outcomes. The account links entitlement principles of justice to the demand that persons' liberties not be infringed. The principles of just initial acquisition and just transfer specify ways in which a person can acquire objects without infringing upon the liberty of others, and such that his being non-consentially deprived of these objects henceforth infringes upon his liberty. Thus a person's right to acquire objects only *via* these procedures and his right to the objects so acquired reflect respectively others' rights not to have their freedom infringed upon and his own right to liberty. (The principle of just restitution reflects the justified infringement of the liberty of those who have violated rights.) This provides the barest rough sketch of the matter. The point, however, is that here is an account of how features of the specified procedures translate into rightful results. In contrast, we shall see, one of the striking things about Rawls' invocation of pure procedural justice is the absence of any Rawlsian explanation of why the complex of procedures he fixes upon should have any moral weight.

In radical contrast to such an entitlement theory, Rawls' theory consists primarily of principles embodying the goals of equal liberty, fair equality of opportunity, and enhancement of the position of the worst-situated archetype, which provide standards for judging the outcome of social and economic practices. With respect to economic results, the Difference Principle is most prominent as an independent criterion for judging the justice of any procedure's results. No social outcome is just unless the goal of the highest possible "social minimum" is achieved. In general, the Rawlsian principles of right are to guide the construction of social and economic institutions, including the "competitive and open market," with an eye to the satisfaction of the goals which those principles express. Thus, in a characteristic remark—this one from his discussion of economic institutions—Rawls maintains that:

> Whether the principles of justice are satisfied, then, turns on whether the total income of the least advantaged (wage plus transfers) is such as to maximize their long-run expectations (consistent with the constraints of equal liberty and fair equality of opportunity).[7]

It is difficult to escape the conclusion that the presence of these independent criteria for evaluating a system's results and for guiding the construction of institutions and social patterns is incompatible with the idea of pure procedural justice.[8]

Can any vindicating explanation be given of Rawls' continued claim to pure procedural justice? An explanation, though not a vindicating one, lies in the special sense Rawls sometimes gives to "pure procedural justice." Rawls maintains that if the several principles of right that govern what institutions and practices are to be adopted do not themselves specify just bundles of holdings for actual individuals and, instead, leave this task to the actual operation of these chosen institutions and practices, then regard for these specifications amounts to commitment to pure procedural justice. Thus, after a discussion of the sorts of institutions demanded by his principles, Rawls repeats that "a central feature of this conception of distributive justice is that it contains a large element of pure procedural justice." And what justifies speaking of this form of justice is that "no attempt is made to define the just distribution of goods and services on the basis of information about the preferences and claims of particular individuals."[9] The details of the definition of the just distribution are left to the operation of the institutions adopted. It is precisely because rights to particular holdings are "subsidiary rights," that is, claims not implied by basic principles of justice, that they are thought of as requiring real world processes for their generation and as, thereby, reflecting pure procedural justice.

For Rawls, what is crucial to pure procedural justice is that "distribution of advantages are not appraised in the first instance by confronting a stock of benefits with given desires and needs of known individuals." Instead, a "system of public rules" is adopted on the basis of abstract principles of right. The operation of this system of rules creates and satisfies "legitimate claims" that no abstract set of principles could identify. "Thus in *this kind of procedural justice* the correctness of the distribution is found on the justice of the scheme of cooperation from which it arises and on answering the claims of individuals engaged in it."[10] But, I shall contend, this kind of procedural justice does not warrant the label "pure procedural justice."

A series of crucial questions is left unasked by both Rawls and Martin. What is it about certain real world practices in virtue of which they yield subsidiary rights? Is there anything distinctive to the institutions and practices that are chosen as conforming to Rawlsian principles that accounts for the justice of the specific holdings that individuals come to possess under the operation of those institutions and practices? If the answer to the latter question is affirmative, the chosen procedure itself has moral weight. It will be because this procedure (or distinctive parts of it) have been gone through that the outcome is just whatever it turns out to be. Only in this case, where the procedure itself is morally weighty, would one have a genuine instance (albeit restricted by, for example, the Difference Principle) of pure procedural justice. Only if there is some morally valuable feature of the practices themselves to translate into just results, into subsidiary rights, can we speak of (restricted) pure procedural justice.

Rawls, however, is not in a position to give an affirmative answer to this latter question. There is no feature of the economic institutions and practices that he favors beyond their conformity with Rawlsian ends and the fact of their adoption that he can cite as a basis for the justice of the particular holdings that such operations would yield. Thus, Rawls has no warrant for invoking, even within a restricted sphere, the idea of pure procedural justice. The related error of Martin's essay is its failure to detect this problem for Rawls. Indeed, Martin repeats Rawls' error in thinking that the available Rawlsian bases for adopting a semi-market system and for the legitimacy of such a system's yield vindicates the use of "pure procedural justice."

Martin writes as though the promotion of "the procedural fairness inherent in an open and competitive market" is itself a fourth Rawlsian goal to be listed alongside the enforcement of the Equal Liberty, Fair Equality of Opportunity, and Difference Principles."[11] Further, a special, valued feature within semi-market practices is suggested by the contrast, in Rawls and echoed in Martin, between the choice of semi-market economies versus command economies and the choice of private versus public ownership of "the means of production."[12] The former choice is presented as more funda-mental—a matter of principle, not just greater congruence with extrinsic ends. The implication is that, even were command eco-nomies better in terms of these extrinsic goals and even were they adopted for this reason, their operation would lack a type of authority that would be had by semi-market procedures in the establishment of subsidiary rights. Finally, there is the idea, ex-pressed by Martin, that the institutions by which Rawlsian principles are built into the basic social structure "represent a set of *middle principles* standing between the two principles and the actual operation of a society."[13] Such projected middle principles seem not to be merely rules of thumb for applying abstract principles of right. They appear to be conceived as guiding the actual operation of society by filling in some of the moral details within the framework determined by those more abstract principles. In this way, they seem to be assigned some degree of independent moral weight.

But the true Rawlsian account of individuals' subsidiary rights need never appeal to intrinsic, independent virtues of the quasi-market procedures that fill the institutional gap. There are simply two parts to the account of the subsidiary (economic) rights. First, some set of institutions and practices is to be adopted as most congruent in the long run with the medley of goals expressed in the principles of right. And here there are good reasons for the choice of a set that gives a large role to market relationships. Market economies are more efficient than non-market ones. They make available larger pies and, thereby, larger possible smallest slices. They pose less threat to civil and political liberties than do command economies. By making use of market mechanisms, a Rawlsian-minded regime can save itself the immense (if not hopeless) task of rationally allocating capital, labor, and consumer goods across society. A competitive market in labor provides a self-adjusting system of incentives and compensations for training costs.

It is the efficiency of the market and its status as an alternative to cumbersome and freedom-threatening central planning that recommends it so strongly to Rawls. The competitive market as such is not esteemed as an instance of pure procedural justice. Rather, what is salient is the idea of the *perfectly* competitive market as "a perfect procedure with respect to efficiency."[14] Various forms of economic regulation are conventionally put forward by Rawls as means of moving the market toward, or compensating for the absence of, so-called "perfect competition."[15] The goal is efficiency and the Rawlsian purposes that efficiency facilitates—not any "inherent fairness" in competitive markets. It is the whole complex of the market, plus its regulation, plus the enforcement of the various principles of justice, that is thought of by Rawls, albeit mistakenly, as an expression of pure procedural justice.

As we have already seen, the second part of Rawls' account of "subsidiary" rights is, very simply, that the actual operation of such a just complex generates expectations that are "legitimate." Individuals' economic rights are simply claims to the fulfillment of these specific legitimate expectations. As Rawls puts it, "In a well-ordered society individuals acquire claims to a share of the social product by doing certain things encouraged by the existing arrangements."[16]

But the well-orderedness of such a society is entirely a function of the satisfaction by its arrangements of Rawls' hierarchy of goals. The legitimacy of particular claims depends entirely on this extrinsic feature of the society's institutions and practices. There is no quality of the practices themselves that translates into just results. No characteristic of the procedures that individuals go through—other than the aggregative causal characteristic of yielding a social and economic profile that satisfies independent Rawlsian criteria— accounts for the justice of any individual's holdings. So there is no reality within the Rawlsian system that corresponds to individual's entitlements existing as a matter of pure procedural justice.

Notes

1. John Rawls, *A Theory of Justice* (Cambridge, Mass.: Harvard University Press, 1971), pp. 225–26.
2. Martin, "Rawlsian Economic Justice and The Proper Bounds of Government Regulation," in this volume, p. 114.
3. *Ibid.,* p. 122.
4. *Ibid.,* p. 123.
5. Rawls, *Theory of Justice*, p. 86.
6. Robert Nozick, *Anarchy, State and Utopia* (New York: Basic Books, 1974), esp. pp. 150–73.
7. Rawls, *Theory of Justice*, p. 277.
8. Martin notes the demand that results conform to the Difference Principle. But, instead of seeing that the role of the Difference Principle as providing an independent standard undercuts the whole idea of pure procedural justice, he merely concludes that one particular practice, the market in and of itself, cannot be an instrument of pure procedural justice. This leaves the way open to the suggestion that the Rawlsian "solution" is simply to "build certain institutions into the market or its immediate context, set certain goals down side by side with market goals, . . . and try to do justice by the whole mix" (Martin, "Rawlsian Economic Justice," p. 119.). In the course of this addition of goals, the problem of explaining how Rawls can lay claim to pure procedural justice seems to be forgotten.
9. Rawls, *Theory of Justice*, p. 304.
10. *Ibid.,* p. 88; emphasis added. Some passages do not fit this (putative) conception of pure procedural justice. For example, Rawls says that "the role of the principle of fair opportunity is to insure that the system of cooperation is one of pure procedural justice" (*Theory of Justice*, p. 87). Here it sounds as though fair opportunity contributes to the purity of the system's operation rather than being a background condition the satisfaction of which is necessary to the system's justice.

11. Martin, "Rawlsian Economic Justice," p. 120. The emphasis on procedural *justice* is reduced from an early draft of Martin's essay. "Procedurally just" is often replaced by the more ambiguous "procedurally fair." And we are no longer told that the status of basic economic institutions is reserved for the open and competitive market "on the grounds of pure procedural justice." But the idea that market processes have independent moral weight remains—both as part of Martin's reading of Rawls' claims and of what Rawls can reasonably claim.

12. In a separate essay much should be said about Rawls' belief that "there is no essential tie between the use of free markets and private ownership in the means of production" (*Theory of Justice,* p. 271). If prices are governmental allocative devices (combined with governmental orders to firms to compete, to match marginal cost and revenue, etc.), then one does not have a genuine market economy. To have such an economy, prices must arise out of the interaction, both actual and anticipated, of separate and independent economic units. But such an independence is incompatible with anything that deserves to be called "public ownership."

13. Martin, "Rawlsian Economic Justice," p. 117.

14. Rawls, *Theory of Justice,* p. 272.

15. On the distortions in economic theory and policy recommendations due to this notion of perfect competition, see F. A. Hayek's "The Meaning of Competition" in his *Individualism and Economic Order* (Chicago: University of Chicago Press, 1948) and "Competition as a Discovery Procedure" in his *New Studies in Philosophy, Politics, Economics and the History of Ideas* (Chicago: University of Chicago Press, 1978). Note Rawls' claim that, in accordance with perfect competition, "whatever the internal nature of firms . . . they take the prices of outputs and inputs as given and draw up their plans accordingly. When markets are truly competitive, firms do not engage in price wars or other contests for market power" (*Theory of Justice,* pp. 272–73). Need it be said that price "wars" and contests for market "power" in a world of ever-changing inputs and outputs and ever necessary entrepreneurial activity is the very essence of competition?

16. Rawls, *Theory of Justice,* p. 313.

Part III

The Adequacy of Cost-Benefit Analysis

Although most people would agree that, at least in part, good government is government in the public interest, government officials have the difficulty of determining just what in fact is in the public interest. One commonly accepted tool for determining the public interest is cost-benefit analysis—a tool that is based on utilitarian moral theory. Given this utilitarian base, it is not surprising that some moral philosophers have argued that cost-benefit analysis is inadequate as a basis for determining government policy. The classical critique is Alasdair MacIntyre's "Utilitarianism and Cost/Benefit Analysis: An Essay on the Relevance of Moral Philosophy to Bureaucratic Theory." MacIntyre's critique of cost-benefit analysis can be summarized as follows: Cost-benefit analysis is inadequate because it fails to consider a large number of the possible options; because it has no satisfactory scale for weighing various options; because it has no standard for determining whose values are to count in the weighing and assessing of harms and benefits; because it has no way of determining how far into the future consequences should be considered; and because it cannot deal adequately with unpredictability.

Most of the papers in this section are at least in part a response to MacIntyre's criticism. Vincent Vaccaro writes from the perspective of a government employee who has worked with cost-benefit analysis problems. Vaccaro believes that MacIntyre's critique is less formidable when cost-benefit analysis is not viewed as *the* basis for government policy. Vaccaro points out that in practice cost-benefit analysis is always constrained by non-economic criteria. The chief difficulty with cost-benefit analysis, Vaccaro believes, is that the problem lies more with the person who does the analysis than with the technique itself. People mistakenly blame "the computer" when in fact they should blame the systems analyst. Similarly, people blame cost-benefit conclusions when they should blame the cost-benefit analyst. Vaccaro then raises three other objections to cost-benefit analysis as practiced: first, that the definition of efficiency is narrowly limited to Pareto optimality; second, that the question of distributional equity is not adequately handled; and, third, that many cost-benefit analyses are costly and slow. Vaccaro concludes by arguing that future discussion should focus on the need to determine the rights and principles that are fundamental to public policy formulation in the United States today and the need for non-economic and quasi-economic techniques or approaches to cost-benefit analysis.

Tom Beauchamp believes that many criticisms of cost-benefit analysis have as their target its use as a regulatory device and, hence, that such attacks are misguided when directed against the technique itself. In his defense of cost-benefit analysis, Beauchamp distinguishes between the strict and the loose sense of the term. By focusing on the loose sense, Beauchamp believes he can show that cost-benefit analysis is an effective tool for policy analysis. He concludes with a defense of both cost-benefit analysis and utilitarianism. His most preeminent argument takes as its starting point the fact that policy decisions must be made by some method or other. The advantages of cost-benefit analysis really come to the fore when it is compared with other available means for making policy decisions.

David Braybrooke and Peter K. Schotch recognize that traditional cost-benefit analysis can be legitimately criticized for not taking account of peremptory considerations (like justice, rights, honor) and for not putting needs ahead of preferences. Braybrooke and Schotch then try to develop a cost-benefit schema that is not subject to these objections. First, a cost-benefit analysis could not get started if a proposed policy violated a peremptory consideration like justice. Such a proposed policy would have to be rejected completely or held up for revision. At the second stage a policy must meet the minimum standard of provision for every need of every person being considered. It is at the third stage, where preferences are considered, that traditional cost-benefit analysis comes into its own. They conclude by pointing out some of the advantages of this account, particularly regarding the problem of the measurement of the danger to human life.

In responding to Beauchamp and Braybrooke-Schotch, John Byrne does not concentrate on the technical feasibility and limits of cost-benefit analysis. Rather, Byrne questions the theory of policy making that those who employ cost-benefit analysis adopt. Those who would use cost-benefit analysis believe that social problems can be resolved by rational objective analysis; the irrationalities of power politics could be eliminated. However, if policy making could be based on cost-benefit analysis, the democratic role of consent would be replaced by the administrative state. Byrne then provides arguments to show that policy making based on cost-benefit analysis has no need for a participative citizenry, that the concept of freedom would change its meaning, and that a new means for measuring governmental success is created. Finally Byrne details the normative underpinnings of cost-benefit analysis.

VINCENT VACCARO

10 Cost-Benefit Analysis and Public Policy Formulation

Unfortunately for many of us the mention of cost-benefit analysis conjures up a series of negative images: McNamara's whiz-kids and the Southeast Asia war, a Benthamic calculus in the hands of an uninspired bureaucrat or an analytical tool running roughshod over the analysts and the projects under review. Against such a hopelessly bleak backdrop, it almost seems ludicrous to ask whether cost-benefit analysis is adequate to serve as the basis for determining government policy.

Now having said this I shall attempt to discuss the role that cost-benefit analysis does and should play in determining government policy. At the very beginning, let it be clear that I do not believe that cost-benefit analysis alone is adequate as *the,* and I repeat *the*, (sole) basis for determining government policy. Certainly there are other factors and forms of analysis that are germane in determining what policy should prevail on one issue or another. However, cost-benefit analysis does provide "a conceptual structure and set of techniques for relating means to ends, for arranging the various costs associated with each course of action, and for describing, comparing, and assessing possible outcomes"[1] and therefore warrants a central role in the formulation and execution of government policy. At this point, I

Before actually beginning this chapter, readers are advised of the two following points: (1) Because many of you are not familiar with the techniques or steps involved in a cost-benefit analysis, the Appendix has been prepared for background reading. If you need a quick introduction or refresher, I recommend you start with it. (2) Because the bibliography for public sector economic analysis in the writings of philosophers is extremely limited. I have included a significant amount of documentation. Thus readers are advised that the text can easily be read without reference to the notes. However, for readers who desire to know more about the topics discussed herein, the notes should provide a handy sketch of where to look and what you can expect to find.

hasten to add that the version of cost-benefit analysis that I shall be discussing is cost-benefit analysis as *practiced* within governmental agencies (primarily at the federal level) and not as a theoretical construct abstracted from its application within the political process.

I shall begin my treatment of the adequacy of cost-benefit analysis by discussing some basic but often confused points about cost-benefit techniques. As a familiar departure or reference point, I shall cite certain remarks of Alasdair MacIntyre concerning parallels between utilitarian moral philosophy and cost-benefit techniques.[2] Although section I will consist of a defense against objections concerning any form of end-state analysis, there are certainly particular problems with cost-benefit analysis. Section II will be taken up with a discussion of some of these. Finally, because I view this chapter as somewhat of a starting point for a philosophical discussion of *techniques* in policy analysis, I shall make a few points regarding four issues that need to be addressed and contributions that philosophers may make.

I

Let me begin by citing some of the apparent weaknesses of cost-benefit analysis as a procedure or an instrument of policy science. Although Alasdair MacIntyre, whom I quote, is primarily concerned with evaluating the conceptual adequacy of the end-oriented, consequential foundations of cost-benefit analysis, and not an analysis of cost-benefit analysis as a procedure or instrument in policy analysis, his points provide a clear summary of apparent weaknesses of this analytical tool.

(1) There is, first of all, the restriction of alternatives so that the benefits and costs of doing this rather than that are weighed somehow against one another, but neither alternative is assessed against an indeterminately larger range of other non-economically described alternatives.

(2) The use of cost/benefit analysis clearly presupposes a prior decision as to what is a cost and what constitutes a benefit; but even more than that, it presupposes some method or technique of ordering costs and benefits so that what otherwise would be incommensurable becomes somehow commensurable.

(3) The application of cost/benefit analysis presupposes a decision as to *whose* values and preferences are to be taken into account in assessing costs and benefits.

(4) The question of what is to count as a consequence of some particular action or course of action must be answered by the advocate of cost/benefit analysis.

(5) Proponents of the cost/benefit theory must also address the problem of what time scale is to be used in calculating costs and benefits that are used in or excluded from analysis.[3]

I do not intend to answer each charge, but I shall merely make four points that I believe will clarify what cost-benefit analysis is about—points that may not be immediately obvious to those unfamiliar with the theory behind the procedure.

First, make no mistake about it, cost-benefit analysis is "a formal procedure for comparing the costs and benefits of alternative policies."[4] The words are clear—the purpose of the procedure is to compare only one aspect of alternative policies, not the policies themselves. For that reason, it is inappropriate to expect this analytical tool to serve as *the* basis for comparing alternative policies.

My next three points concern the interpretation of data. The second one is that, although cost-benefit analysis does require that the alternatives be displayed and compared in economic terms, it in no way ignores non-economic considerations, and, in fact, the analyst is *expected* to appeal to non-economic criteria and standards at numerous points in the analysis. Properly done, cost-benefit analyses begin with the definition of the objective, followed by a searching out of hypothetical alternatives for accomplishing the objectives and then formulation of the assumptions or "givens." (See the Appendix for a detailed discussion of the sequence of steps followed in completing an analysis.) These steps precede (in theory at least) any attempts to determine, quantify, display, or compare costs and benefits. Although most discussions of alternatives and assumptions normally found in cost-benefit analyses are devoted to eliminating non-competing alternatives or are devoted to structuring the data that will be considered (that is, the economic data), a good cost-benefit analyst will always include discussions of alternatives or assumptions that cannot be assessed by cost-benefit procedures.[5] The exclusion of such alternatives or factors, rather than eliminating them from consideration by the policy-maker, in fact, flags them as alternatives or factors that must be considered simply because they have not been adequately evaluated in the analysis. It is because cost-benefit theory is sensitive to identifying and clarifying critical non-economic issues that it is a valuable tool for those who must establish and implement our public policies and goals.

Third, the measurement of costs, but especially of benefits, involves interpretation of data in terms of economic theory. What constitutes a benefit? A cost? Whose benefit? Over what time scale? Such questions often depend for their answers upon a given theory or interpretation of economics. In MacIntyre's terms, there is a need for techniques or methods that order what would otherwise be incommensurable so that they are somewhat rendered commensurable. This is exactly what is being done by cost-benefit analysts and, rather than being a weakness, I consider it to be a definite strength. Good cost-benefit analysts are extremely sensitive to the problems of "comparing apples and oranges" and have devised numerous methods and techniques that compare or at least measure (through cardinality as well as ordinality) apparent "incommensurables."[6] The important thing to note is that before employing any given cost-benefit technique—for example, option value or donor benefits[7]—a theoretical justification (discussion or at least a citation of references) must be presented and defended, and documentation of alternative measures or assumptions must be included. It is because of the requirement for more accurate measurement and complete documentation and justification that cost-benefit analyses are valuable to the policy-maker.

Fourth, the data available to the analyst may not be complete or the analyst may not be "satisfied" with what the data tells us. Here I am not talking about selecting data to prove a point. This point concerns the professional judgment of the analyst; and here MacIntyre and I are in agreement about the need to go beyond economic theory alone. There are times when a single figure may not accurately depict a given state of affairs or outcome of a course of action—economists will make the point in terms of single versus multiple indicies. Moreover, there may be a question about whether the data is somehow biased by the technique used in gathering or categorizing it—for example, for many public sector, regulatory issues, like urban transit systems, "comparisons of cost-related indicators have been impossible because of wide variations in accounting practices. Different procedures have been followed in assigning costs to different costs categories."[8] Furthermore, estimates about the future[9] or uncertainty about the appropriateness of a given measurement methodology may dictate that a range of values (based on various assumptions) be employed. In this way contingencies can be tested, various expected values for parameters displayed, and intuitive judgments introduced, using a technique called *a fortiori* analysis. Again, the analyst is expected to justify and document all such "interpretations." The introduction of such adjustments flags them as worthy of special consideration by the policy-maker.

In short, considerable care is taken by cost-benefit analysts to satisfy and overcome the weaknesses outlined by MacIntyre. In MacIntyre's own words, "cost/benefit analysis is an instrument of practical reason,"[10] and being just one instrument of reason cost-benefit analysis need not answer all questions regarding alternative policies.

II

Certainly cost-benefit analysis has some serious shortcomings, especially when it comes to government policy. Here are some of the major drawbacks or limitations in cost-benefit analysis as it is now used in determining or evaluating policy alternatives.

The first is a conceptual point and in my opinion it represents the most serious to overcome. Cost-benefit analysis is a formal procedure for analyzing policy alternatives involving the use or allocation of the resources of our economy. Thus, its purpose is to assist policy-makers in their fundamentally economic (not political) task of allocating scarce resources among competing alternatives. In other words, the primary objective in cost-benefit analysis is the achievement of allocative efficiency, which means that there is an "improvement" in the allocation of economic resources.[11] Most cost-benefit theorists base their definition of efficiency on the Pareto criterion: any change in the social state is desirable if at least one person judges himself or herself to be better off because of the change, while no one else is made worse off by the change.

But this still leaves the question of who should benefit from the distribution unresolved. I shall briefly discuss two issues—distributional equity and the normative force of rights or entitlements. First, to the question of distributional equity.

It is a generally accepted principle underlying the words, if not always the actions, of public officials that those less fortunate economically, physically, intellectually, and so on should benefit from the actions of those more fortunately endowed.[12] Because both allocative efficiency and distributional equity appear to be equally intuitive and compelling in our society, attempts have been made to accommodate both within welfare economics and cost-benefit analysis—for example, by introducing a theory of compensation[13] or by weighting the desired equity formula in some way and *then* applying the criteria of allocative efficiency.[14] These "shoe-horning" efforts have not provided a conceptually sound principle of distributional equity needed to co-function with the principle of allocative efficiency. Without meeting this conceptual requirement, cost-benefit analysis alone can in principle never serve as *the* basis for determining government policy in this country.[15]

The question of the normative force of rights or entitlements has recently been raised in discussions of cost-benefit analysis. Simply put, allocative efficiency and its related criterion of Pareto optimality focus upon what constitutes the most economically efficient distribution, but allocative efficiency in no way ensures that those who are entitled to benefit (either morally or legally) from the policy or program will actually be the ones who receive the benefit. Allocative efficiency fails to consider the normative force of rights and entitlements in its calculus and therefore fails to satisfy the minimum criterion for social justice.

Although determinations regarding public policy must respect the normative force of rights and entitlements, I do not see this issue presenting a problem to cost-benefit analysis. Cost-benefit analysis again is "a conceptual structure and set of techniques for relating means to ends, for arranging the various costs associated with each course of action, and for describing, comparing, and assessing possible outcomes." Cost-benefit analysis is not conducted in a legal or moral vacuum. Questions or rights and entitlements and full consideration of their normative force can and should be considered as constraints and are generally introduced in steps 2 and 3 of the analysis. All too often, we tend to forget that cost-benefit analysis is an analytical tool that provides a map of how the policy will be *executed* should it be established, not simply what should be done, and for this reason cost-benefit analysis provides valuable information for the policy-maker (or legislator). Because moral and legal rights and entitlements are to be respected in the formulation of public policy (from the legislative, executive, and judicial viewpoints), their normative force is considered in evaluating costs and benefits of the various alternatives. Again, however, it is the decision-maker who decides, not the model; and the main focus of the public sector decision-maker is practical: will it work?

We now turn to some less theoretical, but equally important, limitations. There is a principle in politics that once something has been implemented or allowed, it is virtually impossible to get it off the books at some later date.[16] For this reason, regulations, such as those issued by the Occupational Safety and Health Administration (OSHA), can only be proposed after the cost-benefit analysis is completed and the results are available for the public scrutiny.[17] Cost-benefit studies are costly—one estimate for OSHA standards is slightly less than $100,000 per cost-benefit analysis—and time-consuming—average time required again for OSHA standards may be as great as twelve months.[18] These economic study requirements are viewed by those directly involved, namely, employees and unions for cases such as coke emissions, polyvinyl chloride, or benzine, as "obstructionist devices," mere delay tactics that administratively grant companies the license to harm and endanger the lives of employees through continuous exposure during the period in which the study is being conducted (clearing the shelves, so to speak). An equally interesting point is that the money being expended in conducting the cost-benefit analysis could well be used more efficiently. (Note that the cost of the cost-benefit study is not included in the cost-benefit analysis under standard cost-benefit analysis methodology.)

How good are the studies being done? The quality of a study is directly related to three factors: the strength of the economic theory underlying cost-benefit analysis; the quality of the data available; and the quality of the analyst.

On the first point, as I have mentioned above, there are still many shortcomings and weaknesses of cost-benefit analysis, but the conceptual foundation and critical issues regarding the concept of cost and benefits, the measurement of benefits, estimating the worth of aesthetics and quality of life, cost-estimating methodologies, and the like are being debated and greatly improved. I have presented some of what is underway in section I.

On the second, the availability of data—especially regarding cost—is critical. Unlike the problem of measuring benefits, which is still enmeshed in conceptual difficulties, the primary problem with estimating costs is accessibility. Most cost figures in coke emissions, car emissions, carcinogenic effects, and the like belong to the industries being regulated or threatened with regulation. If the analyst must go to the industry to get the data, the question of its accuracy or completeness is always open. In cases such as the health effects of asbestos or benzine, the problem of projecting twenty or thirty years into the future or extracting data from the past rears its head.

On the third point, one of my pet concerns is: How good are the analysts? The entire gamut is covered, from exceptionally good to grossly incompetent. I think that it should be obvious by now that cost-benefit analysts must be innovative and creative thinkers who can deal effectively with economic and non-economic issues and not merely self-serving or obsequious, number-crunching drones. Some would suggest that outside consultants from highly respected research institutes would provide the safeguards needed (objectivity, professionalism, and perspective). And often they do. But I have come across an interesting example of how not to do a cost-benefit analysis. This study involved a proposed rapid transit system in a major U.S. city and was conducted by staff members of a major "think tank."[19] The result was that the cost-benefit ratio was favorable only because many of the benefits were incorrectly calculated due to errors in estimating inflation, anticipating unemployment reductions, decreasing expenditures, double counting, and including arbitrarily non-quantifiable benefits;[20] because many costs were underestimated or omitted entirely; and because the estimates of passenger usage were overly optimistic. My conclusion is simple: if we are going to use cost-benefit analysis as an effective tool in policy determination and formulation, we must attract and train intelligent and sensitive people to perform the analyses. The criteria used in selecting and developing analysts still leave a lot to be desired.

My last point is that all the work of the economic theorists, data gatherers, and cost-benefit analysts is useless if the policy-maker either cannot or does not take the time to read and understand the analysis. Many decision-makers,[21] unfortunately, would like to see cost-benefit information expressed as a simple ratio on a one-page memo. The problem is that by themselves cost-benefit ratios do *not* provide sufficient guidance to enable one to pick out the best alternative. The proper way to view the cost-benefit ratio is in terms of the incremental ratio of costs to benefits of alternative policies. That is not a simple task by itself and does not include all the non-economic issues "flagged" by the analyst, a point I raised in section I.

III

Several issues arise regarding the economic evaluation of public policy formulation that I shall now touch upon briefly. I shall not in this section attempt to do more than introduce some concerns and hope to provide a springboard for future discussions.

First, a need exists for determinations concerning those rights and principles that are fundamental to public policy formulation in the United States today. I have already discussed the issue of the adequacy of the Pareto criterion, the notion of distributional equity and the normative force of rights. In addition, there are a host of other issues that appear to be assuming the status of "informal" rights or principles, if I can coin a phrase: for example, the quality of the working environment, say, regarding benzine and coke emissions, the "no safe" principle regarding carcinogens in foods, esthetic integrity of rivers, forests, and the like, the quality of leisure or retirement, quality of life for the handicapped, and the "no benefit is too small or too costly" slogan regarding health care. Analysis of these concepts has barely begun. Likewise, it is about time that the United States formally establish certain national priorities, say, for air pollution abatement or minimum income, and require that these priorities be weighed in all regulatory or other cost-benefit analyses. Without some agreement about the meaning and relative importance of such issues, economic and other analytical methodologies will always produce "disputed" results. (National priorities are not that far removed from national needs, and "national needs" are defined in sixteen broad areas that provide a coherent and comprehensive basis for analyzing and understanding the U.S. budget for fiscal year 1980.[22])

The second regards the value of competing or supplemental (reinforcing) economic approaches, such as cost-effectiveness analysis, risk assessment, risk-benefit analysis, cost-benefit analysis, and to a limited extent inflationary impact assessment and regulatory analysis. Each approach has its own conceptual framework and evaluates policy alternatives in light of that framework. For example, cost-benefit analysis requires that decision-makers establish both societal goals and the means for achieving the goals as a basis for accomplishing cost-benefit comparisons. Cost-effectiveness analysis begins with the assumption that societal goals are established and reduces the *analytical* task to issues of cost and technical feasibility. Risk assessment, on the other hand, attempts to estimate how likely it is that some hazard will occur, how many people will be affected and in what way, and what steps can and to some extent should be taken to avert it. Its bottom line is an estimate of the extent to which the public fears or is willing to tolerate a particular risk (or is willing to tolerate lower levels of risk). Decisions must be made (presumably at the federal level) regarding what analytical technique or methodology is most appropriate for a given type of policy question.[23] Such (federal) decisions will also provide a basis for ensuring industry-wide, consistent collection of desired data.

A third issue deals with the need for non-economic and quasi-economic techniques or approaches. Here, one might include technology assessment, regulatory analysis, legal analysis, environmental impact assessment, policy evaluation, and political impact assessment. In addition, even ethical analyses[24] are being proposed, and, in my opinion, such ethical analyses will provide needed insight into establishing national priorities and may possibly provide guidance in determining weights to be assigned in ordering the priorities. Through discussion of each type of analysis, the strengths and weaknesses of each, and clarification of the interrelationship between and compatibility with the various methodologies mentioned above, it may someday be possible to reach agreement concerning what constitutes an adequate analysis of a public policy issue.

The last issue is one of talent. As I mentioned in section II, the quality of the policy analysts of whatever type depends as much upon the insight and creative judgment of the analyst as it does on the analytical methodology or the data. For this reason, policy analysts must have perspective, interdisciplinary interests, and an ability not merely to analyze but to put parts back together into a coherent whole. Policy analysis is demanding, because it requires the analyst to clarify objectives, make assumptions, choose to include or exclude information, select the proper analytical technique, and consume, interpret, and in certain cases translate qualitative information in one field into quantitative data in another. The pressures on the analyst are great, and the professional demands are tremendous. Unfortunately, too many "analysts" (considering the widespread effects of policy analysis) fall short of the minimum level of competence we would hope for at the federal level. Simply put, we appear to be more worried about the methodological techniques than the analysts applying them. Considering the stakes, the establishment of government policy and the multi-million-dollar price tag, neither can be ignored.

Appendix

This appendix is designed to provide those unfamiliar with cost-benefit analysis with a clear picture of what is involved in such an analysis. The wording I shall use in describing the process comes from a Department of Defense cost-benefit program put together while I was a member of the Department of the Navy's Cost Review and Analysis Division. To help you follow the process, I have taken the liberty of copying a page from the DOD Handbook on Economic Analysis as Figure 1.

The cost-benefit process has six major steps or elements: (1) establishing and defining the goal or objective desired (in setting the objective, you have also established what criteria will be relevant in the analysis); (2) searching out hypothetical alternatives for accomplishing the objective; (3) formulating the appropriate assumptions (usually this refers to "givens" and relates to

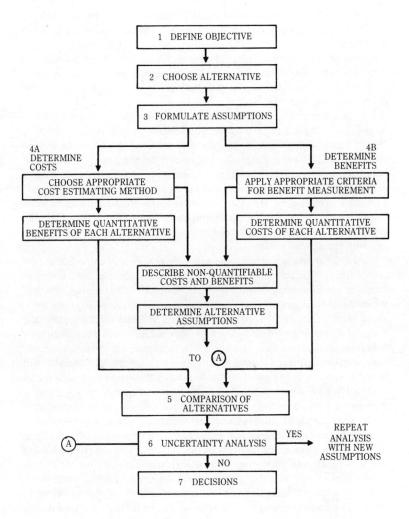

Figure 1. The process of cost-benefit analysis.

Source: Department of Defense Economic Analysis Handbook (2d edition), January, 1975.

future occurrences, for example, the economic life of a bus); (4) determining the costs (the inputs) and the benefits (the outputs) of each of the alternatives; (5) comparing the costs and benefits for each alternative and ranking the alternatives; and (6) testing the sensitivity of major uncertainties on the outcome of the analysis. From the process comes a *basis* upon which the decision-maker *can* make a decision. The decision is in no way the *outcome* of the analysis. Now that is worth repeating: the decision is in no way the *outcome* of the analysis.

Briefly, a few points of clarification and amplification need to be made. In Step 2, searching out the hypothetical alternatives, one may find himself or herself faced with certain constraints or limitations that must be accommodated—for example, the project will be completed by 1983, 50 percent of the funds will be available during the last year of the project, and so on. Step 3 concerns assumptions. As I mentioned, assumptions usually refer to "givens" and relate to the future. However, one must avoid using assumptions when research tools are available for gathering factual information. For example, assumptions about coke emission levels should be avoided if the exact levels can conveniently be obtained.

Step 4, determining the costs and benefits, is the crucial and probably the most controversial step. If we simplify significantly, there are two common methods for estimating costs. One is the Industrial Engineering Method, which consists of consolidating the estimates from various separate work segments into a total project estimate. For example, to determine the cost of a bus needed to provide transportation for citizens confined to wheel chairs, we could obtain separate estimates for the bus's engine, air conditioning unit, seats, exterior, lift mechanisms, and so on, which when added together will give the estimate. When one is unable to gather together all parts to come up with a total or where detailed data do not exist, estimators will use a Parametric Cost Estimating Method. Here the total cost of an alternative is based upon ascribed physical and performance characteristics and their relationship to highly aggregated component costs. In English, all this means is that certain definable characteristics that influence cost are assigned: there will be twenty subway stations that will require elevators for the handicapped, special light signals for the deaf, PA systems for the blind, and so on. Some will require drilling through rock at a certain rate of progress per week; some will require purchase of land, redesign of present platform layout, and the like. For these cases certain Cost Estimating Relationships can be drawn: drilling through rock is ten times more expensive than through sand; the land in section 1 will be twice as expensive as in section 2, but one-tenth that of section 6. It is also important that our estimates of cost take into account inflation, present value, sunk versus incremental costs, and the like.

Assessing benefits is even more complicated than estimating costs. Again, simplifying, the following step-by-step procedure is common: determine, list, and define relevant benefits; establish sources of information for benefit determination (at times a survey method proves helpful); collect and display information for benefit determination; and summarize, evaluate, and present benefit determination for alternatives of the analysis. Some general categories under which benefits may occur include (for an industrial project): production, productivity, operating efficiency, reliability, accuracy, maintainability or controllability, manageability, integrateability, availability, service life, quality, acceptability, ecological impact, economic cost, morale, safety, and security. The words documentation and justification are the watchwords here.

Step 5 involves the process of comparing alternatives. This may seem to be a relatively simple step, and it is, where one alternative strictly dominates all others. It gets more complicated if benefit levels or cost levels are fixed, in calculating costs or benefits versus time, in ranking alternatives, and the like. All of these involve decisions by the analyst involved. (Remember the point here is to compare the increments between alternatives, that is, what benefits are obtained or lost with each change in cost.)

Lastly, Step 6 allows for the treatment of uncertainties. There are even such "things" as unknown unknowns—but after all this mumbo-jumbo unknown-unknowns may be a bit much. At this point, contingencies or changes are tested, ranges (low, medium, or high) can be introduced to cover uncertainties, and intuitive judgments and weight assigned to factors are considered.

After uncertainties are calculated, the data are ready for presentation to the decision-maker. At this point in the analysis, I recommend a summary of non-qualified factors, any intuitive judgments deemed relevant by the analyst, and a distribution impact statement, that is, an assessment of who will receive the benefits and to what degree. These factors should also be clearly spelled out in any executive summary of the complete cost-benefit analysis.

Notes

1. Henry Rowen, "The Role of Cost-Benefit Analysis in Policy Making," in Henry M. Peskin and Eugene P. Seskin, eds., *Cost Benefit Analysis and Water Pollution Policy* (Washington, D.C.: Urban Institute, 1975), p. 363.

2. Alasdair MacIntyre, "Utilitarianism and Cost/Benefit Analysis: An Essay on the Relevance of Moral Philosophy to Bureaucratic Theory," in Tom L. Beauchamp and Norman E. Bowie, eds., *Ethical Theory and Business* (Englewood Cliffs, N.J.: Prentice-Hall, Inc., 1979), pp. 266–76.

3. *Ibid.,* pp. 271–3.

4. Henry M. Peskin and Eugene P. Seskin, "Introduction and Overview," in Peskin and Seskin, *Cost Benefit Analysis*, p. 1. A similar definition is found in Peter G. Sassone and William A. Schaffer, *Cost-Benefit Analysis: A Handbook* (New York: Academic Press, 1978), p. 3: Cost-benefit analysis is "an estimation and evaluation of net benefits associated with alternatives for achieving defined public goals" (my emphasis).

5. "Whatever cannot be expressed in terms of the common-denominator metric at the heart of the analysis is either excluded from consideration, simply noted outside of the analysis itself for the decision-maker's possible use, or at most incorporated into the analysis in the form of a constraint—a qualitative requirement, subject to which the project is designed so as to maximize benefits minus costs" (Burton A. Weisbrod, "Appendix A: Concepts of Costs and Benefits," in Samuel B. Chase, ed., *Problems in Public Expenditure Analysis* (Washington, D.C.: Brookings Institution, 1968), pp. 257–62.

6. For an interesting discussion of "measuring the incommensurable," see James Griffen, "Are There Incommensurable Values?" *Philosophy and Public Affairs* 7, no. 1 (Fall 1977): 39–59.

7. See the discussion of option value and donor benefits in Robert H. Haveman and Burton A. Weisbrod, "The Concept of Benefits in Cost-Benefit Analysis: With Emphasis on Water Pollution Control Activities," in Peskin and Seskin, eds., *Cost Benefit Analysis*, pp. 59–64.

8. *Improving Transit System Performance: Procedures of the September, 1977 National Conference* (Report no. UMTA-DC-06-0184-77-1; Urban Consortium for Technology Initiatives and American Public Transit Association, Washington, D.C.: National Technical Information Service, 1978), p. 63.

9. For example, estimates concerning cost of technology necessitated by new regulatory requirements, e.g., the requirements for air standards and auto emissions and for increased fuel efficiency for automobiles in the 1980's, are generally based upon existing technology and not on the cost-saving technology that inevitably is developed as a *result* of the new standards or requirements. See Mary Jane Bolle, "Cost-Benefit Studies for OSHA Standards: Use and Misuse" (Congressional Research Service, Report no. 77-56E; Washington, D.C.: Library of Congress, Aug. 22, 1977), p. 21.

10. MacIntyre, "Utilitarianism," p. 270.

11. Haveman and Weisbrod, "The Concept of Benefits," p. 39.

12. In Rawls' terms, the difference principle: "the intuitive idea that the social order is not to establish and secure the more attractive prospects of those better off unless doing so is to the advantage of those less fortunate" (John Rawls, *A Theory of Justice* [Cambridge, Mass.: Harvard University Press, 1971], p. 75).

13. See Haveman and Weisbrod, "The Concept of Benefits," pp. 40ff; Nicholas Kaldor, "Welfare Propositions of Economics and Interpersonal

Comparisons of Utility," *Economic Journal* 49 (1939); J. R. Hicks, "The Foundations of Welfare Economics," *Economic Journal* 49 (1939); E. J. Mishan, *Cost-Benefit Analysis* (New York: Praeger, 1971), p. 316; and I. M. D. Little, *A Critique of Welfare Economics* (2d ed.; Oxford: Clarendon Press, 1957), p. 109.

14. See Haveman and Weisbrod, "The Concept of Benefits," pp. 61–64.

15. For a discussion of issues involving efficiency vs. equity and U.S. constitutional principles, see Michael S. Baram, "Regulation of Health, Safety and Environmental Quality and the Use of Cost-Benefit Analysis," *Final Report* Washington, D.C.: Administrative Conference of the United States (March 1, 1979), pp. 32–35.

16. For some areas of government policy, say, health, safety, environmental quality, and education (at least recently), once something is allowed it is viewed by supporters or recipients as if they were now public or private rights that must be revoked, not merely as standards or licenses to be attained or followed.

17. Office of Management and Budget Circular no. A-107, "Concerning Requirements for Inflation Impact Statements," specifies that the required certification shall be provided by the proposing agency "at the time it first certifies it" (para. 5c). Some of the requirements for Inflation Impact Statements include, and I quote A-107:

    a. Agency heads are responsible for the development of criteria to determine which *proposed* legislation, regulations, or rules originated by the agency are "major" and therefore require evaluation and certification. In developing criteria, each agency head shall consider, among other things,

    (1) cost impact on consumers, businesses, markets or Federal, State, or local government;

    (2) effect on productivity of wage-earners, businesses, or government;

    (3) effect on competition;

    (4) effect on energy supply or demand.

    b. Each agency shall develop procedures for the evaluation of proposals identified by application of approved criteria. The evaluation should include, where applicable,

    (1) an analysis of the principle cost or other inflationary effects of the action on markets, consumers, businesses, etc., and, where practical, an analysis of secondary cost and price effects. These analyses should have as much quantitative precision as necessary and should focus on a time period sufficient to determine economic and inflationary impacts.

    (2) a comparison of the benefits to be derived from the proposed action with the estimated costs and inflationary impacts. These benefits should be quantified to the extent practical, and

(3) a review of alternatives to the proposed action that were considered, their probable costs, benefits, risks, and inflationary impacts compared with those of the proposed action.

c. Agencies should comply with the requirements of this Circular with existing resources and personnel.

Those who desire to keep their analytical requirements completely up to date should see President Carter's refinement, now called "regulatory analysis," issued in Executive Order 12044 of March 23, 1978.

18. Bolle, "Cost-Benefit Studies," pp. 5–6.

19. I have not included any reference to the study or the institution, because I believe the quality of this particular study is the exception rather than the rule.

20. When challenged about the inclusion of a $25 million benefit *annually* for "style of urban life," the analyst replied, "others were entitled to their opinion of the value of this benefit."

21. Even more critical is the tunnel-visioned interpretation of the cost-benefit ratio that is often given by bureaucratic middle managers. Rather than viewing the cost-benefit ratio for what it is, a tool for policy comparison, it has in many cases become a road map or benchmark for program design and implementation. Note that it should play a fundamental role, however, in program evaluation.

22. *The United States Budget in Brief*—Fiscal Year 1980 (Washington, D.C.: U.S. Government Printing Office, 1979), p. 25. It is interesting to note that part 3 of the *Brief* is entitled: "Meeting National Needs: The Federal Program by Function." Also of interest is an annual publication of The Brookings Institution, entitled *Setting National Priorities: The 19—Budget,* which consists of discussions of certain critical national program areas.

23. For instance, the cosmetics industry is vehemently opposed to the use of cost-benefit analysis as a basis for evaluating the industry's practices and policies. It believes that risk assessment is most appropriate and that prospective customers or users should be advised of health risks and then allowed to make their own choices (willingness to pay).

24. Albert R. Jonsen and Lewis H. Butler, "Public Ethics and Policy Making," *Hastings Center Report,* Aug. 1975, pp. 19–30. "It is clear that, as in the past, economics and politics will play major roles in health policy decisions. Until recently, ethics was not even in the cast of characters. But awareness that political and economic decisions have underlying ethical assumptions is rapidly growing" (Carol Levine, "Ethics and Health Cost Containment," *Hastings Center Report,* Feb. 1979, p. 13).

TOM L. BEAUCHAMP

11 The Moral Adequacy of Cost-Benefit Analysis as the Basis for Government Regulation of Research

In recent years, especially in the regulatory agencies of government, cost-benefit analysis has been increasingly appreciated as a means of decision-making. Those interested in applied moral philosophy have been intrigued by recent federal regulations that mention risk-benefit or cost-benefit analysis in connection with the role of local institutional review boards that assess research protocols. By federal requirement these protocols are to be assessed for their moral adequacy in protecting human subjects of research. Use of this technique has spread well beyond the regulation of research, of course, and even beyond the regulatory branches of government. For example, some corporate social audits are based on cost-benefit principles. Because of the interests of business and government in cost containment, there has been an unfortunate tendency to view cost-benefit reasoning purely as an instrument of expediency. Yet, as the institutional review board and corporate social audit examples indicate, cost-benefit and risk-benefit analyses can be employed explicitly as a means to moral ends—for example, the ends of protecting human subjects of research and the fulfillment of corporations by what they regard as their broad social responsibilities. The government has sometimes legally mandated the use of cost-benefit analysis for these moral ends, as in the case of its requirements for institutional review boards.

A number of complaints have been registered against this use of cost-benefit analysis for regulatory purposes. It has been variously argued that it is *impossible* to use cost-benefit analysis, that it is an *immoral* utilitarian device, and that it is *impractical* as a regulatory guideline. In this chapter I argue that these complaints are groundless, that cost-benefit analysis is a perfectly reasonable instrument for regulation, and that, on at least some occasions, it is mandatory from the moral point of view.

The Nature of Costs, Risks, and Benefits

Before discussing further either the nature of cost-benefit analysis or regulatory requirements regarding cost-benefit comparisons, we need to come to terms over the nature of costs and benefits themselves. What, then, are costs and benefits?

"Costs" are popularly conceived in financial terms, but in cost-benefit analysis a cost can be any disvalued item that affects human health and welfare. In biomedical contexts the specific costs most often mentioned are not quantifiable and already ascertained financial costs but rather are risks. Accordingly, "risks" rather than "costs" is sometimes most appropriately used when making a comparison to benefits. Here "risk" refers to a possible future harm, and statements of risk are estimates of either the probability of such harms or the magnitude of the potential harm. When expressions such as "minimal risk" or "high risk" are used, they refer to the chance of experiencing a harm (its probability) plus the severity of the harm (its magnitude) in the event of occurrence.

The contrasting term "benefit" may be used merely to refer to cost avoidance, but more commonly it denotes something of positive value that promotes health or welfare. Unlike "risk," "benefit" is not probabilistic; thus, probability of benefit is the proper contrast to risk, just as benefits are comparable to harms rather than to risks of harm. Accordingly, cost-benefit relations are more precisely expressed through the language of the probability and magnitude of an anticipated benefit and the probability and magnitude of an anticipated harm.

There are many different kinds of costs and benefits. There are costs in the form of risks of physical and psychological harm, but there are also risks of damage to other interests such as reputation and property. The most likely types of harms to patients and subjects of research are those of pain and diminished psychological or physical ability. For participants in research that does not hold out the prospect of direct therapeutic benefit to them, the benefits involved are anticipated benefits to society from the research.

Two Concepts of Cost-Benefit Analysis

The simple idea behind cost-benefit procedures is that one can array costs and benefits, at the same time identifying uncertainties and possible tradeoffs, in order to present bureaucrats, judges, policy-makers, and business executives with specific, relevant information on the basis of which a decision can be reached. Such analysis proceeds by "measuring" different units—for example, the number of worker accidents, statistical deaths, dollars expended, and workers fired. In the ideal, cost-benefit analysis converts these units of measurement into a common one, usually a monetary unit. At the present time, however, at least two very different senses of "cost-benefit analysis" abound in literature on the subject, and it is essential that these two different understandings be distinguished.

The Strict Sense of Cost-Benefit Analysis

In the textbook portrayal of cost-benefit analysis given by some economists, which I shall call its "strict sense," cost-benefit analysis requires that costs and benefits should be quantified and compared by some acceptable device of measurement. If different quantitative units are used, cost-benefit analysis should in the end convert seemingly incommensurable units of measurement into a common unit such as money, or at least should bring as many units as possible to commensurate status. This goal of an ultimate reduction gives the method tremendous appeal, because judgments about tradeoffs can be made on the basis of perfectly comparable quantities. Costs and benefits can in principle be "weighed," "balanced," and shown to be "in a favorable ratio."[1]

This tight sense of cost-benefit analysis is largely the one used by critics of cost-benefit when it is employed as a tool for moral evaluation. Alasdair MacIntyre, for example, has complained that utilitarians using cost-benefit procedures encounter problems in the quantification and comparison of different cost-benefit units, problems in predicting with precision the consequences of actions, and problems in the specification of whose values, preferences, and assessments are to count and how much they are to count.[2] His complaints seem to me to presuppose the strict sense of cost-benefit analysis and to fail if a looser sense is used.

The Loose Sense of Cost-Benefit Analysis

A different and looser sense of cost-benefit analysis—the sense I believe generally presupposed by regulatory agencies of government —rests on the commonsense conviction that costs and benefits should be systematically arrayed and compared, while uncertainties and tradeoffs are similarly outlined, in order to present decision-makers with material and impartial information. Although it is desirable to use quantitative units such as the number of accidents and dollars expended, cost-benefit judgments can and must be made when quantitative data are unavailable. This loose sense is now the most common conception in legal and bureaucratic documents. The following description offered by the Committee on Public Engineering Policy of the National Academy of Engineering nicely expresses this loose sense of cost-benefit analysis: "*Benefit-cost* . . . refers to an evaluation of *all* the benefits and the costs of proposed action. It is a much broader concept than that of the traditional cost-benefit analysis involving only economic factors."[3]

This way of understanding cost-benefit analysis does not reduce it to the triviality that in decision-making we should weigh advantages against disadvantages. The intent is that objective data be assimilated in order to provide decision-makers with a constraining, more than purely subjective, framework. As an example, consider the decision to allow the Concorde to land in the United States. Secretary Coleman's decision was based on the method of political compromise. If he had been required to refer to a cost-benefit analysis, such a compromise route would not have been permitted, for there would have had to have been a comprehensive array and comparison of costs and benefits on which the judgment would have to have been at least partially based.

This use of the term "cost-benefit analysis" obviously does not require that all costs and benefits be fully quantified and reduced to commensurable units. Rather, the method requires that principles and standards for calculating costs and benefits that are operative in cost-benefit decisions be stated in detail so that unclarity in the judgmental process is reduced. It will rarely be possible to use precise quantitative techniques in the ultimate assessment of whether a medical treatment or research protocol is justified, and those who use "cost-benefit analysis" in the loose sense agree that we must candidly face up to the difficulties that are presented by a purely quantitative model of weighing risks and benefits. They hold that the proper model for evaluations of scientific research is the systematic, nonarbitrary, and nonintuitive comparison of benefits and risks. Such a model demands that justifications of a research protocol be thorough in the assimilation and evaluation of information about all aspects of the procedures under consideration, and that those assimilating the data be explicit in stating operative standards and principles as well as quantitative measurements for considering and weighing alternative procedures. When carefully spelled out, cost-benefit analysis in this loose sense can render the entire process of evaluating clinical procedures and research protocols more thorough and precise, while enhancing the quality of information transmitted through consent forms.

The Anti-Regulation, Anti-Cost-Benefit Movement

Numerous critics of government regulation demanding cost-benefit assessments have come forward in recent months, especially as imposed on biomedical, behavioral, and social scientists. Philosophers such as Alasdair MacIntyre, social scientists such as Joan Cassell and Murray Wax, and representatives from the biomedical world such as Al Jonsen have all complained in their respective domains about cost-benefit analysis and the use of utilitarian reasoning as its moral foundation.[4] The complaints of this diverse group largely reduce to the following six: risks and benefits cannot be non-arbitrarily and reliably measured and compared; risks and benefits are generally incommensurable and cannot reliably be balanced; risks and benefits cannot be reliably predicted; risk-benefit assessments can easily dispense with individual rights in favor of practical expediences; "risk" and "benefit" are evaluative terms that presuppose the values of those who employ them (in labelling something a cost or a benefit); and risk-benefit assessment fails both to account for distributive justice and to determine whose values are to count in assessing risk and benefits for groups.

By almost all accounts risks and benefits of biomedical research *can* often be stated, though only sometimes in precise, quantified form. The sternest criticisms of risk-benefit assessment have thus come from those involved in fields of research where it is most difficult to specify risks and benefits in detail and with predictive accuracy. Anthropologists, for example, have recently argued that their research is only distantly related to the opportunity for risk-benefit calculations found in the world of biomedicine. A typical example of this complaint is the following statement by Joan Cassell:

> Because investigators are unable to predict exactly what is going to happen during the course of research interaction, it becomes self-contradictory for investigators to secure "informed" consent before the research is initiated. In addition, as we move across the spectrum from biomedical experimentation to participant observation, calculable harms become less serious and benefits less immediate. As a result, weighing potential harms against benefits before research is carried out becomes an exercise in creativity, with little relevance to the ethical dilemmas and problems which may emerge during the conduct of the research. In such research, utilitarian risk-benefit calculations become even less appropriate in judging the value or ethical adequacy of a research project.[5]

This view or some generalizable part of it has been embraced by philosophers, biomedical researchers, social science researchers, and biomedical and behavioral therapists. The general view is so widely shared that it would be fairly described as the contemporary orthodox view—or at the very least as one of the major reasons for resisting provisions in federal regulations that require risk-benefit assessments. Quite obviously I cannot deal thoroughly with each of the six complaints that go to make up the orthodox view. Nor would I wish in a blanket fashion to rebut all six claims. Many of the complaints clearly have merit when properly qualified. However, I believe the anti-regulatory views that they express (or in some cases suggest) are almost uniformly misguided, as in the anti-utilitarian sentiment that underlies much of the criticism of cost-benefit analysis.

Reasons Favoring Cost-Benefit Analysis

A showing that risks are justified by probable benefits is widely accepted as one reason to think a procedure acceptable. Investigators conducting research are expected to describe for members of institutional review committees the risks and benefits for potential subjects prior to the subjects' consent to participation in the research. Investigators are customarily required not only to array the risks and benefits but also to determine whether the benefits justify the risks imposed on subjects. With only slight reformulation this same approach can be applied to the treatment of patients, to the delivery of health services, and wherever individuals might be threatened by actions detrimental to the environment. With this in mind, let us now consider reasons favoring the inclusion of (government-required) risk-benefit assessments in the review of scientific protocols.

First, it is entirely appropriate that many types of risk be studied by review boards prior to the approval of research. Beyond the obvious physical and psychological harms that may occur from research maneuvers, there also may be harms to groups, harms to reputations, serious inconveniences, the placement of seeds of distrust, and so on. These harms may result from even the most innocuous forms of research—for example, disclosure of data collection, interviews with family members, and participant-observation of groups. Historically the major reason for requiring advance and continuing IRB (Institutional Review Board) review of protocols was the need to protect subjects from harm. The IRB system has now been in place long enough so that we know how such levels of harm can be stated and rationally debated, at least for biomedical research.

Second, objections to Health and Human Services regulations or other forms of regulation rest largely on false impressions of the intent, extent, and content of presently operative or presently proposed federal regulations. While it is true that the latest proposed regulations (Aug. 14, 1979) do require "review of human subject research irrespective of risk," they also "exempt from coverage certain kinds of social, economic, and educational research, [and] either exempt or require only expedited review of certain kinds of research."[6] Survey research, public observation research, archival research, and specimen research, for example, are specifically exempted. No one would, I think, suggest that no level of risk whatever is presented by use of these methods. Public observation and survey research, for example, notoriously have presented circumstances where anonymity was inadequately protected, resulting in harm to reputation and even to arrest. Presumably the justification of exemptions or waivers is the low level of risk generally presented to subjects. Anti-regulationists have long argued that the low level of risk presented by certain methodologies justifies nonregulation. But notice the commitments of this point of view. This justification based on low risk assumes that fairly complex, highly predictive risk-benefit calculations can be carried out across whole fields of research. Those who presently oppose risk-benefit regulations thus seem to me to be in the precarious position of denying that risk-benefit assessments can be done by IRB's in the case of single protocols in order to protect human subjects *yet can and ought to be done in order to exempt certain whole categories* of research.

Third, and relatively, expedited review (involving approval perhaps by only one member of an IRB) would be considerably improved in efficiency by a thorough arrayal of risks and benefits, especially if trivial levels of risk can be demonstrated. Such showings would lead to speedy review and approval of research, and would do so on the principled basis that protocols presenting levels of higher risk deserve more thorough review than do protocols presenting low amounts of risk. It should not go unnoticed that pending federal regulations take precisely this approach for whole research methodologies or fields: certain categories of low or trivial risk research are exempted altogether from review.

Fourth, thoroughly arrayed levels of risk in a protocol may quite appropriately justify waivers of informed consent, or at least may reduce the disclosures involved. Traditionally those who write about research ethics have not tied abbreviated procedures for consent to low levels of risk. This seems to me a mistake, as the need for consent may often (though not always) be decisively determined by the level of risk. In survey research, for example, if risks to participants is trivial and respondents fill out the forms provided, I see no reason whatever for formally obtaining the consent of the respondents. The same would be true for telephone interviews, participant observation studies, and the like. Those who oppose further extensions of federal regulation into the domain of consent would actually benefit, then, by acceptance of this need for prior statement and scrutiny of risks.

Fifth, I suspect that one of the reasons for strong resistance to risk-benefit arrayals by nonbiomedical scientists is the difficulty of projecting and arguing for beneficial outcomes of their research (unless any addition to knowledge whatever is considered a benefit, and even then it would have to be weighed against possible harms). Social scientists have no highly valued standard such as health against which the possible harms of their research can be compared. Hence they presumably would have difficulty convincing IRBs of the significance of their research, if significance itself is to be gauged in cost-benefit terms. Social researchers are not used to defending their research by reference to its benefits, and thus feel uncomfortable in having to defend their work in these terms.

There seem to me two fallacies in this line of reasoning, if it be taken as grounds for rejecting regulations requiring risk-benefit assessments. First, as a matter of empirical fact, little social research has been rejected by IRB's on risk-benefit criteria.[7] Second, it seems to me entirely appropriate that research holding out both little prospect of benefit and prospect of significant harm ought to be rejected by IRB's. While I realize that this contention raises the more general and difficult questions of whether the ultimate justification of research is social benefit, I would certainly defend the view that the mere promise of knowledge is not sufficient to justify publicly funded social research independently of considerations of benefit.

In Defense of Utilitarianism

We have seen that many critics tie the method of cost-benefit reasoning to utilitarianism, and then take criticisms of the one to stand as criticisms of the other. While there is no doubt a family resemblance between utilitarian and cost-benefit reasoning, they clearly are distinguishable. For example, one could advocate cost-benefit studies for nonutilitarian reasons. Clearly a nonutilitarian moral theory could hold that acting on cost-benefit considerations is a *prima facie* duty that must compete with nonutilitarian principles that limit or defeat cost-benefit conclusions. However, I do not wish to pursue these matters here. I wish instead to defend utilitarianism against several charges that have been brought against its use as the moral basis of cost-benefit requirements.

Alasdair MacIntyre, in his essay "Utilitarianism and Cost-Benefit Analysis,"[8] mirrors many of these objections. He argues that bureaucrats and executives are always faced with a large range of alternative courses of action, a range so vast that all the possible options could never be seriously considered, that there is no scale on which alternatives can be weighed, that utilitarians leave undecided whose values are to count in the weighing and assessment of harms and benefits, and that predictability over time-given social changes due to inherent unpredictability, inflation, conceptual changes, and unknowable historical developments can rarely be accurately achieved.

These arguments and the arguments against utilitarianism mentioned throughout this chapter seem to me objectionable for several reasons. First, they demand perfect predictability of utilitarians, something that no scientific or moral theory could possibly provide. Moreover, we have seen it to be unnecessary and unreasonable when the loose sense of cost-benefit analysis is at stake. Utilitarianism certainly is a *consequentialist* theory, but one need not be able to foresee all future consequences over a time frame that includes all possible contingent conceptual and historical shifts. Nothing beyond a criterion of *reasonable* predictability that is serviceable for cost-benefit analysis has ever been demanded by utilitarians. To take an elementary example, in the famous controversy over whether the chemical TRIS should be used in manufacturing children's pajamas, cost-benefit determinations were made regarding the benefits of TRIS as a flame retardant and the risks of TRIS as a cancer-causing chemical. (TRIS had been ascertained to be a carcinogen.) On the basis of available evidence, the risk of cancer seemed to far outweigh the risk of being burned. Such projections were then used as aids in reaching a determination about the acceptability of manufacturing TRIS for any purpose.[9]

Second, the opponents of cost-benefit analysis specify no alternative approach that leaves us with a workable methodology for public policy purposes. The most powerful reasons favoring the adoption of cost-benefit analysis is its serviceability for helping us decide as objectively as possible which alternative to pursue in dilemmatic cases. That it provides the most reliable method and perhaps the only method for reaching this goal is a powerful justification in itself, even if the method does occasionally lead to decisions involving injustices or other than perfectly just outcomes. Any ethical system, utilitarian or nonutilitarian, needs *some* principle as a means of balancing possible benefits against harms, benefits against alternative benefits, and harms against alternative harms. The moral life is not so uncomplicated that ethical theory can merely exhort us to produce benefits and avoid harms. Balancing beneficent and nonmaleficent objectives is essential, and to the extent that an ethical theory fails to provide a balancing principle, to that extent is it deficient.

Finally, in assessing the promise and failure of utilitarianism as the soft underbelly of cost-benefit analysis, the utilitarian view of acts and rules put forward by recent rule utilitarians should be kept in mind. Utilitarian rules, according to rule utilitarians, function to provide what in the cost-benefit literature are often called "constraints" on the use of *single,* non-rule-constrained cost-benefit studies (that is, act and not rule contexts). For example, in this literature it is said that there are physical, legal, social, institutional, and environmental constraints on the use of cost-benefit analyses. Such a utilitarian rightly would say that there are moral constraints as well, as determined by utility-based moral rules. If a particular cost-benefit study would lead to actions or scientific research projects that seriously violate a moral rule, rule utilitarians would not accept the actions or the projected research. Thus, cost-benefit analyses are not to be isolated from the restraining control of moral rules.

Opponents of cost-benefit analysis would perhaps reply to this argument as follows: At least some cost-benefit analyses will reveal that a particular measure will prove highly beneficial as compared to its costs, and yet provision of this benefit might function prejudicially in a free-market economy by denying basic services to the poor. But, as a matter of justice, the poor ought to be subsidized, in terms of either health and welfare services or financial awards, no matter what cost-benefit analyses reveal. But, for the reasons just advanced, it would not always be permissible to follow the dictates of single, short-range cost-benefit calculations. There is a lower limit on the risk of harm that can be permitted by the utilization of immediate cost-benefit calculations, and no utilitarian would deny it. Sophisticated utilitarian analyses propose that general rules of justice ought to constrain particular actions or uses of cost-benefit analysis in all cases. Moreover, choices between justice-regarding reasons and utilitarian cost-benefit reasons should seldom, if ever, occur. Utility in the form of cost-benefit analysis itself provides one appropriate principle of distributive justice, even though utilitarian moral rules (of justice and so on) constrain single, cost-benefit outcomes. Therefore, utilitarian considerations of justice (rules of justice grounded in utility) will suffice should individual or single cost-benefit conclusions be shown morally to be unacceptable.

These considerations in defense of utilitarianism do not, of course, speak directly to the complaints of anti-regulators. They are intended solely as a construal of utilitarianism that renders it free of the charge of being a moral monstrosity.

Notes

1. See, e.g., Richard Layard, ed., *Cost-Benefit Analysis* (New York: Penguin Books, 1972).

2. Alasdair MacIntyre, "Utilitarianism and Cost-Benefit Analysis: An Essay on the Relevance of Moral Philosophy to Bureaucratic Theory," *Values in the Electric Power Industry* (Notre Dame, Ind.: University of Notre Dame Press, 1977).

3. Committee on Public Engineering Policy, National Academy of Engineering, *Perspectives on Benefit-Risk Decision Making,* vols. 3–4 (1972).

4. MacIntyre, "Utilitarianism"; Joan Cassell, "Risk and Benefit to Subjects of Fieldwork," *American Sociologist* 13 (1978): 134–43, and "Ethical Principles for Conducting Fieldwork," paper delivered at the 1978 annual meeting of the Association of Humanist Sociology of the American Anthropological Association; Murray Wax, "On Fieldworkers and Those Exposed to Fieldwork," *Human Organization* 36 (1977): 321–28; Albert Jonsen, "Justice and the Defective Newborn," draft paper to be published in *Annals of Internal Medicine* (1980).

5. Cassell, "Ethical Principles for Conducting Fieldwork," p. 13; see also p. 21.

6. "Proposed Regulation Amending Basic HEW Policy for Protection of

Human Research Subjects," *Federal Register,* Aug. 14, 1979, esp. pp. 47688–47692.

7. See the National Commission for the Protection of Human Subjects of Biomedical and Behavioral Research, *Report and Recommendations: Institutional Review Boards,* including the *Appendix* (Department of Health, Education, and Welfare Publication nos. (OS)78-0008 and 78-0009; Washington, D.C.: The Department, 1978).

8. MacIntyre, "Utilitarianism."

9. See Harold Green, "The Concorde Calculus," an article in the Symposium on Risk/Benefit Assessment in Governmental Decisionmaking, *George Washington Law Review* 45 (Aug. 1977): 901–10.

DAVID BRAYBROOKE AND PETER K. SCHOTCH

12 Cost-Benefit Analysis under the Constraint of Meeting Needs

A central sort of complaint against cost-benefit analysis strikes at its tendency to consolidate under a common measure (utility or dollars) considerations—justice, maybe; rights; risk to human lives—that critics hold require separate attention.[1] The tendency to consolidate is, of course, real: it is in fact the characteristic ambition of cost-benefit analysis to consolidate considerations as far as possible and arrive as far as possible at comprehensive measures of the net benefits to be expected from alternative policies. Moreover, in practice there may well be vanishingly little difference between treating all considerations as commensurable and assuming that, if not all effects can be "monetized," "those that can are a reasonable guide for the

In a previous version of this paper, which was presented by me at the conference held by the Center for the Study of Values, University of Delaware, November 1979, some formal apparatus taken over from a valuable paper by William T. Terrell, referred to below, which E. Ray Canterbery called my attention to, was introduced and then modified to suit (roughly) my purposes. I wish to thank Alexandra Cas for helping me master at that stage (so far as I did) the set-theoretical niceties in play in Terrell's presentation and at issue in my modifications. In several other ways as well, she helped me achieve greater precision in the paper. Colleagues in the Dalhousie Department of Philosophy helped, too, by reacting vigorously, manifesting puzzlement and skepticism in various useful forms, to hearing the paper read in draft form. Peter K. Schotch, in particular, was inspired to reformulate the formal apparatus from beginning to end, and it is this reformulation that figures in the present version of the paper. Though we worked together to arrive at the reformulation, Schotch so much took the lead in inventing expressions, and in conforming the whole resulting presentation to expert logical judgment, that in all fairness he must now rank as joint author. (He has gone on, in a forthcoming paper of his own, to a more advanced formulation of the theory of economic choice in terms of possible world semantics.)—David Braybrooke.

176

decision maker," presumably pointing in the same direction when consolidated as those that cannot be.[2] Sober exponents of the procedure, however, disarm complaints about consolidation by forswearing any attempt to "force all outputs into a common index of worth" when doing so leads the cost-benefit analyst to make "arbitrary value judgments." E. S. Quade, who reprobates such attempts, described in those words, as "unfortunate," cites with approval even stronger denunciation by Hatry. Hatry declares that an "appalling" number of analysts "bury" in their procedures value judgments that should "rightfully . . . be made in the political decision-making process" and that "hocus-pocus" of this sort "in the long run tends to discredit analysis." Quade joins him in holding that "the major trade-offs of cost and effectiveness" should be exhibited to the decision-makers, who should judge directly how they had best deal with effects that cannot be reduced to a common measure without begging important questions.[3] Another restriction on ambition that would go far, should it be heeded, to forestall complaints is implicit in Sassone's suggestion that cost-benefit analysis (in contrast to "social impact assessment") is best suited to evaluating projects that affect "many people, but none substantially."[4] We suspect that the complaints raised by philosophers about cost-benefit analysis map one to one onto the cautions expressed by its exponents.

Nevertheless, one may well believe that not everything is yet understood about how the complaints and cautions are to be managed. In large part, the complaints about consolidation might be laid to rest if it were arranged for cost-benefit analysis to proceed only when due account was taken, first, of peremptory considerations (like justice, rights, honor) and, second, of needs, putting them ahead of preferences. Just what, however, would it mean to take due account of these matters ahead of preferences? And how much room would the arrangements for taking account leave for the characteristic operations of cost-benefit analysis? We have independent reasons of our own for being interested in the first question, which we shall bring forward some formal apparatus from the economic theory of choice to treat; but answers to this question are in fact indispensable to working out answers to the other one. For how can one know how cost-benefit analysis is going to operate under the arrangements prescribed, until one knows what arrangements are implied by the proper relation in deliberating choices between needs, preferences, and peremptory considerations?

We put forward the following as a list of basic needs: some more physically than socially oriented—the need for a life-supporting relation to the environment, the need for food and water, the need to preserve the body intact, the need to excrete, the need to exercise; others more socially oriented—the need for companionship, the need for education, the need for social status and recognition, the need for sexual activity, the need for recreation. There are, of course, plenty of other needs, but the case for meeting them depends on their being derived, more or less firmly, from the case for meeting these or on their satisfying the same criterion. A criterion that fits the list presented here is that something counts as a need if and only if failing to meet it at some specifiable minimum standard of provision leads to observable personal incapacity or derangement of functioning in the performance of the tasks assigned a person in the basic social roles of householder, parent, worker, and citizen, and only if on this basis it can be imputed with presumptive universality to all people who have such roles, though not only to them. One may think of the criterion as governing both what items are to be on the list as matters of need and the minimum standards of provision associated with the different needs. These minimum standards will vary with the physique, temperament, and circumstances of the people to whom the needs are ascribed.

With matters of need we contrast matters of preference only. One infers what people's preferences are from the choices that they make in suitable conditions (and from what choices they say or imply they would make were the conditions suitable). Preferences have the same range as wants and like choices themselves may sometimes answer to needs, sometimes run directly counter to them, and sometimes neither conform nor conflict. Matters of preference only concern goods and services produced in addition to those that are assigned to meeting the minimum standards of provision for needs: fourth and fifth tablecloths; sixth and seventh suits; cut flowers; a complete record set of *Die Götterdämmerung*. But preferences also come into meeting needs. In the first place, people may have preferences that their needs, recognizing them as such, be met, though, on the other hand, in fact, sometimes they do not. We shall not treat these preferences, when they exist and accord with the needs, separately from the needs themselves. In the second place, preferences come into meeting needs because of their bearing on alternative forms of provision that meet the same minimum standards—for example, varied diets as against monotonous ones.

If needs are to be given due attention by cost-benefit analysis, they will have to be accorded a certain priority. What will this priority amount to? It is easy to say "lexicographical priority," but lexicographical priority will not work. Even the most vigorous critics of cost-benefit analysis and the most determined partisans of needs could not rationally wish to end up insisting that the tiniest increment in provisions for needs must outweigh the most sweeping advances in matters of preference.

Lexicographical priority modified to incorporate satiation limits —which we could interpret as minimum standards of provision—is more promising, though in the end we shall not be able to accept this idea either. The following model of lexicographical ordering with satiation limits has been constructed using a paper by William T. Terrell as a point of departure.[5] Assume a person with a set of wants W and facing a set of goods G. The person also has in view a choice field X, which is a set of N-element vectors each a combination of different quantities of different goods from G. In L^*, the ordering to be defined, each such combination x, is evaluated according to a number of different utility functions $u^1(x), \ldots, u^k(x)$, where $k = 1, 2, \ldots, \infty$.

L*-ordering

By a personal *choice structure* we understand a 5-tuple $\zeta = (W, G, X, <, \sigma)$ where:

W (intuitively, the set of wants) is ordered by '$<$' (intuitively "more urgent than") such that (W,) is of order type ω. We shall associate with each want w_i a separate utility function u_i defined below. The function is concerned only with ranking alternatives (combinations in accordance with the degree to which they make an effective contribution to meeting just that want, through the presence of goods suitable to meeting it—in the case of a want that corresponds to a need, through the presence of forms of provision for the need. The number of wants (not all of which do correspond to needs) is possibly infinite, hence the set may have as many members as the set of natural numbers, which is the meaning of having, taken together with the relation $<$, order type ω.

$G = \{g_1, \ldots, g_N\}$ is a finite non-empty set of cardinality N, informally, the set of goods.

X is a subset of euclidean N-space called the *choice field*. It is composed of combinations of goods, represented as N-place vectors each of the form $<x_1, x_2, \ldots, x_N>$, where at each place there is a quantity x_i of a distinct kind of good g_i.

Each want-associated utility function has domain X and codomain R_+ (where R_+ is the set of non-negative real numbers).

σ: $W \rightarrow R_+$ assigns to every want (utility function) a non-negative number σ that in general constitutes the *satiation limit* for that want. Here it will be interpreted as representing the Minimum Standard of Provision for any want that corresponds to a need; it would be the satiation limit for anybody who had a want just to meet the need. Thus, writing σ_i for $\sigma(w_i)$, if $u_i(x) \geq \sigma_i$ then the combination x satisfies w_i at or above the Minimum Standard.

Every choice structure determines an ordering of its choice field as follows:

Vx,y X: $xL*y$ iff (1) $\exists$ j: $u_j(x) > u_j(y)$ and $u_j(y) < \sigma_j$ and
(2) $\sim \exists$ i$<$j: $u_i(y) > u_i(x)$ and $u_i(x) < \sigma_i$.

u_j may be said to *distinguish between* x and y if and only if $u_j(x) \neq u_j(y)$ and either $u_j(x) < \sigma_j$ or $u_j(y) < \sigma_j$.

Thus, no difference between one combination of goods and another matters, in the view of a given utility function (in the view of the person who has the want with which that utility function is associated), except when at least one of the combinations is below the satiation limit for that function (below the Minimum Standard of Provision); then and only then is the utility function in question prepared to compare the two combinations.

We may then put the definition of L*: x is L*-better than y (or L*-before y) iff the most urgent want the utility function of which separates x and y, gives x the higher value.

The way in which L* orders X may be illustrated in figure:

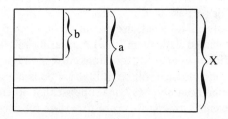

where $x\epsilon a \iff u_1(x) > \sigma_1$, $x\epsilon b \iff \{x\epsilon a$ and $u_2(x) > \sigma_2\}$, etc,
Then $x\epsilon a \iff \forall y\epsilon a$: xL^*y, etc.

The different utility functions are applied successively, in the order of urgency of the wants with which they are associated. The most urgent want thus circumscribes a subset of combinations all of which are at its satiation limit or above; then the next most urgent want circumscribes within that subset a subset at its satiation limit or above; and so forth.

L* orderings cannot be represented by single utility functions. Thus there is no function u such that:

$$\forall x,y: xL^*y \iff u(x) > u(y).$$

For no set of utility functions, say $u_1, \ldots, u_k$, can the vector of values $\langle u_1(x), \ldots, u_k(x) \rangle$ be represented by a single number. Such a procedure would ignore the urgency ordering.

We might try applying an L* ordering to needs and preferences in this way: Classify the wants of a single person (for whom, let us imagine, a cost-benefit analysis is to be prepared) under the two heads of answering to needs and answering to preferences only. Then the utility functions corresponding to the first set are to be taken, in order of urgency, before the utility functions corresponding to the second set, themselves ordered by urgency, are considered. The cost-benefit report will L* order a policy offering a combination x_a of goods ahead of another policy offering another combination x_b whenever x_a does more to satisfy the most urgent need on which a discrepancy between the combinations is encountered. However, once the minimum standard of provision has been met for any need, the utility function representing it drops out; the active alternatives in the choice field will be henceforth confined to combinations all of which meet the standard or surpass it.

Sooner or later, if all needs are met at the minimum standards of provision associated with them, the L* ordering will be established entirely by differences in utility functions corresponding to matters of preference. Some of these will be utility functions having to do with matters of preference only. May one suppose that others will have to do with preferences among forms of provision for needs? We think that without any great difficulty we may: Evaluating a combination x for the degree to which it meets a certain need is a task that can be firmly distinguished from the task of evaluating it for the degree to which the provisions that it offers to meet the need are agreeable ones. Think of a nutritious diet composed chiefly of dried soy beans as compared with one largely founded on such things as a nice white Burgundy, rolled fillet of sole with shrimp stuffing, and lemon meringue pie. In fact, of course, by our assumptions, the utility function representing preferences among forms of provision will count only when all the alternatives are minimally nutritious; but on this point, too, the distinction goes through between this function and the one that looks for degrees to which the need is met.

This solution to the problem of relating needs to preferences is admirably neat. Could any solution offer smoother guidance to a cost-benefit analysis that is to take both into account? We fear, however, that the solution is for practical purposes illusory. Is it really convenient to have the needs ordered by urgency? Or even plausible?

There is a literature of long standing, extending from Carl Menger and before to Abraham Maslow, about hierarchies of needs or wants, in which a higher need or want is attended to only after more basic needs have been met; and it is just this notion of hierarchy that Terrell is trying to capture. Moreover, needs like those on our basic list do differ in respect to how long people can survive unharmed without meeting them: a good deal longer without meeting the need for companionship than without meeting the need for food; somewhat longer without meeting the need for exercise than without meeting the need for water. One can imagine ranking the needs on the list on that basis.

Would it be appropriate to do so, however? If each need is essential to full capacity and smooth functioning, bodily and mental, as all the needs on the basic list supposedly are, they all would seem to have an equal claim to being met in a sufficiently long period of consumption. (It would not be a very long period—perhaps a month.) From the point of view of social policy, which operates over periods that long, it would seem only sensible to accept them all as having an equal claim. It would be highly advantageous, too, since any attempt to rank them (for such periods) is bound to start up controversies, perhaps interminable ones.

Suppose one requires that the cost-benefit analysis not undertake to order combinations by preferences until it is dealing with combinations all of which meet all the needs on the list at minimum standards of provision. We might represent this requirement by ordering the set of utility functions corresponding to needs ahead (by the relation of urgency) of the whole set of utility functions corresponding to preferences. Then we stipulate that a discrepancy favoring a combination x_a on any of the utility functions drawn from the needs set, when x_a and x_b do not differ in respect to other needs or they both meet or exceed the minimum standards of provision, would order x_a over x_b, so long as x_b falls below the associated minimum standard.

However, one no longer has an L* ordering, for one has lost the connexity of L* in failing to provide for ordering all combinations that differ one way in respect to one need and the other way in respect to another. The loss will hurt if one wants to be sure of imposing an ordering on the whole choice field X; or, if, without having that ambition, one nonetheless cannot by any reasonable procedure avoid ordering combinations that fail to meet different needs.

Should one prepare to order the whole choice field X? To do so, one must accept as alternatives combinations in which every good in the set of available goods G is represented by a quantity—indeed, all such combinations. A finite human mind will find it difficult to take in the content of even one such combination if the zero-quantities are to be seen as associated with different goods. It will also be quite unprepared to compare widely divergent combinations none of which have been experienced. In addition, in the case of L*, one must have supplied—and order, for application in strict succession—a very large number, in fact infinitely many, utility functions, each corresponding to a distinguishable want. Clearly, one is not going to get to the end of constructing the ordering in question. Why should one insist on going down that road, and on making sure of its being open at the end?

So we shall proceed from the L^* ordering presented above to a revised conception of choice, which will give due priority to needs, taking them all together, and hence will be called the "due priority conception."

Again, the alternatives presented for choice will be assumed to be combinations of goods, rather than goods themselves. This assumption has some drawbacks. People naturally think of themselves more readily as choosing goods than combinations, though they can no doubt be brought to recognize how combinations are at issue once they are reminded that choosing an attractive good answering to one want may affect their being able to choose any good at all answering to another. Moreover, when we move on to transpose the due priority conception to social choices, it will appear that neither combinations nor goods are entirely satisfactory analogues for the alternative policies dealt with in social choices. Policies are likely to combine features, which may even be familiar species of goods (consider a policy of providing recreational facilities); so far they look not like goods, but like combinations. However, they are, by contrast with the all-encompassing combinations in the choice field X, drastically limited in the variety of their features; with their rivals, they answer to one want or to a limited set of wants. In this aspect, they are much more like goods—so many alternative routes for the new highway, or so many different devices for checking the growth of traffic congestion.

Persisting, nevertheless, with the assumption that the alternatives in view are combinations, we may take some comfort in the fact that both the L^* ordering and the due priority conception (sharing this feature with the L^* ordering) make some provision for attention to separate goods in their provision for separate utility functions. When the chooser is preoccupied with what occupies the place in the N-place vector answering to a given want w_i and to the associated utility function u_i, then he is in effect preoccupied with goods rather than combinations. So both analogies have some footing; and it is sensible that the analogy with combinations should predominate, since both in the choice of global arrangements and in considering the ways in which special projects relate to various features of their context, it is natural to think of combinations being in view.

The Due Priority Conception

Let us partition the set of wants into three subsets S, E, and P, concerned respectively with peremptory considerations, needs, and matters of preference only.

Now we order those subsets, so that

$$Vi, j: w_i \epsilon S \text{ and } w_j \epsilon E \cup P => w_i < w_j$$
$$Vi, j: w_i \epsilon E \text{ and } w_j \epsilon P => w_i < w_j$$

We proceed to reduce the choice field. Only that part of the unreduced choice field that is actually searched is to be taken into account at all, and the set of combinations actually brought to light in this survey is to be further reduced to the *eligible field*. Attention to peremptory considerations and to needs is reflected in the insistence that the set of combinations belonging to the eligible field contain no combinations x such that for some $w_i \epsilon S \cup E$: $u_i(x) < \sigma_i$. If we suppose that the initial actual search and the reduction to the eligible field still leave (for example, by offering possibilities of interpolation between combinations actually identified) a great number of combinations still to be inspected individually, or if we suppose that invoking all matters of preference only to survey the combinations left is an impossibly demanding task, we may infer that in effect (by further satisficing) the eligible field will be reduced further. Only a limited number of matters of preference will be considered.

Confining the eligible field to combinations all of which fulfill all peremptory considerations and meet all needs (here, needs of the person; later, after transposition to social choice, needs of everyone in the Reference Population) is something that may be accomplished by a straightforward stipulation or by means of an analysis relating wants to goods. To aid this analysis we introduce the two functions:

$$A: G \rightarrow 2^W$$
$$H: W \rightarrow 2^G$$

A associates with every good the set of wants to which that good answers. (For every want there are just two alternatives: it is in the set related to that good; or it is not.) H associates with every want the set of goods required for the satisfaction of that want. These functions may be introduced as additional ingredients to some personal choice structure ζ, or we may think of a particular ζ as determining such functions by means of the want–utility function correspondence. In the latter case restrictions on A and H constitute restrictions on the class of wants (and perhaps also on σ). In view of the wants-goods relationship we may describe the restructuring of the choice field to account for needs, say, as follows:

Let $u_1, \ldots, u_k$ be the utility functions associated with needs and $H(u_1), \ldots, H(u_k)$ be the corresponding sets of goods. Evidently $\bigcup_{i=1}^{k} H(u_i)$ constitutes the class of goods that are needed. Thus the eligible field, X', will contain only combinations x', such that in the first k places goods in the above union appear and those just in sufficient quantity (whether all one form of provision in one of the places or a mixture of forms) to meet Minimum Standards of Provision. (Further quantities of those goods may appear in places $k + 1$ and after, valued there by utility functions representing preferences only.) When we now consider an L* ordering of X', or a comprehensive utility function over it, we see that preferences are given their head in ranking various *forms* of provision for needs, as well as preferences in other matters.

Although the conception just discussed has been presented as governed, not by an L* ordering, but on lines further away than an L* ordering from lexicographical priority for individual needs, there is a way of looking upon it that moves back to L* ordering and thus back closer to lexicographical priority. We could conceive of choices by any decision-maker whose preferences answer to the due priority conception of choice as governed by an L* ordering that gives first place to a utility function representing a single want directed at having peremptory considerations (other than needs) satisfied, and second place to a utility function representing a want directed at having all the needs on the basic list met at the accepted Minimum

Standards of Provision. The remaining wants might follow, with each assigned a utility function of its own.

Let us now consider how cost-benefit analysis should proceed if it is to serve choices conceived in the manner outlined in these axioms. Mindful that it is utterly unreasonable to expect any one instance of cost-benefit analysis to cover all relevant matters, we shall present a general schema within which one may imagine particular instances of analysis being offered and subjected to criticism. If the schema came to reflect common practice, particular instances would in time come to be shaped by anticipating the stages of criticism laid out in the schema.

To get to the schema from the axioms we must provide as the axioms do not for the aggregation of costs and benefits falling to the lot of more than one person. The axioms, we shall assume, will apply to each person considered or at risk in the choices of social policy that we shall be concerned with. Aggregation will be easier than some people would expect: We have three sorts of considerations to allow for—peremptory rules or principles, needs, and preferences. Only preferences raise the traditional difficulties about interpersonal comparisons, and once (as here will be the case) they are relegated to a properly subordinate place in the evaluation of policies there will be less to lose from any arbitrary feature in the procedure of aggregation for them.

There are three stages of discussion in the schema. In the first, proposed policies are subjected to peremptory considerations, like justice (in various aspects), rights, honor, standing obligations, respect for life. (We shall not inquire how far these considerations are reducible to one another, or just which should be accepted as morally binding.) Suppose a proposal P_i is found to violate someone's rights. Then either it is rejected completely or held up for revision: the feature that occasions the violation is removed, perhaps; or a feature is added that fully compensates the victim. Now, whether a policy conforms to a peremptory consideration is, given a sufficiently well-defined consideration, a matter of fact that can be ascertained by comparing the features of the policy with the requirements set forth in the consideration. Is it prescribed, without regard to alternatives, for example, as a sacred obligation established in a solemn treaty with the Indians? Is it prohibited, again without regard to alternatives, as an injury inflicted upon innocent people? Or is it permitted, without being prescribed, seeing that it is not prohibited by the consideration in question? To settle these issues, no variation in subjective preference or utility has to be allowed for (though of course no peremptory consideration would ever be respected if some people's preferences were not in the end in favor of respecting it). It is possible to get into trouble about subjective preference or utility, and hence into trouble about interpersonal comparisons, with provisions for compensation; but one need not suppose that the decisive point in compensation is whether the victim is satisfied. The decisive point may be held to be whether the compensation accords with prevailing notions of what a fair compensation in such cases would amount to—in other words, with a further peremptory consideration, conformity to which is objectively ascertainable.

In the second stage of the schema, policies go on to be considered for their impact on minimum standards of provision for needs. We shall suppose that they are not released from this stage until it is clear that they are consistent with meeting every need brought up, at the accepted minimum standard of provision. If too many needs are brought up, discussion at this stage may be so protracted that policy-making will be paralyzed; perhaps, as well, too few proposed policies will survive protracted discussion to cover the basic tasks of the policy-making institution, public or private. A strong incentive thus arises to keep the list of needs from proliferating freely.

(One should remark that there is an equally strong incentive to keep the number and scope of peremptory considerations as small as possible. They have to be allowed for, as the history of attempts to uphold utilitarianism without them shows. They significantly restrict freedom of choice, however; and multiplied without limit, they would quickly take all the freedom away—on occasion perhaps without leaving any eligible alternative in sight. Organizations and governments as well as individual persons require that freedom to adapt to opportunities and improve their situation. They also require it if they are to make full use of reason in discovering and seeking what is best for them. To deny them freedom by invoking peremptory considerations, though sometimes morally unavoidable, runs against reason in another sense, too: peremptory considerations are likely to be matters of intuitive conviction, adopted before arguments begin, rather than matters on which argument can be offered.)

Dealing with needs, there is also an incentive to keep the tests for impact as simple as possible: Subtler tests, aiming to establish the degree to which a policy falls short of meeting a need, will generate problems of measurement that can be avoided by asking simply whether or not the minimum standards of provision have been met. These vary, for any given need, from person to person: people of the same size and in the same circumstances vary widely in the amount of food that they need; and this amount varies, too, if their circumstances are not the same—if one person is doing very much heavier work than another, for example. Having established that a given policy meets one person's need for food, but falls short in this respect of the minimum standard of provision for another, how is one to decide which to weigh more? How is one to weigh meeting one need against failing to meet another, especially when more than one person is involved? We propose to avoid all such problems by holding that to pass the test of being consistent with needs a policy must meet the minimum standard of provision for every need of every person being considered (which, on a utilitarian view, would be everyone at risk in the policy-making).

This approach may seem much too constrained. However, if the list of needs is kept manageably small and the minimum standards of provision are kept low enough relatively to resources, it is in fact a perfectly practical position. For most societies in history—certainly for Canada and the United States today and for some time past—resources have been available to meet for the whole population and with a good deal to spare all the requirements implied by the stated criterion of task performance (and by its extension to children and old people who are not asked to perform the tasks). It is true that in some cases—for example, in respect to safety, conventional standards arbitrary to a degree are applied to determine the risk accepted with the minimum provisions. Moreover, if we match resources not just against the needs on the basic list, but against the needs derived from those needs taken together with prevailing social arrangements (which, for example, disfavor efficient mass transportation), the amount of resources to spare diminishes drastically. Nevertheless, such societies have ample room, within the scope of available resources, to meet basic needs and a good number of derived ones. So long as they do, it will be reasonable, given agreement on a reasonably short list of needs basic and derived, to insist that policies which jeopardize meeting the minimum standards of provision for anyone be sent back for revision. It will not be for lack of resources that the policies have so far failed the test.

It is worth emphasizing that in making full use of the Revisionary Process, which is a prominent feature of real politics, the present schema offers a substantial improvement on standard approaches to economic choice, personal or social, and to cost-benefit analysis. For at the outset these approaches assume that the alternatives (for example, the combinations in the choice field X or the goods in the set G of goods) are all given, and set out to order them all. In reality, only a limited number of alternatives are given with a given issue. From the criticism of these alternatives analysts and politicians infer what features further alternatives must have to have a chance of serving as a compromise acceptable at least to a decisive coalition of participants, and invent alternatives to suit, some of them visibly direct descendants of the original alternatives, revised on the crucial points. Operating within the schema and participating themselves in the Revisionary Process, analysts will have significantly less opportunity for "driving politics deeper into the technical analysis" and "veiling the real choices from the public's eyes."[6]

One effect of the position taken that all needs of everyone in the reference population are to be met before policies pass the second stage is to treat meeting needs not as a meliorative consideration, which may be satisfied to a higher or lower degree and is thus conclusive only relatively to a set of alternatives, but as a peremptory one. (Roughly the same point might be made by speaking of converting a teleological consideration into a deontological one.)[7] This conversion hardly represents a startling innovation, however: the intimate relation between meeting needs and achieving justice, the most important and central peremptory consideration, prepares us all to accept it. Moreover, if the list of needs is kept manageably small, and the minimum standards of provision manageably low, treating needs as a peremptory consideration is consistent with keeping the number and scope of peremptory considerations in check.

Meliorative considerations do not disappear from the sort of analysis that would operate within the schema. They come into their own in the third stage, where attention is given to preferences.

What sort of attention are preferences to be given? Now, it is open to people to insist that they be given lexicographical attention, which would mean, in view of the absurdities involved in a pure lexicographical ordering, asking for a L* ordering with satiation limits (here exactly corresponding to their name). No doubt there are people who feel strongly enough about some matters of preference to make this demand: in common with other intellectually inclined members of the upper middle class who do not have jobs directly dependent on the construction industry, we feel this way about the preservation of historic buildings, city views, and other amenities. But one may doubt whether many people would insist on L* ordering for many matters of preference. In the third stage, the high ambition of cost-benefit analysis, to consolidate considerations and reduce them to a common measure, may be held to come into its own. Here let us (in principle) discover what net gains (or losses) in utility are offered by alternative policies; here let us (in fact) measure what their net benefits will be in dollar terms.

Of course, there are objections to doing any such thing. Some of them are skeptical objections, arising from the problem of other minds. We shall not pause to toy with objections of this sort. There is a more substantial, equally familiar objection arising from the unequal distribution of income: It is reasonable to postulate that the marginal utility or significance of income declines as it increases; thus we may well believe that a $100,000 gain to a person who already has $200,000 a year will not offset losses of $1,000 each to one hundred persons who have incomes of $2,000 a year. However, we have no satisfactory interpersonal measure of utility, so we cannot tell just what the discrepancy amounts to. One might try, even so, weighting gains and losses according to the incomes of the people who were to feel the gains and losses, acknowledging that the weights would be arbitrary; they might be arbitrary, but consistently with being so they could do something to correct for the greater scandal of accepting equal weights. We could simultaneously press for a more equal income distribution just because, among other things, it favors sounder evaluations of policies and a more rational choice among them. Meanwhile, one could refuse to take the results of cost-benefit analysis (carried through the third stage of the schema) as guiding in cases where the gains or losses tended to aggravate objections to the distribution of income.

To some extent, the schema already embodies this precaution. For even the flagrant example given above—the $100,000 gain to the person with $200,000 a year and the $1,000 loss to each of the hundred people with $2,000—is mitigated in effect by the implication that, having gotten through the first two stages of the schema, the policy in question is not objectionable on grounds of contravening justice, rights, honor, and so on, and is consistent with meeting all needs—at any rate, all the needs scheduled for consideration in the second stage—at the accepted minimum standards of provision. (If it is objectionable in either of these connections, it must be sent back for reconsideration at the earlier stages of the schema.) One might wonder whether anything so flagrantly at odds with intuitive notions of justice could in fact pass the first two stages of the schema. However, if it does, the untoward results in the third stage will not arouse misgivings to the same degree as they would if thorough discussion in the first and second stages were not a condition on taking results in the third stage as guiding.

One particular in respect to which the precautionary discussion of the first and second stages makes a striking difference is danger to human life. One does better to try to put a dollar value on the human lives that may be at stake in various policies (lives that will be lost building a bridge; lives that will be saved by certain measures of sanitation) than simply to ignore those lives on the ground that they are too sacred to be priced. Will not one do better still, however, to treat the value of human lives as incommensurable with the other gains and losses that are to be evaluated in the third stage of the schema? The first and second stages of the schema, especially the second stage, make sure of such treatment. For, if the proposal for the bridge (say) implies that the needs of the bridge-workers will not be met at minimum standards of provision—and this question will be faced in the second stage—then the proposal will be rejected or sent for revision. The criterion of task performance will capture the needs falling under the narrower criterion of survival. Similarly, a proposal to omit the measures of sanitation would be related to the human lives at stake through the test of needs in the second stage of the schema. It would not be won or lost (so far as a cost-benefit analysis was taken to furnish guiding results) by consolidated dollar measures in the third stage, in which gains in trivial matters might more than offset the dollar value of the lives lost, treated equally trivially, as a matter of preference.

How much difference will there be between the two approaches in the end, however? Bridges do get built; and useful measures of sanitation are sometimes omitted or postponed. Hence (as those analysts who are prepared, more or less ingeniously, to set a dollar value on human lives will point out with some emphasis) policies are in fact adopted that involve a loss of life (even in peacetime; we are saying nothing about war). Evidently, if the public does not believe somehow that the benefits make them worthwhile, it is willing to accept decisions that can be justified only by accepting this as an implication.

In this and other connections, we do not try to meet the need for a life-supporting relation to the environment fully, or the need to preserve the body intact; we accept as minimum standard provisions for these needs provisions that imply some degree of risk to life and limb. If we did not, we would not cross streets, much less drive around in automobiles, to say nothing of building bridges and skyscrapers. But would not the risk to life be taken into account in a cost-benefit analysis that put a dollar value on the lives at stake in a given project? The probability of losing a certain number of lives in the course of carrying out the project times the dollar value of those lives considered apart from any risk would give the cost to be borne. The analysts might be in a position to infer from decisions about past projects of a similar kind what dollar value for lives was currently being used and what the probability of losing lives on such projects was.[8]

Assume this is the case: Why is it a better way to take the danger to life into account to make sure that the project involves no more than an acceptable risk to life, without trying to put a dollar value on the lives at stake? It might even seem a worse way: If the probability used is in fact the figure for the acceptable risk to life on such projects—in other words, the degree of safety accepted as constituting in part the minimum standard of provision for the need for a life-supporting relation to the environment and the need to preserve the body intact—then taking the dollar value of the lives that will (probably) be lost into account operates as an additional safeguard, by constituting an additional cost to be offset. It goes beyond simply checking for an acceptable level of risk.

Nevertheless, we think there are good reasons for proceeding otherwise. Under the procedure in question, the risk to life is not singled out for attention. It may not even appear in the report of the analysts. If one assumes that the undertakers of the project will be required to insure themselves against claims for compensation in respect to lives lost, one may be pretty sure that the probability figure used is a realistic one, and not understated, as one might fear; it would be the business of the insurance companies to make sure that it was not underestimated. But then the expenses of insurance are in fact going to represent the dollar value of the expected loss of life (plus profit to the insurance companies) and the alternative that we are recommending will not be waiving the attempt to put a dollar value on the lives at stake after all.

True, it is this that turns out to be the more stringent alternative; it is this that demands other things as well. It demands that the risk in the project at hand be compared with the risk normal for the industry; and it opens the way for comparing that risk with the risks prevailing in industry generally. If the risk to life is higher than is normal for the industry, the project would not pass the second stage of the schema; if the risk in the industry is strikingly higher than it is in industry generally, the opportunity would present itself to take measures to reduce the risk in the industry, beginning with current projects.

We have shown, we think, how the complaints about consolidation can be laid to rest by arranging for cost-benefit analysis to heed peremptory considerations and take due account of needs—providing, among other things, for keeping risks to human life within the limits ordinarily accepted. At this point, however, and on this very issue of risks to human life, one might wonder how many practical, level-headed people will want to press the complaints after all. For are we not willing to run—or at least to let other people run— significantly greater risks to human life if the benefits look big and attractive enough? With a new form of transportation (airlines at their beginning) the benefits may be travelling faster, farther, more often; with a daring new construction (a great new bridge), the chance, the dream of successive generations, to get directly from

Brooklyn to Staten Island and from Staten Island to Brooklyn. It looks, at any rate so far as respect for human life goes, as though an unrepentant cost-benefit analysis might sometimes accord better with our practice than complaints about consolidation.

Even if that accord were a fact, it would not necessarily discredit the complaints; for our practice might play fast and loose with fateful considerations like human life. The evidence that the value put on human life varies so much—gigantically—from one context to another suggests very strongly that the issue of the lives at stake is not faced in any regular or coordinated way. Undoubtedly, wide variations between industries and among branches in the same industry have to be allowed for respecting what is accepted as normal risks; and one must allow, too, for the fact that employees and clients voluntarily accept higher risks in some cases than in others. One may still suspect that the prevailing risks are often greater than they would be if an issue were made of them under some such arrangement as the schema.

Proceeding through the schema, one might raise on occasion the question whether great benefits of other kinds would warrant accepting a higher danger to life. Does this possibility undermine the idea of minimum standards of provision, and hence the rationale of attending to needs in the second stage of the schema? We do not think so. The possibility does not generalize easily over the whole list of needs. In some sense of probability, there is perhaps a probability— an infinitesimal probability—that a varied diet of the sort that a given person is used to will not meet his or her need for food or that a glass of the finest product of the city waterworks will do nothing to meet his or her need for water. However, surely a significant practical distinction can be made between the minimum standards of provision for the need for food and water, the need to excrete, the need for exercise, the need for companionship, the need for recreation, the need for sexual activity, in all of which cases provisions for practical purposes certain of their effect can be supplied, and the minimum standards of provision for the need to have a life-supporting relation to the environment and the need to preserve the body intact, where it is impossible practically to remove visible risks entirely. Nor is it to be supposed that the conventionally accepted risks that figure in the minimum standards of provision for the two last-named needs are continually up for negotiation; certainly they are not continually up for adjustment embracing greater risks. The standards are treated, so far as they can be, on the same footing as the minimum standards of provision for other needs; that is the point of recognizing as needs the needs with which they are associated.

A greater difficulty, which we do not have space to treat, is how to keep the number of needs scheduled for consideration in the second stage of the schema manageable. A clue to putting this difficulty in perspective is the fact that the schedule will vary from issue to issue. It may be carried far from the basic list if something like unanimous consent of the discussants is obtained. Such consent, of course, is fateful, as is shown by the consequence that the needs in question become peremptory considerations. An eminent political scientist of our acquaintance feels that the consent has been asked for and given so promiscuously that the concept of needs is playing havoc with political debate. He is opposed even to studying the concept, for fear that studying it will lend it something like a respectable endorsement. We think, however, that the concept can always be brought back from overextended applications and restored to a firm footing; and there it properly acts as a constraint on cost-benefit analysis among other things without preventing us from enjoying the advantages of the latest intellectual techniques.

Notes

1. See, for example, Alasdair MacIntyre, "Utilitarianism and Cost-Benefit Analysis," as reprinted in Tom L. Beauchamp and Norman E. Bowie, eds., *Ethical Theory and Business* (Englewood Cliffs, N.J.: Prentice-Hall, 1979), pp. 266–82, esp. pp. 271–72.

2. Cf. Peter G. Sassone, "Social Impact Assessment and Cost-Benefit Analysis," in Kurt Finsterbusch and C. P. Wolf, eds., *Methodology of Social Impact Assessment* (New York: McGraw-Hill, 1977), pp. 74–82, at p. 79. Sassone is describing practice, not necessarily endorsing it.

3. E. S. Quade, *Analysis for Public Decisions* (New York: Elsevier, 1975), p. 108. Hatry's statement is cited from an article, "Measuring the Effectiveness of Non-defense Public Programs," *Operations Research* no. 18, 5 (1970): 774.

4. Sassone, "Social Impact Assessment"; earlier in the same article, furthermore, Sassone himself fully acknowledges the existence of important "incommensurable" considerations.

5. W. T. Terrell, "The Theory of Economic Choice—Coming Full Circle? a paper given at the meeting of the Southern Economics Association, November 1977. Terrell cites an article by Richard H. Day and Stephen M. Robinson, "Economic Decisions with L** [sic] Utility," in James L. Cochrane and Milan Zeleny, eds., *Multiple Criteria Decision Making* (Columbia: University of South Carolina Press, 1973), pp. 84–92. Day and Robinson in turn trace L* ordering back to articles by J. Encarnación.

6. S. H. Hanke and R. A. Walker, "Benefit-Cost Analysis Reconsidered: An Evaluation of the Mid-State Project," in Richard Zeckhauser *et al.,* eds., *Benefit-Cost and Policy Analysis* (Chicago: Aldine, 1974), pp. 392–416. (Originally published in *Water Resources Research,* vol. 10 (1974), no. 5, pp. 898–908.)

7. For further discussion of the distinction between peremptory and meliorative considerations, see David Braybrooke and Charles E. Lindblom, *A Strategy of Decision: Policy Evaluation as a Social Process* (New York: Free Press, 1963), pp. 150–54. For the relation to the distinction between deontological and teleological considerations, see n. 8 to ch. 7, pp. 256–57. Cf. on this point Bernard Williams, in J. J. C. Smart and Bernard Williams, *Utilitarianism For and Against* (Cambridge: Cambridge University Press, 1973), pp. 87–88.

8. Suppose all the benefits and all the other costs taken into account have been enumerated. There remains, for one project, a cost related to loss of life of so many dollars, a (a constant); for another, a corresponding smaller cost, b. Twelve hundred men and women are employed on the first project; eight hundred, on the second. Let x be the probability that any given person will lose his or her life during the project; and y be the dollar value imputed to an individual life. Then we have two simultaneous equations,

$$(1)\ x\,(1200)\,y = a,$$
$$(2)\ x\,(800)\,y = b.$$

Quade (*Analysis for Public Decisions,* p. 113) points out that there is an astonishing variation in the valuation of lives from one kind of project to another: "In highway design the implicit valuation of a life saved is usually something like \$5000 to \$10,000; in the design of an ejection seat for a new fighter-bomber . . . more than a million dollars." These are lives at stake in the outcome of projects; we do not know whether the same variation occurs for lives at stake in the course of carrying them out.

JOHN BYRNE

13 A Critique of Beauchamp and Braybrooke-Schotch

A rubber plant is currently emitting 25 units of sulfur dioxide into the air daily. Our best estimate of the medical effects is that three people become sick for each unit of pollution, and that it costs fifty dollars to treat each patient. The cost to the firm is as follows:

Amount of Reduction	Cost of Removing Unit	Total Cost of Removing Pollution by This Amount
1st unit	$40	$40
2nd unit	$60	$100
3rd unit	$100	$200
4th unit	$200	$400
5th unit	$350	$750

QUESTION: What is the optimal amount of pollution from society's point of view?

—Freshman Economics Exam
University of Maryland

Let's see now. Damage to the three sick people costs society $150. Therefore the firm should spent up to $150 to eliminate each unit of pollution. The chart shows that after the third unit of pollution is removed, the cost begins to outweigh the benefit. Okay, remove three units; let the twenty-two remaining people keep getting sick, and pay them each $50. Next question.[1]

I. Introduction

In its brief existence, cost-benefit analysis has managed to attract considerable criticism. At the same time, the use of this technique has

198

increased enormously in terms of both the number and range of problems engaged. This increase is nowhere more evident than in the public sector, where nearly every new federal regulation and program is subjected to this type of analysis as a condition of its adoption. Such a state of affairs raises the obvious question of how cost-benefit analysis has been able to withstand the extensive criticism directed at it while simultaneously the scope of its use has expanded.

The Beauchamp and Braybrooke-Schotch articles in this volume offer two important arguments why this technique should prosper in the public sector. While disagreeing about the conditions that impel and provide opportunities for the use of cost-benefit analysis, these writers arrive at a common basis of advocacy based on the perceived relevance of cost-benefit analysis to the modern problems of governance that are regarded as the dilemmas of an administrative world. Both articles manifest an expectation that issues of public policy can and should be resolved through the exercise of right reason. In this context, cost-benefit analysis is offered as a viable means of approaching otherwise amorphous issues of governance in an orderly manner and discovering by calculation of net or proportional benefits the rationally superior public action.

The tenability of these arguments rests upon the tenability of displacing policies with administrative forms in deciding issues of governance. Indeed, the advocacy of cost-benefit analysis by these writers represents an implicit, if not explicit, endorsement of the administrative state. Curiously, however, neither Beauchamp nor Braybrooke and Schotch address the question of the desirability of such a displacement. They appear to presume that a world made safe, so to speak, for cost-benefit analysis is inherently good and preferred. The normative question of the desirability of cost-benefit analysis and the system of governance that it requires is a fundamental one and cannot be resolved by presumption. If the tenability of cost-benefit analysis hinges upon the emergence of the administrative state, then ultimately the use of this technique to decide public policy hinges upon the preferability of this system of governance. My argument against the use of cost-benefit analysis in deciding questions of public policy is built here—around the question of the normative "costs" of cost-benefit analysis and the displacement of politics that is essential to its effective use.

II. Beyond Power and Politics: The Rule of Reason

The most critical issues surrounding the use of cost-benefit analysis in the public sector are normative. For the most part,[2] however, debate about this technique has been restricted to concerns about its technical feasibility and limits. Much of the current criticism as well as advocacy of cost-benefit analysis is preoccupied with the appropriateness of this technique to certain classes of problems and the value implications of its use in the analysis of these problems. It is within this constrained interpretation of the issues surrounding the use of cost-benefit analysis that Beauchamp and Braybrooke-Schotch frame their arguments. From their perspective, if there is a normative dilemma posed by the use of cost-benefit analysis, it derives from the nature of the problem to which the technique is applied rather than from the logic of the technique itself. For them, the key questions regarding the use of cost-benefit analysis are: to what range of problems is cost-benefit analysis applicable? and under what conditions is its contribution optimized?

To Beauchamp, the practical conditions of *realpolitik* urge the use of cost-benefit analysis. He sees the contemporary problem of governance as one of establishing rules of reason by which to decide issues of public concern in an otherwise untidy world of power and politics. While cost-benefit analysis cannot deliver the ultimate rules of governance, Beauchamp nonetheless considers this technique important and valuable for the opportunity it provides for arriving at a rational accommodation of the moral conflicts of an irrational world. In this respect, cost-benefit analysis represents an attractive answer to the problems of modern governance offering the prospect of escape from power and politics. Beauchamp claims that cost-benefit analysis is a pragmatic necessity in "real" moral life where rights frequently conflict. It provides a "morally adequate"[3] means of decision-making that evaluates political decisions against the standard of collective welfare, a standard that "at least on some occasions is mandatory from a moral point of view."[4] Against the charge that such a standard would lead to the denial of basic rights if the costs of so doing were less than the collective benefits, Beauchamp responds with the familiar rule-utilitarian position that cost-benefit analysis should not be immunized from the restraining control of moral rules.[5] He maintains that the force of moral rights will not be contravened if a "loose sense" of the cost-benefit technique is adopted in which the objective is to determine whether a particular action is "acceptable," "reasonable" *within* the boundaries of morality.[6]

While recognizing that the value of cost-benefit analysis relates to its capacity to yield rational solutions of moral problems, Braybrooke and Schotch see no means of using this technique within the contemporary world of politics. For these writers, no minor modification of the world as it is will suffice. What is needed is a revolution in human history, such that the "peremptory consideration" of rights and "basic human needs" that civilizations have so consistently failed to provide will now be assured. What is sought is nothing less than a world of guarantees in which the problems of civilization are rendered moot and the human condition no longer precarious. To achieve such a world, the conflicts of political and economic life are to be transcended through the exercise of right reason. Braybrooke and Schotch propose a system of governance as problem-solving in which issues of collective concern are scrutinized for their involvement, respectively, of questions of rights, needs, and preferences. Rights and needs are to be addressed by means of threshold analyses. In the case of rights, "whether a policy conforms to a peremptory consideration is to be treated as a matter of fact that can be ascertained by comparing the features of the policy with the requirements set forth in the consideration."[7] Response to potential rights violations is to take one of two forms: either the policy is not to be enacted until and unless the cause of violation is removed, or the policy is to be enacted on the condition that fair compensation of victims, again to be regarded as a matter of fact, can be assured by a compensation scheme that presumably would have to satisfy the criterion of cost effectiveness as well. Observance of minimum needs thresholds is also to be required of any proposed policy. Such thresholds are to be established from objective analysis of "minimum standards of provision."[8] Any remaining public policy problems are considered in this scheme to stem from conflicts of preferences. Within an institutional framework that provides for prior checks for violations of basic rights and needs, cost-benefit analysis has the role of resolving subjective "interest" conflicts according to the criterion of maximization of objective social benefit. For Braybrooke and

Schotch, then, cost-benefit analysis represents a particular stage of analysis within a general framework of objective analysis of moral problems.

Thus, to those who charge that cost-benefit analysis is a "moral monstrosity"[9] in an imperfect world where harms and benefits are seldom quantifiable, Beauchamp responds that the technique's strength is that it furnishes a rational alternative to the visceral and ideological, which too often dominate in an imperfect world. While those who disdain cost-benefit analysis for its philosophical crudeness are answered by Braybrooke and Schotch, who locate this method within a general framework of objective analysis of morals. For all three, cost-benefit analysis promises to elevate policy-making above the inefficiency and irrationality of politics. But they also recognize that if this problem is to be exploited, certain conditions having to do with how social problems and their possible solutions are conceived will need to be met.

Despite certain differences in the way these frameworks conceptualize the possibilities and limits of cost-benefit analysis, a common set of conditions for the optimal use of this technique is projected. Both frameworks approach the social world as one in which problems occur relatively independently of one another and are bounded in scope. The Braybrooke-Schotch scheme extends this independence condition to the moral dimensions of social problems as well, expecting that rights, needs, and preferences can be separately addressed without distorting the nature of the problem. To this condition about the nature of social problems, these writers add important conditions regarding the nature of their solution. Each treats the set of alternative solutions to a particular problem, where such a set exists, as an analytically finite and commensurable one. This means that if solutions exist, there is always a superior one. Where no solutions are known,[10] no rational engagement of the problem is available in either scheme and no public action can be justified under them. A third set of conditions concerns the issue of valuation. In both schemes, the costliness of a particular problem and the implementation of its solution as well as the worth of any advantages that might result (beyond the elimination of the particular social problem itself) are regarded as objectively knowable. Of special importance, these values are thought to be available to the analyst without recourse to individuals or communities who might be affected by the contemplated public action.

If these conditions can be met and much of the debate surrounding cost-benefit analysis is absorbed by this question, a distinct political opportunity emerges. Insofar as social problems can be treated as independent and bounded in scope, their solution regarded as a question of optimizing net benefit, and the availability of objective measures by which to evaluate competing solutions confidently assumed, government by right reason would seem to be within our grasp. Historic social conflicts such as those concerning the distribution of wealth and the public provision of basic rights and needs, as well as more recent ones like the protection of the environment, worker and product safety, and balanced economic growth, would all appear to reduce to discovering and implementing the best alternative and therefore to be resolvable through procedures of rational calculation. This is because, in a world made safe for cost-benefit analysis, conflict is the result not of irreconcilable substantive differences, as much of political theory has traditionally argued, but of the use of faulty "decisional premises."[11] Correcting those premises that distort our understanding of the true costs of public services or that encourage suboptimal supply (either over- or under-) of such services should lead in a world fashioned from the postulates of cost-benefit analysis to the virtual elimination of social conflict. And indeed this is precisely what is envisioned by Beauchamp and Braybrooke-Schotch with the advent of the widespread use of cost-benefit analysis. Thus, Beauchamp in his discussion of the conflict of rights brought on by the potential for harm to human subjects of research argues that social problems such as this stem not from substantive differences between the needs and rights of separate classes of individuals but from the absence of sensible rules that would ensure that individuals in their capacities as, for instance, subjects and researchers could accurately calculate the costs and benefits of their mutual actions. Braybrooke and Schotch arrive at similar conclusions with regard to the problems of civilization as a whole. For example, they suggest that the basic need for nourishment is a problem of right reason rather than civilizational conflict. The issues are not those of the haves versus the have-nots, the needs of the future versus those of the present, or other such intractable problems, but instead ones associated with the establishment of objective minimum standards of provision. Hunger, with due apologies to Jonathan Swift, is a problem of truly modest dimensions: "People of the same size and in the same circumstances vary widely in the amount of food they need; and this amount varies too, if their circumstances are not the same—if one person is doing very much heavier work than another, for example."[12] Social problems—the conflict of rights, the provision for basic needs—are not *per se* problems in their view. The dilemma is located instead according to these writers in the matrix of information and constraints that mold the selection of actions or ends. Alter these and our problems change, if not disappear altogether.

Engaging the social world from the vantage point of cost-benefit analysis is an exciting proposition for these writers. It heralds the possibility of the triumph of reason over power and the displacement of politics with analysis. Perhaps because this possibility is so attractive for them, they tend to be unpersuaded of the tenuousness of the conditions necessary for cost-benefit analysis to be effective. But regardless of whether the tenability of these conditions is conceded, the basic objections to a world made safe for cost-benefit analysis remain.

III. What's Wrong with Being Reasonable

The worlds projected by Beauchamp and Braybrooke-Schotch would require a profound transformation in the basis of governance. Fundamentally, these worlds call for the abandonment of rule by consent in favor of the rule of reason. The replacement of consent with reason as the foundation of governance is intended to dispense with the inefficiency and irrationality of politics, but in fact it dispenses with democracy in favor of the administrative state. The issues that normally give rise to questions of democratic participation and consent are simply without salience in the transformed world of cost-benefit analysis. Indeed, the ideals of democracy could not be tolerated in the new world and only its veneer would survive the transformation.

The world of cost-benefit analysis has no need of a participative citizenry. The processes of public decision-making depend in this world upon the identification of objective values. It is only with their identification that rational solutions can be found. To involve the citizenry in the process of identifying values could only result in contamination of the process, for all they can offer are subjective assessments of their idiosyncratic circumstances. To operate effectively, the world of cost-benefit analysis must be insulated from and pre-emptive of the participation of its citizens.

But if participation is precluded, what is left of the idea of citizen? Little more than a glorified notion of consumer. In a world of cost-benefit analysis, governance is a consumptive good. Citizens decide whether and to what degree they are satisfied with the products of governance but they have no responsibility for the production of governance or even overseeing its production. Indeed, the expectation is that citizens have no substantial interest whatever in such matters.

Without an active citizenry, indeed with an active intolerance of democratic participation, can such a world be democratic? To characterize the world of cost-benefit analysis in such a way would be to inflict much violence on the term. The classic association of democracy and freedom disappears in that world. For "free" in the new world refers neither to the absence of constraints on choice or action nor positively to the pursuit of collective goals such as the elevation of the intellectual and moral character of society, the promotion of social equality, and the like. Such definitions presuppose the cost effectiveness (at least) of freedom, a judgment that must necessarily be questioned. Instead, freedom in the world of cost-benefit analysis refers to the appreciation of objective existence. It is the knowledge that decisions about one's future are based upon and limited to the facts that makes one free in this world. This is not to say that the worlds projected by Beauchamp and Braybrooke-Schotch would not be populated by those sensitive to democratic ideals of freedom. Rather, it is to argue that a world fashioned from the postulates of cost-benefit analysis is indifferent to concerns with democratic freedom.

If the world of cost-benefit analysis displays little or no concern for democratic freedoms, it likewise shows little regard for the need to ground governance in principles of justice.[13] As with ideals of freedom, those of justice do not find a central place in the administrative state. Again, the absence of a central place is not indicative of an aversion within the mechanics of cost-benefit analysis to matters of justice, but rather an indifferent regard to them; what is fair, moral, respectful, can only be incidental to what is of maximum net benefit. Cannot such qualities either be monetized and included in rational calculations or, as Braybrooke and Schotch suggest, treated as peremptory considerations? In one sense, they can be and these writers take some pains to demonstrate how. But their suggestions appear to be negatively rather than positively motivated as a response to the charge by critics that such matters cannot be adequately incorporated and as a result little attention seems to have been given to the desirability of doing so. For the issue only begins with the question of whether these dimensions can be incorporated in the cost-benefit calculus. It must also be ascertained: first, with what relative confidence can they be included, especially in comparison with what are considered the non-normative dimensions of policy issues; and, second, at what cost to our understanding of the role and importance of these considerations could this be done?

But in a more fundamental sense, ideals of freedom and justice receive reduced attention because they do not bear the essential quality of objectivity. With some confusion, Braybrooke and Schotch make this point with their observation that "peremptory considerations [rights and principles of justice] are likely to be matters of intuitive conviction, adopted before arguments begin, rather than matters on which arguments can be offered."[14] The labelling of rights and principles of justice as intuitive borders on the bizarre. It presumes that the inability to bring closure to debate on questions of freedom and justice is somehow undesirable and moreover that the peremptory status typically accorded these matters is ultimately unrationalizable, even if necessary. But the central point, despite this confusion, is clear: matters on which debate can be objectively decided and closed are of superior interest and importance in the world of cost-benefit analysis.

But if in the administrative state the achievements of governance are not judged by the extent to which the governed are free and public actions just, then what is to be the measure? The success of government, I submit, is to be measured in the world of cost-benefit analysis by whether it works efficiently. In a society governed by right reason, government is held accountable for the delivery of cost-effective policy. Substance can have only secondary importance unless and until it yields to objective definition. Government has little to do with the goal of ensuring that public actions are moral, normatively preferred, fair. While such qualities may perhaps be deemed desirable, their "intuitive," more exactly, normative, foundations prevent them from being included as central commitments in the constitution of rational society.

If such a foundation of governance is to be called democratic, it is democracy without a substantive basis of accountability. What matters is not what is achieved, but the premises upon which actions are taken and the efficiency of their execution. All that can survive of democracy are its symbols and its formal procedures. Most prominent among them, representational voting would in all likelihood remain in the world of cost-benefit analysis. For this mechanism conveniently solves a sticky problem for the new system of governance. As earlier noted, cost-benefit analysis is predicated on the assumption that if normative dilemmas exist, they exist as attributes of the problems engaged and not as attributes of social analysis itself. This being the case, though, how are the problems for analysis to be selected without bias in the world of cost-benefit analysis? Clearly, any selection must be normative, for it necessarily will favor one normative dilemma over another. To have some apparatus of analysis determine which problems are investigated and which are not, therefore, would obviously undermine the very basis of authority on which rational society operates. But "democratic" voting removes at least the appearance of such a problem by transferring normative responsibility to the citizenry and its subjective proclivities. The insidious result is that a democratic mechanism is used to relieve the administrative state of democratic responsibility.

The intolerance of the administrative state to participation and debate on questions of values is traceable directly to the distinctive attribute of this system of governance—its lodging of authority in reason rather than consent. There is no place in the workings of this system for majority votes and minority objections to interfere in, much less withhold legitimacy for, public actions dictated by rational analysis. Cost-benefit analysis and the system of governance it implies depend upon right reason to convince us of the sensibleness of policies selected by its use. In this respect, the achievement of a world in which the contributions of cost-benefit analysis to policy are optimized is the achievement of irresistibility for the decisions and actions of government. It is a world in which we must abandon political choice and participation to gain efficient and unassailable social order.

If this is the price for reasonable government, for being reasonable in our public decisions and actions, and for being able to rationalize moral problems, it is unbearable.

IV. The Normative Underpinnings of Cost-Benefit Analysis

Ultimately, the Beauchamp and Braybrooke-Schotch defenses of cost-benefit analysis amount to efforts to divest social problems of their normative character. In this regard, I have argued that the central question is not, "Are such efforts tenable?" but rather, even if they were, "Would it be a desirable thing to do?". In view of the demands such efforts make on the nature and aims of governance, I see no basis whatever for their claim that advancing the cause of cost-benefit analysis in public policy-making will yield a preferred social world.

It might be suggested, however, that the link between cost-benefit analysis and undemocratic principles of governance is not absolute and that under certain conditions that Beauchamp and Braybrooke-Schotch failed to see this mode of analysis could indeed be compatible with democratic principles. But here I must come to the defense of Beauchamp and Braybrooke-Schotch. For in my view they have accurately identified the necessary analytic conditions for the effective use of cost-benefit analysis. The problem here lies not with the elaboration of analytic conditions but with the fact that cost-benefit analysis is itself normative. That is, the source of its undemocratic tendencies is not to be found in repairable or replaceable conditions under which it is used but in the unrepairable and irreplaceable conditions required for its use.

The conditions necessary for the effective use of cost-benefit analysis in matters of public policy are normative. They favor certain conclusions about the social world over others, and certain actions in that world over others. These conditions are neither neutral nor trivial. They cannot be represented as mere analytic devices to focus attention on certain relevant attributes of social problems because they introduce systematic bias that can only be removed by violating the requisite conditions for the use of this technique.

The condition that social problems are independent and bounded in scope found in Beauchamp's and Braybrooke-Schotch's versions of cost-benefit analysis is neither dispensable nor non-normative. The necessity of this condition is that, without it, closure on cost-benefit calculations is forfeited. If social problems are largely interdependent, then the costs and benefits of certain actions to resolve these problems cannot be assumed to mainly aggregate in the first few orders of effect. It means also that what might appear in terms of direct costs and benefits to be the superior solution may not be after indirect effects are accounted for.[15]

Closure is an important advantage accruing from the use of methods such as cost-benefit analysis because it means that complex problems can be to a significant extent simplified. But when this simplification is at the expense of an accurate portrayal of the nature of the problem, then it is no longer an advantage. Nonetheless, the dangers of simplification that are always potentially present in the case of requirements such as that social problems are independent can be judged quite insignificant if the sorts of problems one is talking about have little collective salience. But exactly the opposite is the situation here, for cost-benefit analysis is being urged not as a valuable technique for evaluating individual or business alternatives, but public ones. In this context, such a condition is dangerous.

The condition of independence among social problems can be translated as a presumption that what economists call Pareto-optimal moves[16]—actions that can bring net benefit to at least one person without inflicting incompensatable harm on one or more other persons—are always available in the public arena. That is, insofar as social problems are largely independent and bounded in scope, one is assured that efforts to resolve such problems will not result in the exacerbation of attendant problems for which no acceptable compensation is available. The dilemma is not only that such moves are seldom actually available and that, to use the economists' term again, substantial externalities often exist. If this were all, then additional screening procedures on the types of policy problems engaged could "resolve" objects to this condition.[17] Rather, the problem is that this condition precludes the possibility of addressing social problems for certain purposes as generic, caused by a common, overlapping set of conditions that, when social problems are treated in isolation, escapes attention. This condition represents a presumption that the problems of society, economy, polity, are best addressed piecemeal. Basic change must be presumed to be always less preferred than a series of marginal ones. The disturbing implication is that social problems need not be engaged from the vantage point of collectivity, that issues of governance do not concern the whole of society. Instead, they are to be regarded in the narrowest of terms as involving only the facts of those measurably affected one way or another by the persistence of the specific problem at hand.

The condition imposed by the cost-benefit framework on the nature of solutions to social problems is equally necessary from the standpoint of the validity of cost-benefit analysis, yet highly normative in the context of public policy. The condition that alternative solutions, when such exist, be finite in number and commensurable is essential if any calculation is to take place. Indeed, a singular advantage of cost-benefit analysis—the precise comparison of rival solutions—hinges on the commensurability and finiteness of alternatives. There can be no assurance of a superior alternative without this condition.

Again, if the object of this analysis were the evaluation of problems with little collective salience, the possibility of numerous exceptions to this condition might properly be judged inconsequential. But in addressing issues of governance, the "exceptions" to this condition are of enormous importance. Commensurability and finiteness among political positions presumes that political conflict is ultimately reconcilable. It promotes the view that issues of public policy are indeed largely administrative, having to do with organizing public action in such a way that it efficiently services only nominally contending interests. But on what grounds is one to suppose that political conflict is not real? Certainly, such a question is not an empirical one, but a normative one. The reasons for accepting this understanding of collective conflict must derive from certain desired attributes of decisions based on it. What might these be? If conflicting political solutions are ultimately commensurable, then there is no need to depend upon subjective individuals to discover the right solution, with all the inefficiency that would involve both in terms of time and resources. Indeed, relying on contending parties to develop solutions to their problems is a clearly inferior course to follow when a commensurable calculus is available to ferret out the inevitable exaggerations of each side. Thus, one stands to gain efficiency and precision by the commensurability condition. Such gains, however, can be looked at just as easily as enormous costs. To say the least, this view of political solution is extraordinarily antagonistic toward democratic choice and participation, for it would tend to discard as costly proposals to seek solutions based on consent and to be highly suspicious of subjectively, that is, normatively arrived at solutions. Equally serious, the commensurability condition is, like that of independence, a blinder to the possibility that radical changes are needed to solve social problems. The view that what is needed are solutions that are "zero-sum" and therefore irreconcilably conflicting must be ruled out if commensurability is to be maintained. But in many ways the most serious implication of this condition is that, where proposed solutions cannot be compared, public action cannot be defended. This suggests that from the perspective of cost-benefit analysis issues of governance are not, or at least should not be, the intractable problems of civilization. If such a view is intended to act as a proscriptive limit on public action, what an extraordinary limit it is. To employ this method effectively, the most consequential problems must be forsaken for the most manageable. If instead it is intended only as a restriction on the use of cost-benefit analysis[18] the silence of this technique on the fundamental questions of governance belies claims of its significant value in grappling with social problems. Under either interpretation, the dilemma with accepting this condition is that it puts a substantial premium on public inaction and discourages significant concern for the most difficult social problems. Combined with the suspicion it casts upon democratic choice and its prejudice against the possibilities of radical change, this condition must be regarded as a massive endorsement of the status quo.

Finally, consider the imperative of objective value. Even if social problems generally satisfied the conditions of independence and commensurability, the promise of cost-benefit analysis could not be fulfilled without this condition. The central claim of cost-benefit analysis is the availability of measures of collective value that are not rooted in or influenced by human subjectivity. It is this value condition more than either of the others on which claims that cost-benefit analysis is non-normative are based. But despite the claim, the basic measures used in cost-benefit analysis do not represent objective measures of collective value.

The most prevalent measure of value employed in cost-benefit calculations is prices. Whether it is the cost of equipment and salaries of personnel necessitated by a new environmental rule mandated for industry, or the budget savings of government programs eliminated by a change in the rule, cost-benefit calculations rely heavily on prices to measure alternative possibilities. But are prices objective measures of collective value? Certainly only in the rare circumstance of perfect competition would conventional price theory suggest that this would be the case. And even there, assumptions regarding income distribution equity, economic mobility, information cost and availability, and the like would be required to assure at least approximate equality of starting positions. Such assumptions cannot be made in this world without serious distortion. In the absence of such assumptions, however, the meaning of prices as measures of value is greatly complicated. In a world where all are not equal, those more equal than others have a greater opportunity to influence prices. Such differential influence can have profound consequences. For example, if one considers the problem of condemnation to clear land for a new highway, can one use existing housing prices as an objective measure of the costs of such condemnation? The all too predictable consequence of their use, of course, is that slums become the optimal places for building highways. Similarly, in monopolistic and oligopolistic markets in which firms can pass on increased costs to them in the form of higher prices, should the higher price be used to determine the cost of a new regulation even though in a more competitive context comparable increases might not occur? Many such examples could be cited, but these should suffice.[19] Prices in an unequal world cannot so readily be taken to represent non-normative measures of collective value.

In addition, the use of prices raises the problem of individual versus collective as the unit of measure. The presumption even in the ideal circumstance of perfect competition is that the sum of individual valuation equals the collective determination of value at a specified level of production. Yet much of this century's contribution to economic theory suggests that this equality is often tenuous. The theory of public goods and externalities and, most abstractly, welfare theory point to vast areas of "social" production in which aggregate and collective value need not be synonymous.[20] Indeed, to represent them as such may, according to these arguments, yield socially inefficient as well as inequitable results. The areas in which aggregate-collective equality cannot be preserved, of course, coincide almost completely with the domain of governance. If, therefore, cost-benefit analysis is to be employed in resolving such issues, either its use must be curtailed to the exception where aggregate expressions of value can be taken to stand for collective value, or this theoretical dilemma must be ignored. If the former, cost-benefit analysis once again retreats to an excuse for public inaction, while, if the latter, the purported objectivity of its measure of social value is reduced to dogma.

The other principal measure employed in cost-benefit calculations in determining supposedly objective valuations of social problems and action are probability distributions. These include demographic distributions of age, race, sex, occupation, epidemiological distributions of disease, symptoms, and the like, economic distribution of goods and services production, use, and cost, and so on. They are intended to furnish the analyst with projective information on likelihoods of certain outcomes. One of the central problems with their use, however, is that they incorporate patterns of social inequality and abuse into the cost-benefit calculation. Thus, as an example, if the problem were to which of two medical research programs public funds should be allocated to yield maximum net benefit, and one program was concerned with a disease found prominently among whites, the other among blacks, likelihoods would suggest that, *ceteris paribus,* the first program would prove of higher net benefit because whites tend to live longer than blacks in this country. Yet such a determination would amount to an endorsement of an economic and social system that was an essential factor in determining this differential. Again, numerous examples could be offered identifying normative issues associated with the use of supposedly objective probability distributions.[21] In these various instances, as with those regarding the use of prices, the value condition required for the effective use of cost-benefit analysis cannot be represented in the context of public policy formulation as neutral and non-normative.

Cost-benefit analysis as a tool for evaluating issues of governance injects considerable and significant normative content. This content largely favors incremental change and often no change at all. Significant social problems of inequality and injustice are under-valued or not valued at all by this procedure, which nonetheless carries substantial distrust for solutions arrived at by democratic choice and participation. This mode of analysis projects values arrived at mainly by individuals without regard to their collective consequences as social values or defers to provide any assessment at all.

Such content is by no means neutral in its support of the ideals of the democratic versus the administrative state. Yet most conse-quential of all is the failure of advocates to recognize the normative tendencies of cost-benefit analysis in public policy. If this failure persists and social problems continue to be treated instead as the culprits in stymieing efforts to achieve rational solutions, then we run the risk of becoming ignorant of and refusing responsibility for the moral consequences of our public actions.

V. Conclusion

In sum, the advocacy of cost-benefit analysis in the evaluation of issues of governance is based on two flawed premises: first, that the basic dilemma of modern governance is how to arrive at rational definitions and ultimately solutions of complex social problems; and, second, that cost-benefit analysis provides one important method for achieving rationalization of our problems and that it can furnish non-normative solutions to our normative social problems. Cost-benefit analysis is not neutral, does not offer non-normative solutions, and cannot rationalize social problems without considerable violence to our understanding of these problems. The problems of modern governance, moreover, are not mainly administrative and in need of rational definition. They are political, as they have always been, and require the exercise of political will and choice. While such solutions will necessarily be by some measures inefficient, temporary, and confused, this is a small price to pay compared with what has so far been offered as "non-political" alternatives. The rational utopia projected by advocates of cost-benefit analysis ultimately depends upon surrender to the irresistibility of right reason to garner converts. In this respect, the use of cost-benefit analysis to decide matters of governance is by no means a modest proposal that we "enjoy the advantages of the latest intellectual techniques."[22]*

Notes

1. Mark Green and Norman Waitzman, "Cost, Benefit and Class," *Working Papers for a New Society* 7 (May-June 1980): 39. Incidentally, sixty-six persons, not twenty-two as the text observes, are likely to get sick as a result of this cost-benefit calculation.

2. Prominent exceptions include Alasdair MacIntyre, "Utilitarianism and Cost-Benefit Analysis: An Essay on the Relevance of Moral Philosophy to Bureaucratic Theory," in Tom L. Beauchamp and Norman E. Bowie, eds., *Ethical Theory and Business* (Englewood Cliffs, N.J.: Prentice-Hall, 1979), pp. 266–82; and Robert H. Socolow, "Failures of Discourse," in Harold A. Feiveson *et al.,* eds., *Boundaries of Analysis* (Cambridge, Mass.: Ballinger, 1976), pp. 9–40.

3. Tom L. Beauchamp, "The Moral Adequacy of Cost/Benefit Analysis as the Basis for Government Regulation of Research," in this volume. Beauchamp also characterizes this technique as a "means to moral ends" (p. 163).

4. *Ibid.,* p. 164.

5. *Ibid.,* 172–73.

6. *Ibid.,* See pp. 166–67 for a discussion of his "loose sense" c/b; and pp. 169 and 172, respectively, for his identification of "acceptable" and "reasonable" as the primary criteria on which a "loose sense" c/b is based.

7. David Braybrooke and Peter K. Schotch, "Cost-Benefit Analysis Under the Constraint of Meeting Needs," in this volume (p. 187).

8. *Ibid.* See pp. 179–81 for their development of the notion of "minimum standard provision."

9. Beauchamp, "Moral Adequacy," p. 174, regards his contributions as "a construal of utilitarianism that renders it free of the charge of being a moral monstrosity."

10. Actually, where the probability distribution of the solution set cannot be accurately estimated.

11. This term is used by March and Simon to describe the basis of organizational behavior and is the core idea for their definition of organizational-administrative, as distinct from political, authority. As will become

clear shortly, it is my view that cost-benefit analysis owes as much to bureaucratic, organizational, and administrative theory as to utilitarianism for a rationale of its use in deciding issues of governance. The relevant literature in this regard includes: Max Weber, *The Theory of Social and Economic Organization,* trans. A. M. Henderson and Talcott Parsons (New York: Oxford University Press, 1947); James G. March and Herbert A. Simon, *Organizations* (New York: John Wiley and Sons, 1958); and Herbert A. Simon, *Administrative Behavior: A Study of Decision-Making Processes in Administrative Organizations* (3d ed.; New York: Free Press, 1967). Representative critics of this literature to whom I owe a considerable debt include: Sheldon Wolin, *Politics and Vision: Continuity and Innovation in Western Political Thought* (Boston: Little, Brown, 1960); Charles Perrow, *Complex Organizations: A Critical Essay* (Glenview, Ill.: Scott, Foresman, 1972); and Sanford A. Lakoff and Daniel Rich, eds., *Private Government* (Glenview, Ill.: Scott, Foresman, 1973).

12. Braybrooke and Schotch, "Cost-Benefit Analysis," p.189. In a display of attention to detail, these writers subsequently (p. 189) qualify this view of the problem of hunger as almost exclusively applicable to the developed West.

13. Indeed, one proponent of cost-benefit-type reasoning has argued that rights and justice should be administered so as to maximize their market value, thus substituting economic performance for justice as the primary aim of government. See Richard A. Posner, *Economic Analysis of Law* (Boston: Little, Brown, 1972), and also his "Utilitarianism, Economics and Legal Theory," *Journal of Legal Studies* 8 (1979): 103–40.

14. Braybrooke and Schotch, "Cost-Benefit Analysis," p. 189.

15. This condition is remarkably similar to March and Simon's "empty" environment (*Organizations,* 176) in which few actions are interrelated and consequently planning for certain actions is relatively more feasible.

16. Actually, Pareto optimality is typically defined as states of benefit-without-harm, compensatable or not, while Kaldor-Hicks optimality is used to refer to net benefit states achieved with compensation.

17. Even though such resolution would reduce the contribution of c/b to deciding the most trivial social problems.

18. Beauchamp argues that the condition of commensurability be treated only as a constraint on the use of cost-benefit analysis, while Braybrooke-Schotch regard it as a constraint on governance itself.

19. For additional discussion of this point, see Edwin Baker, "The Ideology of the Economic Analysis of Law," *Philosophy in Public Affairs* 5 (Fall 1975): 3–48; and Green and Waitzman, "Cost, Benefit and Class."

20. The dilemma in using market values as proxies of social value and market-based reasoning to devise government policy is examined in detail in J. M. Buchanan and G. F. Thirlby, eds., *L.S.E. Essays on Cost* (London: Weidenfeld and Nicolson for the London School of Economics and Political Science, 1973).

21. For a brilliant theoretical statement of the problem of using probabilities in modelling human decision and action, see G. L. S. Shackle, *Uncertainty in Economics* (London: Cambridge University Press, 1955).

22. Braybrooke and Schotch, "Cost-Benefit Analysis," p. 196.

*I am indebted to Daniel Rich and Norman Bowie for their helpful comments and criticisms. Preparation of this paper was supported by the Center for the Study of Values and the College of Urban Affairs and Public Policy, University of Delaware.

Part IV

The Government's Responsibility to Inform the Public

In the final section of the book, the reader's attention is directed toward a specific problem: the government's responsibility to inform the public. Many of the previous articles concerning the legitimate function of government and the obligations of representatives to constituents will be relevant here.

Although most persons agree that our government does indeed have a responsibility to inform the public, detailed arguments for this view are relatively few in number. In his chapter, Professor Hugo Bedau considers three non-utilitarian arguments on behalf of the government's responsibility to inform the public. All three arguments have individual autonomy as their ground. The first, which is constitutionally based, rests on the right to self-government. The second, based on the work of Lon Fuller, rests on the conditions that make the rule of law possible. The third, which represents Bedau's own distinct contribution, rests on the idea of "man as a rational creature for whom knowledge is an object of delight for the possessor." These arguments provide three principles of governmental responsibility to inform the public: First, the government has the responsibility to inform the public of all the laws it enacts, including regulations it promulgates and judicial processes it initiates, as well as its own deliberations in the formation of policy, subject only to such exceptions as may be required by national security and individual privacy. Second, the government has the responsibility not to interfere with the public's efforts to inform itself about governmental activities (for instance, legislative and regulatory hearings) relative to establishing and enforcing the law, or to interfere with the public's efforts to inform itself about its own activities. Third, the government has the responsibility to foster the arts and sciences, and especially general education in support of the natural cognitive aspirations of all persons.

In the final section of his paper, Bedau considers when these principles of governmental responsibility to inform the public can legitimately be overruled. He identifies two such considerations: privacy considerations, which protect a person against slander and libel, and secrecy, which is necessary for the national interest. Whether or not Bedau has identified the only two legitimate considerations will be a matter of some debate.

Professor Joseph Margolis also attempts to provide a set of principles to determine the government's responsibility to inform the public. In fact, the principles he proposes are not so dissimilar from Bedau's. Margolis is careful to point out, however, that his principles are relative to the context of the democratic state; his principles do not apply to all political systems. In addition, his principles lack fixed criteria of application. Well-intentioned persons may all appeal to the same principles in defense of incompatible decisions that apply them. Margolis contends that neither the relative nature of his principles nor their lack of exactness in application are difficulties for his principles; all political principles are of such a nature.

If Margolis is right, certain conclusions follow regarding the contributions that political philosophy can make to this issue. Perhaps philosophers can arrive at a set of acceptable principles for determining a democratic government's responsibility to inform the public. However, philosophy cannot settle all debates regarding what the government's responsibility to inform is in specific cases. What is needed in this latter situation is some acceptable procedure for settling such debates, and philosophers like John Rawls do have something to say about what constitutes an acceptable procedure.

HUGO ADAM BEDAU

14 The Government's Responsibility to Inform the Public

Does a government have a responsibility to inform its citizens? If so, how far does this responsibility reach? To whom among the public and under what conditions? What principles express this responsibility? What principles limit it? What is their deeper source? These are among the questions on which I hope my remarks will shed some light.

I

The idea of a *right* to information—or, if you prefer, a right to be informed—as a natural or human right does not seem to be a prominent feature in our political tradition. There is no express reference in the federal constitution to any such right of the people, or to any corresponding responsibility of government. Instead, all we have is what can be inferred from these two passages: each house of Congress shall keep a "journal of its proceedings and from time to time publish the same excepting such parts as may in their judgment require secrecy" (Article 1, section 5); and "in all criminal prosecutions, the accused shall enjoy the right to a . . . public trial. . . ;[1] to be informed of the nature and cause of the accusation; [and] to be confronted with the witnesses against him" (Amendment 6). There is, of course, explicit reference to the government's responsibility not to interfere with the public's efforts to inform itself: "Congress shall make no law . . . abridging the freedom of speech, or of the press"

221

(Amendment 1). Whatever constitutional right the public has to be informed, or not to be interfered with as it seeks to inform itself, must be deemed to be a consequence of the meaning and interpretation of these provisions.[2]

I think this omission is a predictable reflection of the traditional and perhaps still dominant ideology of the responsibilities of government and the rights of persons across a whole range of issues, of which access to and provision of information is but one. According to this ideology, the sole responsibility of government is to serve as the referee of last resort for the conflict of private interests in the free-for-all of the marketplace. Thus, the First Amendment freedom from government interference is the paradigm of the government's responsibilities to the public in this area. The chief and perhaps sole duty of the government is to keep its hands off efforts by the public (and especially by its servants, news journalists and their publishers) to inform itself in whatever manner, medium, and fashion it chooses to do so. The standard argument (as I shall call it) for this freedom is at least as old as James Madison, who rightly observed that "a people who mean to be their own governors, must arm themselves with the power knowledge gives. . . . A popular government without popular information or the means of acquiring it, is but a prologue to a farce or a tragedy, or perhaps both."[3] According to this argument for the First Amendment rights of freedom of speech and press (and, interlinearly, of access to information), these rights are a necessary condition of self-government.

If this is the entire source and extent of our right to information then this right suffers from three severe limitations. First and most obvious, this right arises from a prior right, the right of self-government. The standard argument has nothing to say on behalf of access to information except as this is a necessary condition of self-government. An aristocratic, oligarchic, monarchical, or totalitarian state might have a responsibility to let the public inform itself in a manner similar to what the First Amendment provides in our constitutional democracy. But the reasons would have to be quite different from the reason Madison offers, since self-government plays little or no role in the constitutions that underlie these alternative modes of government.

Second, the standard argument attaches no weight to any non-instrumental value that access to information, self-expression, and the search for truth might have. It does not so much deny any such value as ignore it. Thinkers in the liberal tradition, however, from Milton to Mill and beyond have always attempted to argue that access to information and self-expression do have a non-instrumental value. To the extent that they are correct there must be a further argument for the rights under discussion, one that supplements the standard argument in important ways. I shall return to this point below.

Third, insofar as information and self-expression are not necessary for self-government, the standard argument has no clear way to resist indifference and interference by government to the release and circulation of information. Under the standard argument, it would be as if the familiar "need-to-know" criterion for access to so-called "classified information" were to apply across the whole of society on all issues. This is especially evident where it can be alleged that social and individual harms will occur from access to information when that information itself is not necessary for self-government. This has both good aspects (it provides a basis for restricting access to information, and to the publication of information, by those who would plead freedom of speech and a right to know simply in order to slander or libel) as well as darker aspects (it also allows a pretext for censorship or other legal processes against those who, like pornographers, would allegedly endanger the social fabric).

A noteworthy feature of the standard argument is that it is silent with respect to whether the government has no more than the passive duty not to interfere with the public's efforts to inform itself, or whether the government also has the duty to make available to the public information in its possession and perhaps the further duty to obtain information in order to disseminate it publicly. The bias is in favor of the passive duty, and it arises from what I have called the traditional ideology of liberal democracy. In the special case where a government grudges the public information about public activities, it is not difficult to see how such a government—consistent with the standard argument—could make it extremely difficult for the public to learn about the government's own activities, not to say its deliberations, intentions, and agenda for policy discussions. However meritorious the standard argument may be, and however short actual governments may fall from complying fully even with its circumscribed requirements, it is an argument that even at its best leaves much to be desired.

II

The standard argument, because of its familiarity and its partial adequacy, at least for those of us who are wedded to the liberal democratic tradition, is in danger of obscuring a deeper line of argument that is no less important for our purposes. This prior consideration (as I shall call it) manifests itself in the constitutional provision of Article I, section 5, and also indirectly in the Sixth Amendment. It has been vividly presented by Lon Fuller in *The Morality of Law,* where he chronicles the successive disasters encountered by the singularly inept ruler, Rex. After struggling to bring to his realm the benefits of the rule of law, Rex decides to improve on his prior practice of ruling without any written laws. Accordingly, he undertakes to rule through an explicit and detailed written code. But it is a code to which he alone has access; its text he keeps entirely secret from his subjects. This yields the not surprising result that his subjects' compliance with the law is infrequent, unpredictable, and wholly accidental. Fuller argues not only that such a failure to publicize the law is unfair to those held liable for its violation and a nullification of the possibility of public compliance with the law but also that "the failure to publicize, or at least to make available to the affected party, the rules he is expected to observe" constitutes an irreparable violation of "the inner morality of the law."[4] This morality, like all moralities, imposes a duty upon anyone who would live under it to make its content—its prohibitions, requirements, and other provisions—known and understood by everyone whose conduct will be assessed by reference to its standards.

Whether one should follow Fuller in the special features of his position on "the inner morality of the law" we need not explore. What is important for our purposes is to see that in this argument we draw upon a deep consideration, one that is both logically and historically more fundamental than the standard argument with its peculiar relevance to the ideology of self-government and the democratic tradition. Perhaps the *locus classicus* of the point under discussion is in the doctrines of St. Thomas Aquinas. According to Aquinas, "promulgation of the law" is so important and inseparable from the very idea of the rule of law that it forms part of the proper definition of "law."[5] One cannot get any deeper than that.

The logical and historical priority of this consideration is unquestionable. It cuts across the forms of government and is common to all that purport to embody and abide by the rule of law. It may also be, though neither Aquinas nor Fuller argues it, that the responsibility of government under the prior consideration—to make information available to the public as to what the law says—is severely limited in scope and content, given the vast amount of information that modern governments have in their possession and the wide range of topics this information concerns. Even so, my chief point so far is only to insist that the standard argument does not exhaust, indeed, it does not even tap, the fundamental considerations that underlie the public's need for information in a society ruled by law.

Still, there is a connection between the standard argument and the prior consideration, and it should not escape our notice. Self-government can be said to begin with an individual's reflective ability to comply with (or disobey) the law, even if we usually think of self-government as applying mainly to a constitutional structure that requires both laws and public officials to survive popular scrutiny and approval in the form of referenda and elections, respectively. Thus, one might see a natural development from the demand for information about the law, as a necessary condition of self-government under the law, to a demand for information about policy and possible laws, and about officials and their conduct in office, and about a whole range of social, economic, and political facts as a necessary condition of self-government, where that ideal is taken in a larger and more encompassing sense. This connection some may find too attenuated to take seriously; I offer it not in order to boil down two lines of argument into one but in order not to neglect a possible common factor worthy of further reflection.

To return to the prior consideration itself: it also lays upon government a duty stronger than the one laid on it by the standard argument. Whereas the standard argument might be understood to require only governmental non-interference, the prior consideration must be understood to require the government to undertake publication and provision of information. What form and frequency this publication must take is, of course, open to various interpretations and subject to economic and administrative constraints. Even so, the prior consideration provides a way of testing a government's commitment to and understanding of the rule of law. To the degree that the government fails to publish and make accessible the text and meaning of its own laws (proclamations, regulations, statutory enactments, rulings, decisions, and revisions of current law), it violates the principle of the rule of law and defeats the chief purpose for which it holds power in the first place.

III

In addition to the standard argument and the prior consideration, each of which generates independent but not inconsistent duties for government with regard to the dissemination of information to the public, there is a third line of reasoning that needs to be yoked to the other two in order to give the full picture of the sources of public right and government responsibility regarding the matters at hand. This line of reasoning is more elusive and more controversial than either of the other two, and it may be that what I am about to say altogether fails to carry any persuasion with it. It is the theme to which I alluded earlier when I noted that liberal thinkers have clearly attached weight to some further consideration beyond the need to have information in order to engage in effective self-government. Roughly, their idea was that man is a rational creature for whom knowledge is an object of delight for the possessor, simply for its own sake, and thus an object of aspiration both for this reason and also because it is a necessary element in whatever plan of life a person develops for himself. Our nature and our circumstances are such that we want and need to know a predictably indefinite range of things, some simply to gratify curiosity and others because they are necessary to achieve some other goal or to fulfill some purpose. If this is true and significant, then any government that blunts, frustrates, refuses to acknowledge, or ignores our nature in this respect is hostile to a deep and fundamental fact about the people it governs and is to that extent derelict in its responsibilities and incompetent to discharge them. A government that does not take into account our native curiosity and unlimited intellectual, scholarly, academic, scientific, historical, and literary interests is failing to take into account a potent factor in the very nature of its citizens.

Direct evidence, at least in our federal Constitution, that our society expects its government to acknowledge such a responsibility is nil. Apart from preambulatory language that refers to "promoting the general welfare," we have no explicit constitutional warrant for the federal government to undertake to finance, establish, and maintain universities, scientific institutes, professional schools, museums, libraries, research laboratories, academies, symposia, conferences, technical journals, and so forth. To be sure, state and federal governments now devote considerable resources to all of these things as a matter of law and policy. But it is a relatively recent development in our history and comes in virtually every instance upon the heels of private, non-governmental ventures that first showed the way. The justifications offered by and to government for its sponsorship of ventures erstwhile confined to the private sector (see, for example, the actual arguments presented to Congress on behalf of creating the National Science Foundation and the National Endowment for the Humanities) have a utilitarian quality rather at odds with the kind of argument I have said can be found in the liberal tradition for governmental sponsorship of such activities. Perhaps this only shows that not every good argument will play in Peoria.

In this context it is useful to digress briefly in order to remind ourselves that, dollar for dollar, it may be that there is no better use for public (not necessarily federal) funds by the government in the discharge of its responsibility to inform the public than to finance the public's own general education. The resources of general education and a generally educated public enable persons to pursue their own intellectual and cognitive purposes so that they can inform themselves about whatever it is they want to know. This is surely a far more economical use of public funds than, say, myriad local government information offices staffed by government employees ready to answer questions on whatever an interested citizen might ask. And more economical, too, than a flood of government publications mailed to each householder on every subject on which the government has publishable information in its possession. (Whether in some not too distant future there might be an argument in this vein for a tax-supported system of computer terminals in every home and at every desk with access to a National Data Bank funded and maintained by the federal government I will not speculate.) To put the point the other way around, it is difficult to imagine a government, seriously bent on its responsibility to inform the public, that has no interest, or only a casual and intermittent interest, in the availability to the general public of general education in literature, the arts, and the sciences.[6]

Yet even as I say this I hasten to add that I share the older liberal ideology to such an extent that I am loath to treat this responsibility of government on a par with either its duty to promulgate its own laws to those who are subject to them or its duty not to interfere with free speech and free press. The reason I hesitate is that this responsibility of government seems to be clearly subsequent and subordinate to its other responsibilities. We can see this from the point of view of the individual rights involved, and the significance of the violation of those rights. You and I have a right that the government shall tell us what its laws are; this is a right prior even to our right to elect the officials who make and enforce these laws. But our right to do both of these things is surely prior and violations of these rights are surely more significant (as I have argued elsewhere in another context)[7] than our right to be assisted by government to satisfy all our cognitive aspirations.

Some might even want to argue that there is no "right" of this sort at all. For one thing, it is a right that governments cannot help but violate or frustrate all the time. There is no way that a government can do all the things generated as its duties once we insist upon claiming such a right. It seems only reasonable either to conclude that there is no duty of government that its failure to act as required would violate, or to concede that, in the rank order of rights, this one is far down on the scale (perhaps alongside the much-derided "right to holidays with pay" advocated in the United Nations Universal Declaration of Human Rights).

Of course, the desire most elected officials have to maintain good public relations with their constituents dictates officials will try to be responsive to individual requests for information, even where the failure to provide the information does no more than frustrate some personal project or whim, lest wounded egos result in depleted campaign chests, vindictive support for rivals, and defeat at the polls.

But this is merely a prudential consideration for those officials subject to its constraints, not a reflection of any duty or responsibility of office or of any right of the public.

As for the argument that the public, having paid for the information in the possession of the government, has a *right* to it, just as anyone who purchases a good or service has a right to what his money has bought—that cuts deeper. It is true that any information in the possession of the government can be made available to the public only after further cost to someone, even if the cost is slight. However, if the person seeking the information is also willing to pay the further costs of transmitting the information to him, there should be a presumption in favor of his being supplied with the information. Even if he is willing to pay; however, his right of access may be constrained by a variety of legitimate considerations (to be discussed below). And, of course, this argument is to no avail when we seek a rationale for public funding of libraries and museums, institutes and laboratories, whose chief tasks are to create, communicate, and conserve information that does not yet exist and has not already been purchased by the public.

IV

By way of summary, we can organize the principles of governmental responsibility to inform the public so far elicited as follows:

1. The government has the responsibility to inform the public of all the laws it enacts, including regulations it promulgates and judicial processes it initiates, as well as its own deliberations in the formation of policy, subject only to such exceptions as may be required by national security and individual privacy (about which, more below shortly).

2. The government has the responsibility not to interfere with the public's efforts to inform itself about governmental activities (for example, legislative and regulatory hearings) relative to establishing and enforcing the law, or to interfere with the public's efforts to inform itself about its own activities.

3. The government has the responsibility to foster the arts and sciences and especially general education in support of the natural cognitive aspirations of all persons.

Thus, the prior consideration becomes principle 1, the standard argument becomes principle 2, and the more elusive aspiration factor becomes principle 3.

What is perhaps the most controversial aspect of government responsibility to inform the public has yet to be mentioned. It concerns the government's duty to inform a private citizen, upon request, of information that the government has in its files about that citizen. The duty of the government so to inform the citizen, and the reciprocal right of the citizen to be so informed, does not stem directly from any of the principles so far identified. This duty and its counterpart right does not stem from the essence of law and the rule of law. It has nothing to do with the individual's capacity to engage in the collective enterprise of self-government. Knowledge of this sort is not a condition of the development and nurture of each person's cognitive capacities or of their enjoyment. Instead, it arises out of the possibility of abuse of powers, of victimizing citizens either intentionally or otherwise and whether they are innocent or guilty of some violation of law. This origin is acknowledged by Congress in its preamble to the Privacy Act of 1974, in which the central role of "the right of privacy" is emphasized.[8] We are to think of persons as having a right to security from the invasion of privacy that possession, let alone disclosure, of information about him by the government without his knowledge and permission would violate. This right of privacy generates both a prohibition of the government's freedom to use certain information in its possession and a duty to inform individuals that it has such information about them.

What emerges from the principles and arguments so far deployed is a picture of the foundations of government responsibility to inform the public in which individual privacy and especially individual autonomy are paramount factors. Autonomy obviously underlies principle 2, insofar as autonomy entails the conditions requisite for public self-government. Autonomy also underlies principle 1; here it is the autonomy of persons who must know what the law permits and requires if they are to comply with it, and who willingly comply with it not only because it is the law but because of its content, what it actually provides. Finally, autonomy underlies principle 3, though here it is the autonomy of a society of individuals whose growth, self-reliance, and self-criticism is to be fostered.

If my argument so far is correct, then we could imagine, in the ideal case, a government that would acknowledge these principles with constitutional and statutory provisions. Constitutionally, there would be self-imposed restraints (such as our First Amendment provides) against governmental interference with speech and publication. There would also be (as there is not in our federal Constitution) a provision requiring government to promulgate the law in a manner accessible and intelligible to the public.[9] Finally, there would be an acknowledgment of government's concern for the state of education, the arts, sciences, and humanities. In the statutes, there would be legislation creating a National Science Foundation and comparable corporations to support and oversee education, the arts, and the humanities, as well as a Freedom of Information Act and a Privacy Act, in which would be detailed the responsibilities of government to divulge to individuals upon their request the information it holds on them in its files.[10]

How thoroughly and accurately our current laws reflect the principles I have proposed here must be left for evaluation on another occasion; the matter is far too complex and requires a discussion much too detailed to be undertaken in the present setting. Nevertheless it is gratifying to note at least a rough fit between what our laws and Constitution now provide and what an ideal system of law would have to provide if the privacy and autonomy of individuals, bearing on the creation and access to information, were to be fully acknowledged.

V

Are there considerations that legitimately defeat or justify overriding any of the principles so far elicited, with the consequence that it would not be wrong for the government under certain conditions to deny to the public information (or the opportunity to obtain the information) that the principles otherwise require? Are there justifications for the refusal or failure to promulgate a law (a violation of principle 1), for example, that arise because there is some still higher, more fundamental, moral requirement with which promulgation in this instance would conflict? There are, of course, administrative considerations of time, money, opportunity, facilities, and so forth that may excuse delay and inefficiency and account for incapacity to perform as required. There are also ample uncertainties in the meaning of each of these principles, so much so that reasonable persons who avow commitment to them can nevertheless honestly disagree over their interpretation and application, with a result in some cases virtually identical to what it would be if the government repudiated these principles and its responsibilities under them. But these are not the really interesting difficulties (even though hundreds of pages of testimony in congressional hearings on the Freedom of Information Act attests to the interest in them).[11] The truly interesting difficulties concern justifiable exception to these principles based on appeal to incompatible principles of a higher or prior importance.

In this connection, it is useful to contrast the sole express limitation mentioned in the Constitution with the list of exceptions enacted in the Freedom of Information Act. The Constitution, as we have noted, refers to withholding publication of portions of the House and Senate Journal insofar as that is deemed necessary. The purposes for which this might be deemed necessary are not identified, although two such purposes come immediately to mind. One is to protect individuals from slander and libel in remarks and the record thereof by congressmen and senators (who are themselves immune from legal restraints in their remarks on the floor of Congress). The other is national security, which could be jeopardized by putting words into the wrong hands under conditions of civil war, foreign invasion, imminent attack, terrorist threat, or other emergency. The constitutional permission for secrecy in portions of the House and Senate Journal can plausibly be used as a basis for argument to cover secrecy and censorship of a wide range of printed and written materials created by the normal activity of government. The tacit principle that underlies the constitutional exception is, presumably, that the government shall not jeopardize the national welfare (interest, security) by divulging or by risking divulgment of information in its possession about its own activities. So stated, I take it that the principle does express a genuinely justifying consideration in favor of secrecy and censorship. If, as the ancients used to say, *salus populi suprema lex,* then it may be that the government's chief responsibility to the people will have to take precedence over its responsibility to inform them, or to let them inform themselves, on particular matters of interest.[12]

The Freedom of Information Act of 1966 as amended in 1974, however, has a long list of categories of information in the hands of government to which the provisions of the Act concerning divulgment "does not apply." They are as follows:

(1) national defense or foreign policy matters regarded as secret and so classified;

(2) personnel rules and practices of a government agency;

(3) anything exempt from disclosure by a statute so declaring;

(4) trade secrets, financial information, and other privileged or confidential information;

(5) inter- or intra-agency memoranda and correspondence not available by law except to a party in litigation with the government;

(6) personnel and medical files protected by personal privacy;

(7) investigatory records compiled by law enforcement agencies;

(8) data on the operation and regulation of financial institutions;

(9) geological and geophysical information concerning wells.[13]

Whether this list of exclusions is too wide or too narrow depends, in the context of the present discussion, on whether these nine categories can be shown to derive from the two considerations so far identified as the only ones appropriate to override the principles governing public disclosure—namely, the privacy considerations that give rise to slander and libel laws, and the national security considerations that give rise to secrecy and censorship. An obvious sinner in the above list is category 3, unless a specific statutory prohibition against disclosure is itself based on one of the two considerations that justify non-disclosure. Somewhat similar reflections are prompted by exemptions 5, 6, and 7. Exemptions 4, 8, and 9, however, seem to arise mainly out of concern to protect private property. Exemption 2 strikes me as the most dubious, since it would surely appear that the "internal personnel rules and practices of an agency" ought to be a matter of public knowledge and subject to public scrutiny lest government agencies be able to draw a cloak of secrecy over their inefficiency, not to mention unlawful discriminatory (racist, sexist) personnel practices. There may be, of course, a rebuttal to this objection, one that draws upon two justifying considerations I have identified. But I have difficulty in imagining what that rebuttal would be and thus I am skeptical of the appropriateness of this exception, especially when private institutions (such as universities) are properly required by law to make known to the government their "internal personnel rules and practices."

VI

One might object to the foregoing discussion in any of several ways. It might be argued that I have set out the wrong principles; that the principles I have identified are not the ones that determine the government's responsibility to inform the public and the limits thereto. A second possible criticism is that while the principles I have identified are correct, my list is incomplete (perhaps very incomplete), as there are other (and maybe significantly more fundamental) principles independent of the ones I have cited. A third line of criticism might be that the principles I have identified, whether correct and complete or not, do not have their source in the ideas and arguments that I have claimed give rise to them. A fourth criticism could be that although I have correctly identified all the major principles and their sources, we can do very little of a practical nature with such principles because they are too abstract or too vague; they need intermediate principles before they can be applied, additional standards, supplementary considerations, none of which I have supplied. I take comfort from the thought that no one can consistently advance all these criticisms—and discomfort from the possibility that nevertheless at least one of them may be well taken.

The first, second, and third criticisms are ones to which I have given some thought. Obviously, if I believed any had merit, I would have revised my views accordingly. So, if there is to be a successful development of criticism along any of these lines, I must at least for the present leave it to others. In regard to the fourth criticism, however, a different response is called for. Anyone who has read from the hearing records on the Freedom of Information Act, in which a wide range of testimony will be found on administrative practice, policy statements by responsible officials, memoranda on drafting problems, and the appellate court record of litigation in FOIA cases, will be bound to conclude that there is a tremendous gap between accepting principles such as I have proposed, even if they are correct and complete at their level, and knowing enough to evaluate whether in actual cases the government has discharged its responsibility in a fair and effective manner in compliance with those principles. J. S. Mill replied to criticism of the principle of utility by remarking, "Whatever we adopt as the fundamental principle of morality, we require subordinate principles to apply it by.[14] The need for lower-order principles is not confined to employment of a fundamental or supreme moral principle. It is equally true where, as in the present instance, we are concerned to apply the first principles that govern conduct in a fairly narrow domain. A host of procedural considerations, ultimately rooted in moral principles themselves, must be brought to bear. Many empirical judgments of varying complexity must also be rendered. In these tasks, philosophers may have little to contribute in contrast to lawyers and experienced administrators. If we want to set out at its fullest the considerations to which we must appeal as we work out the true responsibilities of a government to inform its citizenry, this larger task, which I have only identified here, must also be undertaken and completed.

Notes

1. This right has now been put in jeopardy by the recent decision in *Gannett* v. *De Pasquale,* 443 U.S. 368 (1979).

2. Standard treatises by writers familiar with our constitutional and philosophical tradition, such as Carl Cohen in *Democracy* (Athens, Ga.: University of Georgia Press, 1971), have little to offer by way of adumbration or reflection on this subject as an integral part of their conception of democracy. The same is true of constitutional commentators, such as Edward S. Corwin in *The Constitution and What It Means Today,* 12th ed.; (Princeton, N.J. Princeton University Press, 1958). Even the American Civil Liberties Union, in its valuable treatise edited by Norman Dorsen, *The Rights of Americans* (New York: Pantheon, 1970), nowhere mentions any right to information or right to be informed by government. The one exception known to me (and it came to my attention only well after this paper was completed) is Samuel J. Archibald, "Access to Government Information— The Right Before First Amendment," in *The First Amendment and the News Media* (Final Report of the Annual Chief Justice Earl Warren Conference on Advocacy in the United States; Cambridge, Mass.: Roscoe Pound–American Trial Lawyers Foundation, 1973), pp. 64–76.

3. James Madison, *Writings,* vol. 6, p. 398, a text widely quoted in discussions on freedom of information.

4. Lon Fuller, *The Morality of Law* (New Haven, Conn.: Yale University Press, 1964), pp. 34–39, *passim.*

5. Aquinas, *Summa Theologica,* 1–2, Q. 90, A. 4, *respondeo,* in Aquinas, *Treatise on Law* (Chicago, Ill.: Henry Regnery Co., n.d.), p. 10.

6. Whether there is evidence in our political tradition for any view such as the one advanced in the text may be doubted. Nevertheless, it is worth noting that Jefferson, in his *Notes on Virginia,* made much of the importance of public education and even proposed "an amendment of our constitution . . . in aid of the public education" (Adrienne Koch and William Peden, eds., *The Life and Selected Writings of Thomas Jefferson* (New York: Modern Library, 1944), p. 265.

7. See H. A. Bedau, "Human Rights and Foreign Assistance Programs," in Peter G. Brown and Douglas MacLean, eds., *Human Rights and U.S. Foreign Policy* (Lexington, Mass.: D. C. Heath and Company, 1979), pp. 29–44.

8. Congress refers to this right as "a personal and fundamental right protected by the Constitution of the United States." There is, of course, no explicit mention of any such right in the Constitution or its amendments. Prior to *Griswold* v. *Connecticut,* 381 U.S. 479 (1965), this right was of such doubtful constitutional status that standard treatises (e.g., Corwin, *The Constitution*) make no mention of it whatever.

9. This omission from the Constitution might be remedied, at least in part, by a generous reading of the explicit prohibition against "ex post facto law" (art. 1, sec. 10) and the Supreme Court's developed "void-for-vagueness" doctrine.

10. There would not be, as there is in Great Britain, an Official Secrets Act. For the reasons, see Thomas I. Emerson, "Why We Don't Need an Official Secrets Act," *The Nation,* March 10, 1979, pp. 263–66.

11. See "U.S. Government Information Policies and Practices—Administration and Operation of the Freedom of Information Act," *Hearing Before a Subcommittee of the Committee on Government Operations,* parts 4–9, H.R., 92nd Cong., 2d sess., 1972; and "The Freedom of Information Act," *Hearings on H.R. 5425 and H.R. 4960,* H.R., 93rd Cong., 1st sess., 1973; and "Freedom of Information Act," *Hearings Before a Subcommittee on Administrative Practices and Procedures,* Committee of the Judiciary, Senate, 95th Cong., 1st sess., 1977.

12. Whether under this reasoning the government would have a right to prohibit publication of sensitive information to which a reporter had apparently gained lawful access seems doubtful; hence if the injunction against *The Progressive* in March 1979 to prohibit it from publishing an article on H-bomb construction was justified, it must be on some other ground. For a discussion, see Cynthia Bolbach, "'Born Classified': The Lessons of the 'Progressive' Case," *The Progressive,* Oct. 24, 1979, pp. 1033–1038.

13. See U.S.C.A. §552 (b) (1)–(9).

14. J. S. Mill, *Utilitarianism* (1861), sec. 2, penultimate paragraph.

JOSEPH MARGOLIS

15 Democracy and the Responsibility to Inform the Public

There is only one kind of theory of the state in accord with which a government may be said not to have any responsibility at all to inform the public about matters putatively in its interest. That is the theory that the state is an entity the existence of which (as distinct from its effectiveness) does not depend in any formal sense on "the consent of the governed," or which incorporates a governed population in a relationship that mere consent, implicit contracts, and the like cannot create or sustain. The fascist mysteries regarding the state as an ideal organism and the sixteenth- and seventeenth-century doctrine of the divine right of kings approach, in rather different ways, were just such theories. This in itself is worth our notice, because it shows that the issue of a responsible government need not preclude totalitarianism or absolute monarchy.

In fact, since the theory of the socialist state is often thought to be both totalitarian and committed to the government's informing the public, one might plausibly draw the conclusion that socialist governments have just such a responsibility congruent with the range of their putative totalitarian competence. On the other hand, those cynical about the Soviet Union, for instance, may claim that the totalitarian competence of the socialist state (*a fortiori,* of the government) corresponds to its responsibility to care for, or to take care of a governed population—hence, they may claim either that that responsibility precludes the responsibility to inform an independent public or else that it trivially entails its satisfaction. Thus, for

237

example, the apparent suppression in the Soviet press of news of prominent defectors may be taken either to involve no violation of the responsibility to inform (since there is none) or else actually to constitute a judicious action intended to inform in an appropriate way. On the second alternative, our cynicism must (to some extent at least) be tempered by the subtleties of what should count as relations between, and actions affecting, the state, the government, and the public. These are not nearly as straightforward as we might believe, even in the context of what is generally understood as a democracy or a democratic state. Certainly, an appeal to actual historical practice as opposed to theory will clarify matters only to a limited extent; for our intention in referring to practice is normally to extract some prescriptive instruction about relevant policies—which makes it quite impossible to justify a strong contrast between the facts and our theory of the facts.

Our principal concern, however, lies with Western-style democratic states. The distinction of a democratic state is essentially captured in the following three constraints: the origin and continued existence of the state is thought to depend, in some sense, on the consent of the governed; the competence of the state is, in principle, restricted to a public domain separated from the private concerns of its citizenry; and the domestic and foreign policy of the state is directed toward, and justified primarily in, preserving and enlarging the sphere of the private liberties of its citizenry and in securing a public order within which individual citizens may effectively and equitably act to share in the direction of the government and in the use of their private liberties.[1]

Even in the theory and practice of direct democracy, it was fundamental to Calvinist thought (despite the obvious tendency toward totalitarian competence) to distinguish sharply between private and public matters; though it is more characteristic of more recent representative democracies to extend the scope of the private well beyond thought and belief to a significant range of action as well. At any rate, there is a strong historical tendency for democratic theory and practice to reject totalitarian competence. Among representative democracies, it is a principled objection. The paradigm in this regard is undoubtedly the American Bill of Rights. But, although the analysis of the legitimacy of particular practices and policies regarding a government's responsibility to inform is bound to require a close attention to the details of an actual legal tradition, the conceptual issues involved deserve to be examined in more general terms, detached as far as possible from the temptations of special pleading.

Here, the most instructive aspect of the government's responsibility to inform lies with the unavoidability of practical dilemmas; these follow, in fact, almost directly from the nature of the democratic state itself. Consider, for example, the well-known warning of the U.S. Surgeon-General's about the hazards of smoking. The warning is universally included in all cigarette advertising and packaging but it tends to become invisible just because of its ubiquity, and it is notably bland, disconnected from the dissemination of relevantly detailed information, and not particularly energetically connected with an in-depth educational program designed to dissuade smokers. In fact, Joseph Califano (of President Carter's original cabinet) was thought by many who agreed with his views to have pressed a vigorous anti-smoking campaign by way of an inherently illegitimate extension of the government's responsibility to inform the public about the dangers of tobacco.

The reason is a double one. First of all, if a domain of private competence is reserved for citizens, then governmental initiatives competing with such competence run the risk of being viewed (in the private sector) as potentially illegitimate and paternalistic. The dissemination of governmentally approved information and educative programs may well be construed as intrusive in just this sense, though it is not conceptually impossible that the government act both to provide relevant information and to permit the effective collection of information in the private sector. The possibility that the government might broadcast selected information in order to disorganize the influence of information independently and privately collected cannot be guarded against by appeal to merely formal principles. On the other hand, the prospect of an abuse of privately collected information—for example, in misrepresentation, neglect, or refusal to disclose, or the confusion of advertising—suggests the reasonableness of conceding the government's responsibility as an alternative informant.

Secondly, if a sphere of private competence obtains, and if the government wishes to avoid the charge of paternalism or even a conflict of interest, the government may assume that all relevant information bearing on the interests of its citizens will be duly supplied through the private sector itself. Thus, for example, in the United States, the government requires that candidates for public office be officially certified and listed on public ballots. But it normally has no further role in making available relevant information regarding the competence, experience, probity, and the like of particular candidates. The result, particularly in the United States, is that voters tend to be remarkably uninformed about the qualifications of actual candidates.

Not unreasonably, one might argue that such widespread ignorance constitutes a politically relevant danger to the very life and quality of the state; but it would be terribly difficult to find anyone (in the United States) who would argue that the government was actually responsible for providing the required information. In the Soviet-bloc countries, on the other hand, countries that characterize themselves as "people's democracies," the government holds the initiative both with regard to selecting and recommending candidates for public office and with regard to the direction and control of the press and other public media. Hence, to say the least, the range of personal liberties varies strikingly from "democracy" to "democracy," and the responsibility to inform is either satisfied (in the Soviet-style state) by satisfying the responsibility of state care, or else the criticism and correction of governmental practice is largely generated within, and restricted to, the government itself. There are, normally, no regular channels for gathering reliable information independently of government-approved or government-sponsored sources—as the heroic efforts of a handful of dissenters and an underground press attest. Hence, the settlement of any dispute about the adequacy of a government's informing its independent citizenry requires a fundamental contrast between Western-style democracies and so-called people's democracies. For, to the extent that a government is criticized for having failed to meet that responsibility, (*a*) the competence and private liberties of the citizenry extend to gathering and assessing information independently of the government and to acting unhindered, on its own best appraisal, and (*b*) the state (*a fortiori*, the government) is restricted from paternalistic invasions of that very competence. People's democracies reject both (*a*) and (*b*); understandably, therefore, they tend not to be viewed in the West as genuine democracies. But it is one thing to concede that the discussion of the government's responsibility to inform depends on the assumption of a Western-style democracy, and quite another to criticize the practices of "people's democracies" as failing to meet the constraints of another type of political system.

Nevertheless, even granting a democratic government's responsibility to inform, there can be no simple way to determine in principle that the exercise of that responsibility will or will not collide with its responsibility to respect and secure the domain of private liberties. For example, to require biology texts in elementary and secondary schools (both public and publicly licensed private schools) to include an accurate presentation of evolutionary theory may count as an exercise of the government's responsibility to inform the public; but it may also be construed, in the context of privately financed schools, as invading the right to gather and distribute information in accord with privately promoted educational concerns and convictions. Again, banning the use and the dumping of TCP may count as the realistic enforcement of the government's responsibility to inform; but Monsanto and the industrial firms that have used TCP profitably for forty years could claim that the government lacked scientifically valid information justifying its action and that it disorganized bona fide inquiries requiring considerable care and expense and time— inquiries properly originating in the private sector.

In spite of dilemmas of this sort, it is possible, within the context of democratic theory, to formulate some plausible guidelines regarding the government's responsibility to inform. In fact, we have already touched on a number of relevant considerations that suggest a more systematic account. For example, the very notion of the government's "responsibility to inform" may be construed, non-exclusively, as the government's responsibility to exert a positive initiative in gathering and distributing information, or to act so as not to disallow or to hamper information-gathering and information-distributing activities originating in the private sector. It is, for instance, realistically quite unlikely (though not altogether impossible) that state-run penal institutions can be counted on voluntarily to disclose adverse conditions in the management of prisons and prisoners; but, in that case, it may be argued that the public press, operating within the private sector, should be permitted (within reasonable constraints) to examine prison life and to report its findings. The details of such liberty are, of course, arguable within a particular legal tradition. But the following generalization seems reasonably required by the theory of the democratic state: (1) wherever it supports particular legislation or enforces a particular policy, the government is responsible for informing the public (in the double sense given) about matters, involving such legislation or policy, bearing on the internal and external security of the state and on the exercise of the powers and liberties reserved for the private sector. For example, to institute and maintain prisons entails, on this principle, that the public is entitled to know whether they actually promote domestic security and whether those imprisoned are treated in a way consistent with the function of prisons in a democratic society. To deny access without qualification is, in effect, to violate the conceptual and prescriptive bond between the doctrine of the consent of the governed and the government's responsibility to inform. But once this is conceded, then at least two additional principles seem pertinent: (2) the government's responsibility to inform (in the double sense intended) should be regularly enlarged, consistent with the security and internal order of the state and the protection of rights, and should regularly enlarge the range of competence in the private sector; and (3) information legitimately collected should, consistently with (2), be made effectively accessible within the private sector. The idea is that if the purpose of a democratic state is conceded and if a competent citizenry is assumed, then a democratic government cannot fully justify its own activities unless those activities can be construed as continually supported by the independently informed consent of the governed. Thus, for instance, the courts' unconditional refusal to permit the general public—*a fortiori,* the press—to gather information about prison life through personal interviews with willing prison inmates constitutes a *prima facie* violation of principle (1).[2] But even granting that public access to such information ought not to be unconditional, a democratic society is bound to attempt, over time, to enlarge and to make even more generous the public's access to such information, particularly if it expresses a clear and strong interest in having it.

What we must remember is that, on a democratic theory, the citizenry function both as a source for recruiting informed members of the government and as competent to exercise their rights and powers within the private sector; they can function effectively in neither of these capacities without suitable access to pertinent information. The upshot is that failure on the government's part to act in accord with (1) and (3) constitutes an inadmissible application of the principle of doubt effect.[3] One cannot justifiably invoke the distinction between intended and merely foreseen effects if what is "foreseen" is either entailed by what is intended or else linked to it by causal necessity or overwhelming probability; in such cases, an agent's intention cannot but extend to the foreseen effect as well. Consider again the issue of prison interviewers. The High Court's refusal, for instance, in *Pell* v. *Procunier*[4] and *Saxbe* v. *Washington Post Co.,*[5] to permit either the general public or the press to conduct regulated interviews entails an intention, whatever its putatively intended purpose in upholding the security arrangements and arrangements regarding prisoners' loss of rights within state prison systems, to deny information admittedly within the competent concerns of the citizenry. In a word, the democratic state cannot, in accord with (1), justify an absolute ban on gathering information; and it is bound in accord with (2), to experiment with increasingly generous arrangements regarding pertinent information.

Principle (3) also bears on the accessibility of information already gathered—hence, for instance, on the disclosure of government-conducted inquiries or of private inquiries bearing directly on such issues as public security, health, and order (for example, regarding the American commitment in the Vietnamese war, the management and dangers of the Three Mile Island facility, and the activities of organized crime). But one cannot realistically admit such a responsibility, without, at the same time, recognizing the bearing of legitimate concerns about national security, the danger of public panic, and the effectiveness of police campaigns. Hence, just as (1) precludes all unconditional bans on information, (2) precludes all unconditional claims to information in behalf of the private sector. Herein lies the source, of course, of the practical dilemmas already sampled.

In fact, the issue at stake yields, on reflection, a further principle (partly redundant): (4) neither the government nor the public is entitled to unconditional access to information. The very idea of protecting a sector of private competence entails that the government shall not press to gather information, putatively in the interest of public security, public health, public order, or the like, that would adversely alter the existence or scope or effectiveness of the private sector. In effect, democratic theory entails that the government will yield in the direction of principle (2), and that a reasonably informed citizenry will not seek to gather or disclose information that would constitute, say, a "clear and present danger" to the state's security. On the first issue, perhaps the press's right to refuse to disclose its sources of information may be regarded as a normal constraint on the government's own information-gathering activities. On the second, perhaps the attempt to publish secret information about the details of manufacturing an atomic bomb may be regarded as going beyond the legitimate constraints on the information-gathering activities of the private sector. In recent court cases, it is certainly true that the government's attempt to force reporters to disclose their sources is, on the face of it, contrary to principle (2). On the other hand, bona fide instances of publishing government secrets (say, regarding national security and the like) are bound to be viewed as treason or other high crimes. In the Daniel Ellsberg case, however, the disclosure of the Pentagon papers was too closely linked to the government's now-exposed practices during the Vietnam era and that government's resistence to principle (3) to make a charge of treason stick; and the recent newspaper publication of how to make a hydrogen bomb has proved to have relied on materials entirely in the public domain already (carelessly released, it seems, in compliance with principle [2]). Still, the issues involved are not, for such reasons, rendered any less legitimate. The security of the state remains a necessary condition for the preservation of the liberties of the private sector; and the protection and enlargement of liberties within the private sector are essential to the very purpose of the democratic state.

Having said this much, we need to remind ourselves more closely of the nature of the argument. First of all, claims regarding the government's responsibility to inform clearly presuppose an ideologically favored commitment to a certain type of political state. There is no sense in which the question meaningfully arises outside of a severely circumscribed historical tradition. This is what we have established in linking the question's pertinence to the nature of the democratic state. On the other hand, there are no known decisive conceptual or empirical grounds on which to demonstrate the rational necessity or clear superiority of subscribing to the tenets of the democratic state *vis-à-vis* all contending alternatives. So the question of the government's responsibility to inform is primarily an internal question—a question of reasonable behavior within the assumptions of the democratic state. In this respect, normative speculation about the *praxis* of governments is not altogether unlike theology: the tenets of the true believer set minimal constraints on relevant disputes, and debate proceeds by dialectically determining the least restrictive account of internal principles and practice consistent with such constraints. Inevitably, challenges to the basic tenets themselves fall outside the pertinent concern of such a political theorist or of the theologian. It remains true that, as in theology, relevant speculation may attempt alternative interpretations of the basic tenets of the system in question—here, the system of democratic government. But even such speculation will be pursued in terms of the tradition of interpretation that has developed with the system itself; and, in many cases, it will be indistinguishable from purely internal considerations. This is the point of having attempted to formulate the essential constraints on governments said to accord with Western-style democratic states. Having fixed these constraints, the set of principles offered as rightly guiding the government's responsibility to inform are offered both as fully compatible with the very concept of a democratic government and as the least restricted set possible of such principles.

The second thing to notice is that the principles advanced—any such principles—cannot fail to lack explicit or fixed criteria of application. The reason is partly that the usual disputes center more on the application of principles to cases or, more specifically, on the validity of criteria for the application of principles to cases than on the validity of the principles themselves. In short, as everyone realizes, it is quite likely that all who are committed to the democratic state can subscribe to our principles (1)–(4); but that goes no way toward showing that there need be no deep disputes or no irreconcilable disagreements about the interpretation and assessment of individual cases. On the contrary, there is every reason to believe that debates about the details of what, precisely, *is* the government's responsibility in particular instances are bound to vary considerably in at least two respects: that competing proposals must, realistically, fall within the range of historically perceived options at any given moment; and that, relative to any such moment, conviction, partisanship, and the like tend normally to support dialectically opposed resolutions that cannot be shown, neutrally, to be any the less plausible or reasonable than certain of their competitors. There is, in short, no effective way to ensure one and only one correct judgment about the government's responsibility in particular cases. The result is that *every* such resolution may be fairly judged to be (however sincerely believed) a partisan judgment. Hence, even to construe a particular issue as requiring resolution in terms of specifically opposed alternatives is a substantial expression of political influence; and a favorable *judgment* (as in the courts) must count as part of an effective political *act*. To appreciate the point is to appreciate the implications of attempting to settle "ethical issues in government."

This does not, by any means, signify that judgments about the government's responsibility to inform are logically or politically arbitrary. On the contrary, it is closer to the truth to hold that attempts to derive, from timeless principles or rules of normative political morality or justice, detailed judgments binding in historically distinctive circumstances are themselves politically arbitrary and conceptually odd. One sees this at once, once one sees that, if there are any non-vacuous moral principles (or moral or normative principles of politics) derivable from, or somehow justified by reference to, human nature, it is utterly unlikely that (apart from certain extreme doctrines) the most interesting and viable theories of the political state would be obliged to reject them. And yet, in spite of such agreement, there can be no question that neither such principles nor the more restricted democratic principles already adduced will be adequate to resolve serious disagreements about the responsibility of government to inform in this or that disputed case. In a sense, this is no more than the theoretical side of our previous acknowledgment of the inevitability of practical dilemmas. The correct balance, for instance, between the government's responsibility to protect the security, order, health, and similar objectives of the state cannot, in principle, be discovered; any recommended balance can be shown to be or not to be compatible with the essential constraints of democracy, with principles like the four offered earlier regarding guidelines for governmental informing, and with the historically emergent perception of the relevant context of dispute. But conformity with these conditions is insufficient to entail an exclusively correct resolution; moreover, alternative resolutions may well be incompatible with one another, in the straightforward sense that they cannot be jointly adopted.[6]

A third consideration may be in order here. There is no doubt that the rationale behind political states is normally construed in terms of the principal prudential interests of human beings; and that, furthermore, these will normally be understood in some sort of species-specific way. The democratic doctrine of the rights and competence of citizens within a reserved private sector is an acknowledgment of that fact. But even the totalitarian theory of the state may come to terms with such underlying prudential interests. Hence, as we have in effect already seen, it is quite possible for a totalitarian state to provide alternative views about how, plausibly, a government should manage its responsibilities involving informing the public. It would be conceptually impossible for such a state to admit a responsibility to inform a politically independent public, simply because such an admission would be incompatible with the doctrine of totalitarian competence. In that sense, a totalitarian state subscribes to a different "theology." Nevertheless, assuming the pertinence of species-specific concerns, there is bound to be at least gross-grained analogies between the disputes about the government's responsibility to inform (within the context of democratic theory) and the government's responsibility to take care of its citizenry (within the context of totalitarian theory). This, too, may reinforce the illusion that we may progress toward adequate universal political principles. But the impressions cannot be more than an illusion, since already on the assumption, the partisans of democratic and totalitarian states cannot jointly subscribe to their own political model and to that of their opposite numbers. Also, since their agreement probably converges most compellingly on the nature of human prudential interests, there is no reason at all to suppose that such complex disputes as those regarding the government's responsibility to inform can simply be translated or transformed from the terms of reference of the one system to those of the other.

Finally, if it is not unreasonable to think of moral questions as arising only within the setting of the political and historical life of a society—a conception that, apart from the classical bourgeois tradition, is very nearly universally accepted—then there is every reason to believe that the kind of relativism generated by our question regarding the government's responsibility to inform may be counted on to color as well the attempt at objective debate regarding personal morality.

Notes

1. It may be conceded at once that the notion of the "public," as here used, involves an important equivocation: in one sense, speaking of the relationship between the state and its citizenry, it marks the limits of the legitimate competence of the state as opposed to the "private" preserve that it ensures for its citizens; in another, speaking of the behavior of its citizenry, it marks only the perceivable nature of what citizens do as opposed to the imperceptible nature of their unexpressed states of mind. Hence, what is public in the second sense may well be private in the first.

2. The relevant legal history is conveniently summarized in Lawrence K. Rockwell, "The Public's Right to Know: Pell v. Procunier and Saxbe v. Washington Post Co.," *Hastings Constitutional Law Quarterly* vol. 2 (1975).

3. "Double Effect, Principle of," *New Catholic Encyclopedia*, vol. 4 (New York: McGraw-Hill, 1976), pp. 1020, 1022.

4. 417 U.S. 817 (1974).

5. 417 U.S. 843 (1974).

6. I have developed a comparable account of the moderate relativism of interpretive and appraisive judgments in the context of the criticism of the arts, in "Robust Relativism," *Journal of Aesthetics and Art Criticism* 30 (1976), and in *Art and Philosophy* (Atlantic Highlands and Hassocks: Humanities Press and Harvester Press, 1980). My point in pressing the comparison is that I believe relativism of such a sort is required in all the distinct disciplines concerned with cultural phenomena.

Index